UWARCHIW

# BALLROOM
# DANCING

**Alex Moore**

# BALLROOM DANCING

### TENTH EDITION

## ALEX MOORE

### WITH 100 DIAGRAMS OF THE QUICKSTEP, WALTZ, FOXTROT, TANGO, ETC.

### FOREWORD BY

## PHILIP J. S. RICHARDSON

Routledge • New York

A Theatre Arts Book
Published in the USA in 2002 by
Routledge
29 West 35th Street
New York, NY 10001
www.routledge-ny.com

Routledge is an imprint of the Taylor and Francis Group.

ISBN 0-87830-153-4

Cataloging-in-Publication Data is available from the Library of Congress.

Tenth edition originally published in Great Britain in 2002 by
A & C Black Publishers Limited
37 Soho Square, London W1D 3QZ
www.acblack.com

A & C Black uses paper produced with elemental chlorine-free pulp, harvested
from managed sustainable forests.

Illustrations on pages 6, 12, 70 and 220 by Catherine Ward

Typeset in Minion 11$^{1}$/₂pt on 15pt

Printed and bound in Great Britain by Clays Ltd, St Ives plc

# FOREWORD TO THE FIRST EDITION
## BY
## PHILIP J. S. RICHARDSON

Mr. Alex Moore's name is so well known in the dancing world today, not only in this country but also abroad, that any introduction from me is really superfluous, but, having been invited to write a few words, I may say that I do so with great pleasure.

He was a first-class dancer when I first knew him. Nevertheless, I think that it is as a teacher that he excels. He has a keen analytical mind and, though a staunch believer in the modern technique as laid down by the leading authorities, does not hesitate, as will be seen in several instances in the following pages, to point out cases in which he considers this to be at fault.

Mr. Moore has had considerable teaching and lecturing experience both at home and in other European countries, North America, Japan, Australia and South Africa, and is well able to realize and appreciate the difficulties which confront the beginner.

I am sure that the following pages will prove of great assistance not only to the absolute beginner, but also to the more advanced dancer who wishes to reach the "competition" standard, and to the student preparing for examinations.

## AFTERTHOUGHT – 1950

It is nearly fourteen years since I wrote the above Foreword to the first edition of Mr. Alex Moore's book and, except for one word, I see no need to alter what I then penned. The word "considerable" as applied to Mr. Moore's teaching and lecturing experience seems to me today to be totally inadequate. He has now had very great experience indeed, and as the results of his experience are embodied in the following pages, this volume should be of very great value to the dancer.

P. J. S. R.

## PREFACE TO THE NINTH EDITION

In earlier editions it was necessary for me to suggest many deviations from the standard technique but the majority of these suggestions have now been incorporated in the technique accepted by the leading societies of teachers of dancing. It can be stated quite confidently that the dancing of all first-class dancers is based on the present technique, and although personal expression will account for some slight deviations among our leading dancers, the keen amateur and student cannot go wrong in following the technical descriptions and diagrams given in this book.

In this ninth edition, the standardised version of the International Viennese Waltz has been given.

ALEX MOORE

# PREFACE TO THE FIRST EDITION

When I was invited to undertake this work two difficulties became apparent to me: one, the feasibility of presenting to both amateurs and students something sufficiently comprehensive within the limits of a book of restricted length; and the other, the possibility of ensuring that the work was prepared in such a form and in such a sufficiently interesting manner to satisfy oneself that it could be assimilated by all classes of dancers. The introduction of a new form of Dance Chart may prove of assistance to amateurs in learning the various figures more speedily, but it is sincerely hoped that the keen amateur will regard the book as something more than a means of acquiring a knowledge of steps and variations. It is also to be hoped that no student will be foolish enough to be gulled into the belief that a parrot's knowledge of its contents will be sufficient to satisfy an astute examiner.

If I have succeeded in producing something which will aid the pupil in the study of Ballroom Dancing and create a desire to strive to appreciate the art, I am amply repaid.

It may be that some of my views may not meet with universal approval, but they are given in the conscientious belief that they will assist towards a truer interpretation of the Dance, and its recognition as the finest of indoor recreations.

In suggesting slight deviations from the recognized standard technique of Ballroom Dancing, I in no way wish to dissent markedly from the views of my fellow members of the Ballroom Committee of the Imperial Society of Teachers of Dancing, who have done so much to raise the standard of dancing in this country.

My grateful thanks are extended to my partner, Miss Kilpatrick, for the assistance which she has so freely given to me during the course of the preparation of this book, and to my friend and pupil Mr. Edward Youel for his generous help with the Charts.

ALEX MOORE
KINGSTON-ON-THAMES

# CONTENTS

## SECTION II

## THE WALTZ 96

## SECTION III

## THE FOXTROT                                                 159

## SECTION IV

## THE TANGO                                                   219

## SECTION V

## SECTION VI

# INTRODUCTORY SECTION

Perhaps the most significant point regarding the progress of Modern Ballroom Dancing can be found in the way in which it was able to achieve international prominence in a fairly short space of time. It is now, however, some years since the English dancing public made the great change from the sequence and set dances, and engaged themselves in the turmoil of what was then known as "Jazz". Naturally enough, chaos existed for a number of years, but the standardization of a few basic steps and the gradual clarification of the technique that governs them, have resulted in tremendous progress being made, until, today, the English style of Ballroom Dancing stands pre-eminent throughout the world.

This international interest, achieved without very much publicity, is the natural result of the recognition of Modern Ballroom Dancing as the greatest indoor sport and recreation the world has ever known. As a competitive sport it has aroused the interest of practically every country in the world and the standard of dancing is sufficiently high to challenge our best English dancers.

Teams from all over the world compete in the World

Championship, now held annually in a different country each year.

Primarily, Ballroom Dancing is a mental and physical recreation and as such it can scarcely be said to have an equal. Taken seriously, it can give the young person as much physical exercise as is desired; to the more mature dancer, it can give exercise that is effective without being too strenuous; to the busy man or woman it will provide that mental relaxation which is so necessary to physical health.

To reach a reasonable standard of efficiency is neither difficult nor laborious, and the added pleasure of executing a few simple steps correctly, and with a good poise and balance, will give full compensation for the time spent in learning them.

## SUGGESTED METHOD OF APPROACH

### (1) The Novice

The novice (whose initial desire is to learn sufficient about dancing to be able to move both comfortably and unobtrusively in the ballroom) will only need to assimilate very little of the information in this book. To many people dancing is a hobby, a recreation, or a pleasant means of obtaining healthy physical exercise. Others approach it from different aspects, one of the most important being the mental relaxation that an evening's dancing can give. Obviously, the method of approach must vary in each case. The unambitious beginner need not be alarmed by the seemingly intricate details which follow the simple descriptions of the various figures. They are as unnecessary to him or her as are the intricacies of motor racing to the ordinary car driver.

After reading the general instructions at the beginning of this book, paying especial attention to the Hold, and the Poise and Balance of the Walk, the beginner should turn to the

Quickstep Section, and learn the Walk, Quarter Turns and the Natural Turn. Full use should be made of the charts. They are quite easy to follow, especially if the squares are marked out on the floor. The various steps should be danced with the feet kept flat at first, afterwards a little attention being paid to the Footwork, as the turns will be much easier with some little use of the ball of the foot.

The fundamentals of the Waltz should be learned next, and the best method of approaching this dance is given at the beginning of the section dealing with it.

The beginner who enters the ballroom with just a knowledge of the Walk, Quarter Turns and Natural Turn in the Quickstep, and the Closed Change, Natural Turn, and Reverse Turn in the Waltz, will be able to take part in about three-quarters of the average Ballroom Dance programme.

It must be remembered that a good carriage and the ability to move easily and rhythmically are of utmost importance. There is much more pleasure to be obtained from dancing a few simple figures well than from dancing a dozen indifferently. When an easy and comfortable interpretation of the basic figures has been achieved, the desire to learn further variations will soon follow.

## (2) The Competition Dancer and Keen Amateur

The reader who aspires to competition dancing should remember that a judge's first impression comes from the general appearance of the couple. A good poise and a hold that is stylish and unaffected are most essential, for however well a couple may dance they will never command attention if such important details are lacking. Much useful information on these points is given in the early part of this book, and it should be studied with great care. Footwork, so important because it is so noticeable, should be neat and correct, whilst the subtle difference between "Body Swing" and the rather hackneyed "Contrary Body Movement" is well worth investigating. Finally, the controlled use of Body Sways and Rise and Fall, which should be felt in the body, should be understood, as a really finished dance is impossible without them.

The charts will be found most useful in checking the alignment of the various figures. This feature of dancing is so often overlooked by competition dancers.

There is no short cut to championship rank in dancing. The standard of competition dancing at the present time is so high that there is not the slightest chance of a dancer attracting the judge's eye with a series of tricky variations that are not based on a sound technique.

It is possible to learn much from a book, but lessons from a good teacher are essential: it is so difficult to visualize the general effect of one's own dancing.

The keen amateur who shrinks from the publicity of competition dancing will be well advised to enter the Amateur Medal Tests which are held quite frequently all over the country. These Tests are of a similar nature to the Ice Skating Tests, and bronze, silver, and gold medals are awarded according to the standard of the entrant. There are also tests for the social dancer and ongoing tests beyond Gold for the real enthusiast, affording an excellent opportunity for dancers to test their proficiency. The fees for these Tests are quite moderate, and the board of examiners includes the most famous teachers of dancing in the world. Further notes on the Tests and on Competition Dancing will be found on pages 295 to 305.

## (3) The Student

The student who is training for a professional examination with a view to becoming a teacher of dancing should obviously be able to derive the most benefit from this book, for it contains much technical information necessary for a student's or teacher's examination. A big mistake, however, would be made by the student who thinks that, with a mere book knowledge of the technique of dancing, plus a reasonably good practical demonstration of the standard dances, a competent examiner can be cheated into believing a candidate is fit to hold the diploma of a Teachers' Society.

The secret of the successful study of this book has nothing to do with the ability to remember such technical details as the numbers of the steps on which CBM, Rise and Sway occur. Rather, it is the ability to understand why they occur. The student reader who tackles his or her studies in this way will never have the mortification of going "blank" in the examination room and not being able to "repeat" those lines which have been so carefully committed to memory. The descriptions and technical details should be learned thoroughly, and applied in practice. Where slight alternatives to the standard technique have been given, these should be noted, and, more important still, the reason for such alternatives being suggested should be understood. Remember also that a technical knowledge of dancing is not even a half of the requirements of a successful teacher. The ability to give a good practical demonstration of dancing and to speak firmly and clearly (but not dictatorially) will always inspire confidence.

Note: It is important to work from the syllabus of your chosen society, obtainable from their Headquarters. Remember the figures used in this book are the author's choice.

**The Hold (Man's Back View)**

# THE HOLD

## Gentleman's Hold for the Quickstep, Waltz, and Foxtrot

Careful attention should be paid to the hold in ballroom dancing. A bad hold will not only give a dancer an appearance of bad style, but will also seriously affect the balance and the guiding.

Stand in an upright position with the feet close together. The body should be braced slightly at the waist, but not at the shoulders, which should remain free and at the normal level.

Although the position of the arms is to some extent a matter of individual style, the following hints, together with the accompanying illustration, will help the dancer to avoid anything that is ungainly.

1. The LEFT ARM should slope slightly downwards from the shoulder to the elbow, otherwise the shoulder will be lifted. This part of the arm should be kept well back so that the elbow is in a line with the man's back. A common fault is to allow the elbow to move forward, towards the lady, thus forcing the lady's Right arm backwards.

2. The LEFT ARM should bend quite sharply at the elbow, the forearm pointing upwards and slightly forwards from the elbow to the hand. The forearm may be taken slightly inwards from the elbow, so that the hand is nearer the head than the elbow. This must not be exaggerated otherwise the hold will be too compact and breadth lost. The arm should be definitely angled at the elbow. Held in this way it is much smarter and not so likely to annoy other dancers as when allowed to extend outwards.

3. The PALM of the LEFT HAND should be facing forward in a direction diagonally to the floor. The lady's Right hand should be held in a comfortable and "unfussy" manner. Most men hold the lady's fingers between the thumb and first finger, and then close the fingers over the side of her hand.

4. The LEFT WRIST must not bend. There should be an unbroken line from the elbow to the wrist, with the knuckles of the hand very slightly higher than the wrist. The hand should never bend downwards from the wrist.

5. The RIGHT ARM should slope downwards from the shoulder to the elbow in as near as possible the same line as the Left arm. This will depend to a great extent upon the height of the partner. The Right elbow will be more forward than the shoulder, owing to the hand being on the lady's back. It must not go too far forward nor must it be dropped close to the man's Right side.
6. The RIGHT HAND should be placed below the lady's Left shoulder blade. It should not be placed too far round the lady's back, or the Right shoulder will tend to drop.
7. The HEAD should be held in an easy upright position, and the man should normally look over the lady's Right shoulder.
8. POSITION WITH PARTNER. The man should endeavour to hold the lady in a position in front of him, *very slightly* to his Right side, but care must be taken not to let this position become too pronounced.

## The Hold for the Lady

The hold for the lady must always depend somewhat upon the man, but the following points should be observed:

1. Stand in an upright position, slightly braced at the waist, without raising the shoulders.
2. Stand in front of the man, very slightly to his Right side, but do not exaggerate this.
3. Raise the RIGHT HAND with the fingers together, and allow the man to take it to his normal position. The man generally holds the lady's fingers between his thumb and first finger. When he has taken his position, the thumb is closed over the thumb of his Left hand.
4. The RIGHT ARM may slope slightly downwards from the shoulder to the elbow and then upwards from the elbow to meet the man's hand.
5. The LEFT ARM should rest lightly on the man's Right arm and must not bear downwards.
6. The FINGERS of the LEFT HAND should be grouped neatly on the man's Right arm between the elbow and the shoulder, but nearer the latter.

The hold for the Tango is described in the Tango Section of this book.

## THE POISE, BALANCE AND GENERAL OUTLINE OF THE WALK

To be able to walk properly in a forward and backward direction is the basis of ballroom dancing, and with it are allied such important points as the Poise or Carriage of the body, the Balance, or correct distribution of weight, and the alignment of the feet.

The following notes should be studied very carefully.

### The Forward Walk – Gentleman

*Poise.* Stand in an upright position as described in the notes on the hold. The knees should be slightly relaxed, but not definitely bent. Now let the body incline forwards from the feet upwards, until the weight of the body is felt mainly on the balls of the feet, but not letting the heels leave the floor. In doing this take care not to alter the upright position of the body from the hips upwards. You are now in the correct position to commence the Walk.

*Movement of the Legs and Feet.* Note. For the purpose of this description the Walk is being commenced with the Right foot. There is no rule on this point. The man may commence with either Right foot or Left foot but must indicate his intention to his partner. This is dealt with under the heading of "Leading and Following".

Take the weight on to the Left foot only and proceed as follows. Swing the Right leg forward from the hips, first with the ball of the Right foot touching the floor, and then the heel skimming the floor with the toe slightly raised.

As the Right foot passes the toe of the Left foot, the Left heel will be released from the floor, so that at the full extent of the stride the ball of the Left foot and the heel of the Right foot will be touching the floor. Lower the Right toe immediately so that the foot is flat on the floor.

With the body still moving forward, bring the Left foot forward with just a little pressure on the ball of the foot, and swing it past the Right foot to repeat the whole movement described above.

*Distribution of the Weight in the Walk.* When commencing a Walk from a closed position, the weight must always be brought forward over the balls of the feet before a foot is moved.

In the actual Walk the weight is first on the stationary foot, at the full extent of the stride it is divided for a moment between the heel of the front foot and the ball of the rear foot. It is taken immediately on to the front foot as this foot becomes flat.

Points to remember are:

From a stationary position, always feel that the *body* commences to move slightly *before* the foot. Remember that the speed of the foot is always greater than the speed of the body. If the foot is moved before the body, the weight will be kept too far back and a "sitting down" effect will result.

The KNEES should be easily and naturally relaxed throughout the Walk. The legs are only straight at the full extent of the stride, but even then the knees are not rigid. They are most relaxed as the moving foot passes the supporting foot.

The ANKLES and INSTEPS should be kept free to allow a slight downward "flick" of the foot as the toe is lowered at the end of each forward walk.

The FEET must be kept straight, the insides of the feet at both the toes and heels brushing past each other every time the feet pass.

*Important Note.* Although standard technique demands that some part of the foot is kept in contact with the floor in all forward steps, the majority of advanced dancers do not adhere to this rule. When moving the back foot to a forward position the heel does not actually touch the floor until it reaches the full extent of the stride. The movement thus becomes softer and lighter than could be achieved with the heel in contact with the floor.

## The Backward Walk – Lady

The Backward Walk for the lady is much more difficult than the Forward Walk of the man. The movement for the man is but little removed from a natural walking step, whilst the lady is using her legs and muscles in a manner that is not employed in any other sport or recreation. For this reason it is not always possible for a novice, especially the older novice, immediately to adopt the poise and balance of an accomplished dancer. In the following notes the correct poise and balance are given first; some useful advice to the beginner who has difficulty in maintaining this poise and balance in the early stages is given later.

*Poise and Balance.* Stand in an upright position as described in the notes on the Hold. The knees should be slightly relaxed, but not definitely bent. The upper part of the body and the head should now be poised slightly backwards and to the left. This position in no way assists the balance, but certainly makes the couple look much more attractive. Care should be taken not to lean backwards too much, or an ugly arching of the back will result. Feel the weight mostly over the balls of the feet.

Now let the body incline slightly backwards from the feet upwards, until some of the weight of the body is felt over the heels. At this point, the man's body is commencing to incline forwards, and the backward inclining of the body by the lady must be taken from the man. Although the lady's body is inclining backward she should endeavour to resist the man's forward movement slightly, this resistance being felt at the lower part of the body. It should not be felt entirely at the hips as this will tend to impede the man's forward movement and make outside steps very difficult. The lady should not lean forward, or endeavour to keep her weight forward over the balls of the feet when she is moving backward. If this is done the resistance to the man's forward movement will be felt at the chest, and this will not only check the even flow of the walk but will make the lady feel heavy to her partner.

This poise is the most difficult thing for the lady to acquire, and is only possible if she has such control over the muscles of her legs as to enable her to lower her back heel at an even speed. This is explained in the following notes on the "Movement of the Legs and Feet". The beginner would be well advised to try to master this correct poise, but, as it is sometimes physically impossible with a middle-aged dancer, an alternative poise is given on page 14.

**The Hold (Lady's Back View)**

*Movement of the Legs and Feet.* Note. For the purpose of this description the Walk is being commenced with the Left foot. There is no rule on this point. It is always left to the man to determine and indicate to his partner the commencing foot.

Take the weight on to the Right foot only and proceed as follows:

Swing the Left foot back from the hips, first with the ball of the foot and then the toe skimming the floor. When the Left foot has passed the Right heel, the ball of the Right foot will be gradually released from the floor.

At the full extent of the stride, lower on to the *ball* of the Left foot, so that at this point the ball of the back foot and the heel of the front foot are touching the floor.

Continuing to move backward, move the Right foot back to the Left foot, and at the same time *slowly* lower the Left heel to the floor, *making sure that it does not touch the floor until the Right foot is level with it*. The Right foot is moved back with the heel on the floor, the ball of the foot being lowered as it reaches the Left foot. Continue the Walk with the Right foot.

The most important feature of the Backward Walk is the gradual lowering of the back heel, and it is the careful control of this that ensures the lady keeping contact with the man whilst maintaining a backward poise.

*Distribution of the Weight in the Walk.* When commencing a Walk from a closed position, the weight must always be taken back over the heels before a foot is moved.

In the actual Walk the weight is first on the stationary foot. At the full extent of the stride it is divided for a moment between the heel of the front foot and the ball of the back foot. It is then taken on to the back foot, with slight pressure retained on the heel of the front foot.

Points to remember are:

From a stationary position, always feel that the *body* commences to move slightly *before* the foot.

Do not cling to the floor with the ball of the front foot, but release it gradually as the moving leg goes back.

The KNEES should be easily and naturally relaxed throughout the Walk. The legs are only straight at the full extent of the stride, but even then the knees are not rigid. The greatest relaxation is when the moving foot passes the supporting foot.

The ANKLES and INSTEPS should be kept free. If the ankles are stiff when the foot moves back, the stride will be considerably curtailed.

The FEET must be kept straight, the insides of the feet at both the toes and heels brushing past each other every time the feet pass. The usual fault is for the lady to allow her Left foot to move slightly to the Left instead of straight back. This causes her weight to be thrown against the man's Right arm and gives a definite feeling of heaviness.

## Alternative Poise for the Lady and Hints to the Beginner

The Poise described on page 11 is not easy to acquire, and the novice would be well advised not to attempt to poise herself backward, unless the balance of the body can be controlled and kept in that position without the feeling of pulling away from the partner. A good method of practising the balance of the Walk is as follows:

Take a long step backward with the Left foot and stand balanced with the weight evenly divided between the heel of the front foot and the ball of the rear foot. Now slowly move the front foot back, and make sure that the heel of the back foot does not touch the floor until the Right foot closes. Keep the arms extended sideways and, if necessary, keep the fingers of one hand touching the wall to assist the balance at first. When this can be done with ease, try to move backwards round the room, making sure to check any tendency to topple backwards.

If difficulty is experienced it is advisable not to attempt a backward poise when dancing with a partner, but to stand upright, and endeavour to keep the weight forward as long as possible.

Although, danced in this way, the Walk will not feel so easy to the partner as when danced in the correct manner, it will feel much more comfortable than the heavy "pulling away" effect that must inevitably result when the weight is dropped back to the heel too quickly.

## The Backward Walk – Man

Normally the man does not do a succession of Backward Walks except in the Foxtrot. Although the actions of the feet and legs are similar to those described for the Backward Walk of the lady, the man must remember to retain the same poise of the body as for a Forward Walk. The positions are not reversed when the man moves backward and it would be quite wrong for the lady to adopt a forward poise and take control over the man.

## The Forward Walk – Lady

Although the actions of the feet and legs are similar to those described for the Forward Walk of the man, the lady must not alter the poise of her body. She can materially assist the man's backward movements by pressing forward on forward steps, but any attempt to do this with a forward poise of the body would completely upset the man's balance. The man must retain control whether moving forward or backward.

# CONTRARY BODY MOVEMENT

Contrary Body Movement is the action of turning the opposite hip and shoulder towards the direction of the moving leg, and is used to commence all turning movements.

To the novice, the term "Contrary Body Movement" may appear rather frightening. In many cases, the term "Body Swing" would probably convey this turning action more clearly, for it should be noted at once that an excess of Contrary Body Movement will produce a dance that is more ugly and unbalanced than one entirely devoid of it.

Since it is essential that even the beginner should understand the elementary factors that govern turning movements in dancing, the following points should be noted.

There are four principal ways of turning in dancing. A turn to either the Right or the Left can be made when moving forwards, and also a turn to the Right or Left when moving backwards. The Contrary Body Movement in these turns would be as follows:

1.  *Forward Turn to the Right.* Step forward with the Right foot and at the same time swing the Left hip and shoulder forward.
2.  *Forward Turn to the Left.* Step forward with the Left foot and at the same time swing the Right hip and shoulder forward.
3.  *Backward Turn to the Right.* Step back with the Left foot and at the same time swing the Right hip and shoulder backward.
4.  *Backward Turn to the Left.* Step back with the Right foot and at the same time swing the Left hip and shoulder backward.

It should be remembered that, with the exception of the pivot type of movement, this contrary swing of the body is in no way a "stationary" action. If a forward turn to the Right is being made it is far more important to feel a *forward swing* of the Left side of the body than a conscious twist of the body to the Right.

Although Contrary Body Movement must embrace the turning of both the hip and the shoulder, it is sometimes helpful to try to feel that, in forward turns, the movement is initiated in the shoulders, and, in backward turns, from the hips. This subtle difference in the mental approach of these two different turns should prove helpful to the novice.

Care must be taken not to turn the shoulders independently or an ugly dipping movement will result.

A most important point to remember is that Contrary Body Movement does not alter the direction of a step. A common fault with many dancers is to alter the alignment of a step as Contrary Body Movement is used. An example of this is:

*Facing the Line of Dance with the Right foot free, ready to make a forward turn to the Right.* As the Right foot moves forward and the body turns to the Right many dancers allow the Right foot to travel in a direction diagonal to the wall. This is wrong. It is only the body that turns away from the Line of Dance. The Right foot must move straight forward, or, if anything, cover in slightly in front of the other foot. The same rule applies to backward turning steps, although to step directly behind the stationary foot is not often possible when moving backwards.

## Contrary Body Movement Position

Contrary Body Movement, as described above, is a movement of the body. Contrary Body Movement *Position* is the position attained when either foot is placed across the front or the back of the body without the body turning. It is, therefore, a foot position, but in some cases Contrary Body *Movement* is used at the same time.

Even the novice should remember that every step taken outside partner, or with the partner outside, must be placed across the body in *CBMP* to ensure that the two bodies are kept in close contact.

Contrary Body Movement Position also occurs frequently in the Tango and in all Promenade figures.

# FOOTWORK

The term *Footwork* in Ballroom Dancing now has a definite technical meaning. At one time Footwork was almost entirely governed by Rise and Fall, but nowadays these two headings are separated. *Rise and Fall* now refers to the upward lift and lowering felt by advanced dancers in the *body* (which includes the legs, of course), and *Footwork* has been simplified to convey which part of the foot is in contact with the floor on each step.

Body Rise has been dealt with in the following pages and is of little interest to the beginner. Footwork, however, has a definite practical value, and the simple manner in which it is described will make it very easy for the beginner to gain an elementary knowledge of the correct placing of the feet in all steps. The more advanced dancer and the student should endeavour to understand the basic principles of this method of describing Footwork, and these are given below. They refer to Footwork used in the Quickstep, Waltz, and Foxtrot only. The

Tango footwork is dealt with in the section dealing with that dance.

Only the terms *Heel* and *Toe* are used. The use of the term *Ball of Foot* has been omitted, and *Toe* includes the ball of the foot as well as the higher position on the toes.

The use of the term Heel or Toe is meant to convey which part of the foot is in actual contact with the floor. Note, however, the following rules:

1. A forward walk on RF, then on LF would be described as 1. Heel 2. Heel. The fact that the whole of the RF lowers to the floor immediately is assumed, but not mentioned. It is also obvious that when the LF moves forward, the heel of the RF will naturally leave the floor, as described in the Forward Walk of the man. Again this is assumed, but not mentioned.

2. A forward step on RF followed by a forward step or side step on the LF, *taken on the toes*, would be given as: 1. Heel, Toe 2. Toe.

3. Two backward walks, on LF then RF would be described as: 1. Toe, Heel 2. Toe. This indicates that the Toe of the LF is in contact with the floor first, then lowering to the Heel. On the second step only Toe is mentioned as the R. Heel does not lower until the LF passes the RF to continue with another step.

4. A backward step on the RF followed by a backward or side step on the LF, taken with a *rise to the Toes*, would be: 1. Toe, Heel, Toe 2. Toe. This indicates that the R Heel will leave the floor as the LF passes the RF for the next step. This footwork seldom occurs.

5. A backward step on the RF followed by a side step on the LF, which is taken on the Toes would be: 1. Toe Heel 2. Toe. This indicates that the R Heel is still on the floor until the LF has been placed in position on the Toe. It is, however, most important to remember that when a foot begins to close from a side step, it must be done with the toe in contact with the floor. This means that although the footwork of 1 (RF) is Toe, Heel, as the RF closes towards the LF for the 3rd step, it must close with the R Toe in contact with the floor.

It may be thought by some students that it would be clearer to give the footwork on 1 as Toe, Heel, Toe, but this would be quite wrong as it would indicate that the R Heel leaves the floor as the LF passes it on its way to the second step. To do this would result in an early rise and a stilted movement. The following example will help students to understand this method.

Reverse Turn (Waltz) – Lady; Footwork:

1. Toe, Heel
2. Toe
3. Toe, Heel
4. Heel, Toe
5. Toe
6. Toe, Heel

Although this method of giving Footwork makes it quite clear which part of the foot is in contact with the floor when a step is taken, it does not adequately cover the passage of the foot from one step to another. While this is fairly obvious in forward movements, it is not always clear when moving backwards. Two good rules to remember are:

1. Any time a foot is moved to close to a step that has been taken sideways it moves with the Toe in contact with the floor. Not only should the toe be in contact with the floor but firm pressure should be placed on it. Some advanced dancers tend to let this toe leave the floor as it closes to a side step (for instance, between 1 and 3 of a Lady's Natural Turn, Waltz) and the consequent lack of control results in an untidy closing of the feet.
2. In a succession of backward movements as used in the Foxtrot, if the Footwork on 1. (LF) is Toe, Heel, when the LF moves back for the third step it will move back with the Heel on the floor, and with the Toe slightly raised as in a normal backward walk.

If the Footwork on 1. (LF) is Toe (or Toe, Heel, Toe) when the LF moves back for the third step, it will be move with the Toe in contact with the floor.

Less normal, but quite important terms also used in describing Footwork are *Inside edge of Toe* and *Inside edge of Foot*. Such terms will be found self-explanatory.

Additional notes on the correct use of the feet, especially after a rise, will be found in the following notes on Rise and Fall.

## RISE AND FALL – BODY

The rise and fall used in the feet is covered by Footwork, although it is to be regretted that this method of describing Footwork hardly gives a clear or true picture of the subtle uses of the ball of the foot as well as the toes.

As mentioned in the previous section, Footwork will cover the early requirements of the beginner. Body Rise is something that must be studied by the keen dancer wishing to reach a high standard, as this will add expression to their dancing, and it is not too much to say that no dancer can hope to be first class unless the subject is understood.

It must be remembered that the legs are a part of the body and, in fact, much of the Body Rise used in dancing is the result of the bracing of the muscles of the legs. The reaction to this will be felt in the body far more than any elevation taken from the feet without the co-ordinated use of these muscles. In addition, there are steps where the dancer should feel a slight "stretch" in the trunk of the body, but this upward stretch, if overdone, can have bad results. Normally, as mentioned in the remarks on the Walk, the dancer should be slightly braced at the waist at all times, and any effort to stretch or lift the body higher is likely to result in the shoulders being raised when attempted by inexperienced dancers.

There are three different types of Body Rise used in the Waltz, Foxtrot, and Quickstep, and if the student will endeavour to learn and understand these, the subject will present no difficulties when applying Body Rise to any figure in these dances. It will be noticed in the following examples that the term *No Foot Rise* has been used, and this denotes a later rise in the feet on the inside of all turns. It is a sound point and its use makes the Body Rise far easier to understand. The different types of Body Rise in use are as follows.

## Natural Turn – Waltz

### Man

*Commence* to rise at the end of 1.
Continue to rise on 2 and 3.
Lower at the end of 3.
*Commence* to rise at the end of 4. (No foot rise.)
Continue to rise on 5 and 6.
Lower at the end of 6.

The words "Continue to rise" indicate that most of the rise is felt towards the end of each part of the turn; between 2 and 3 and then between 5 and 6. The term no foot rise makes it clear that the Left Heel is kept in contact with the floor until the Right Foot is in position.

## Natural Turn – Quickstep

### Man

*Rise* at the end of 1.
*Up* on 2 and 3.
Lower at the end of 3.
No more rise.

### Lady

*Rise* at the end of 1. (No foot rise.)
*Up* on 2 and 3.
Lower at the end of 3.
No more rise.

The use of "Up" on 2 denotes an earlier rise than in a Closed Turn in the Waltz, which is due to the faster speed of the Quickstep music. This type of rise is used in all Chassé Turns in the Quickstep. Exceptions are the first part of the Quarter Turns and the Progressive Chassé, where the rise is continued for three steps instead of two steps as in other turns. In these figures, and in a Lock step which also has a rise for three steps, the Body Rise is: commence to rise at end of 1; *continue* to rise for 2 and 3; up on 4. The rise is thus more gradual than in normal Chassé Turns.

## Natural Turn – Foxtrot

### Man

Rise at the end of 1.
Up on 2 and 3.
Lower at the end of 3.
No more rise.

### Lady

*Rise slightly* at the end of 1. (No foot rise.)
Continue to rise on 2.
Up on 3.
Lower at the end of 3.
No more rise.

Once again the use of *up* denotes an early rise for the man, who is on the outside of the turn.

The lady is on the inside of the turn and the slight bracing of the muscles of the L leg at the end of the first step will cause her to rise slightly. This rise is continued as the legs are braced further on the actual Heel Turn. *No foot rise* is used to indicate that the feet are flat even though a slight body rise is used. She will be *up* and feel the body well braced as the third step is taken. Care must be taken to release the Heel of the foot supporting the weight, very gradually, and not rise abruptly to the toes as the third step moves forward.

This type of rise is used in all Open Turns in the Foxtrot, and in the Double Reverse Spin in Waltz and Quickstep. In other words the lady will use this type of rise on heel turns when the man is using a rise.

These specimen rises cover practically all the turns in the moving dances, and careful study will show that they are comparatively easy to understand.

One further point which should be understood by the student is what is meant by the "end of a step". The following notes will be of assistance:

1. *A Forward Step.* The end of this step is when the moving foot is passing the foot supporting the weight, and the heel of the supporting foot will then be released from the floor.

2. *A Backward Step*. The end of this step is when the moving foot is passing the foot supporting the weight.
3. *A Side Step*. The end of a Side Step, such as the 2nd step of a Natural Turn in the Waltz when the feet are to close on the 3rd step, is approximately when the third step has closed half-way towards the second step. The end of a Side Step which is to be followed by a step forward or backward is when the moving foot is passing the foot supporting the weight.

## No Foot Rise

It has been explained in the preceding notes that the term *no foot rise* has been added in cases where a Body Rise is used while the foot supporting the weight of the body is still kept flat. It will help students if they appreciate that no foot rise occurs between 1 and 2 of all *Inside* Turns. (In the Natural Turn in the Waltz, the man is on the outside of the turn on the first part and on the inside of the turn on the second part.) Even in the Progressive Chassé (Quickstep) the man's R heel is still down when the LF is in position on the 2nd step. The one notable exception to this rule is between steps 4 and 5 of the man's Reverse Turn in the Foxtrot. In this figure, although the man is on the inside of the turn he will rise with the *feet and body* between steps 4 and 5. His forward poise and desire to swing forward into the Feather Finish are the reasons for this earlier rise.

In all forward movements in the Foxtrot, such as the Feather and Three Step, the man's forward poise and swing will again result in the lady having no foot rise, although she will feel a body rise by bracing the legs. This does not apply in a Forward Lock in the Quickstep where the direction of the steps is more diagonally forward in relation to the body. In such figures she will have no foot rise on the first step only.

No foot rise for the lady will also occur between steps 1 and 2 of such figures as the Closed Change in the Waltz and the

Cross Chassé in the Quickstep. The forward poise of the man is again responsible for this, even though no turn is being made.

## An Important Note

Although the technique has dealt comprehensively with the Rise and Fall and with the Footwork of all basic figures, one most important point has been completely neglected.

With very few exceptions a Rise is preceded by a softening of the knee of the supporting leg. As an example, it would be quite wrong to assume that in a Natural Turn in the Waltz the first step is taken forward with the leg straight and that the following rise is immediately achieved by further bracing of the muscles of the R leg, or by "lift" in the feet or body.

It is most important to remember that any leading step, forward or backward, is followed by a softening of the knee as the weight is taken on to that step. This will mean that the dancer *lowers* slightly before commencing any rise. This softening of the knee on a leading step is to some extent even more important than the following rise, which in many cases will occur naturally if the correct forward swing and footwork have been used.

The relaxation of the knee must not be sharp. As the weight is taken over a step the knee will soften to prevent any "jar" in the movement. The subsequent straightening of the knee will materially assist the dancer to achieve a soft and flowing movement during the following turn.

The degree of relaxation will very much depend on the speed of the music. Greatest relaxation of the knee is felt on the first step of Waltz Turns. In the Foxtrot it will be noted that there is more relaxation on the first step of a Feather than on the first step of a Natural Turn, where too much relaxation would seriously impede the swing into the turn.

## AMOUNT OF TURN

For examination work it is necessary for students to know the amount of turn made on each figure and, in some cases, between each step. This is of little interest to the beginner as the amount of turn is covered by the descriptions and the diagrams.

It is obvious, however, that a teacher or student training for the profession should be able to state how much turn is made between each step when a turn is used. The use of the fractions *one-eighth* and *three-eighths* may appear complicated at first but they are necessary to ensure accuracy.

It should be noted that the amount of turn is measured from the positions of the feet, which is a little disconcerting at first. It would appear to be easier to take the amount of turn from where the body is facing, but in practice this becomes even more complicated.

An instance of how the amount of turn is assessed can be taken from the first three steps of the lady's Natural Turn in the Waltz. After stepping back diagonally to wall on the first step, her second step is placed to the side with the R toe pointing down the LOD. The amount of turn is, therefore, given as three-eighths of a turn, although the body has turned slightly less.

The keen student will soon observe that although the turn is continued with the feet on the outside of every turn, on the inside of the turns the feet are always placed with the toe pointing to the required position, and no swivel of the foot is used. This can be seen quite clearly in the diagrams and it is very important to observe this rule when dancing. The few exceptions to the rule are noted in the descriptions.

The following example is given to assist students:

## Natural Turn (Waltz), Man – Amount of Turn

¼ turn between 1 and 2.
⅛ turn between 2 and 3.
⅜ turn between 4 and 5, the body having turned less.
Body completes the turn between 5 and 6.

The man is on the outside of the turn on steps 1 to 3, and has a greater distance to travel, hence the continuing of the turn with the feet on this part of the figure. On steps 4 to 6 he is on the inside of the turn and will need no foot swivel.

## ALIGNMENT

The general meaning of the word *Alignment* has been given in the section on Definitions of Technical Terms on page 30.

In the revised technique *Alignment* is assumed to refer to the position or direction the *feet* are pointing in relation to the room.

The alignment of each step is made clear in the descriptions or diagrams of each figure, and has not been given in detail in the technical notes following each description.

Students should note that three terms are used in connection with alignment. They are *Facing, Backing,* and *Pointing.* Facing and Backing are self-explanatory. Pointing is used on side steps when the foot is pointing in a direction different from the way the body is facing. The following example will help students to understand these terms:

## Natural Turn (Waltz), Man – Alignment

1. Facing diag. to wall.
2. Backing diag. to centre.
3. Backing LOD.
4. Backing LOD.
5. *Pointing* diag. to centre.
6. Facing diag. to centre.

Pointing is used on step 5 because the RF is pointing diag. to centre while the body is facing centre.

Pointing is also used in some Promenade steps to give a clearer picture of the position of the foot.

## BODY SWAYS

Body Sways in ballroom dancing are used chiefly for effect, although in a few turns even the novice may find them of practical value. The following notes regarding Sways should be helpful:

Sways should be made by inclining the body to the Left or Right.

Sways can be used on nearly all turns. Exceptions are all Spins, where the turn is too quick to permit Sway to be used with comfort. Sway is also used on figures that curve or wave and in some side figures such as the Cross Chassé.

All turns are initiated by a Contrary Body Movement step, and Sway is taken directly following this step. If the Contrary Body Movement step is with the Right foot, the inclination of the Sway will be to the Right; if with the Left foot, then the Sway will be to the Left, whether this step has been taken forward or backward. The Sway is usually held for the following two steps and will be corrected at the next Contrary Body Movement step. Sways sometimes occur on one step only. Details of the correct steps on which the body should sway are given with the descriptions of each figure.

The main principle of swaying is to incline the body towards the centre of the turn. Thus the practical value of swaying would be found in its assistance in preventing the dancer from overbalancing or overturning. This is most marked in the Waltz, and even the beginner may find that a slight inclination of the body *against* the direction he is moving will prove helpful and assist in preserving balance.

The greatest value of swaying, however, is purely decorative, and the keen dancer will find that a careful study of the correct Sways in the descriptions of the various figures will make the resultant dance much more attractive. To oversway, however, is a much worse fault than not swaying at all.

## LEADING AND FOLLOWING

There being no set sequence of steps in modern dancing, the responsibility of leading from one figure to another rests *entirely* with the man. The lady's part is to follow, whether the man is dancing a figure correctly or not.

Most of the leading for the turns is done by the turning action of the man's body combined with a *very slight* pressure with his Right hand. The Right hand must not be used to pull or push the partner, but rather to keep an even pressure, thus ensuring that the lady feels from the man's body action the amount of turn that is being made. This pressure should be obtained by a slight inward movement of the forearm and not from the hand alone. The base of the Right hand and the Right fingers are only used to turn the lady into, and back from, Promenade Position. The Left hand and arm must not be used in guiding. They must be kept still.

It will be seen that it is of the utmost importance for the lady to keep contact with the man and to keep her body perfectly still from the hips upward, in order to feel the lead for a turn at the proper moment. She must not anticipate – she must not have a mind of her own. She must just follow whatever the man does and not attempt to correct him.

Contact with the partner should not be at the hips only, but from the hips and the diaphragm. If the lady presses her hips forward so that the only contact with the man is at the hips, the lady's body will tend to be poised backward far too much and the forward movement of the man will be seriously restricted.

When commencing to dance it is most important that the man should indicate which foot he is using first. There is no rule; it is for the man to use the foot that seems most natural. To practise this, stand with a partner in the normal commencing position with the feet together. If wishing to commence with the Right foot move the Left foot very slightly to the Left and take the weight on to it. At the same time, move the lady slightly to her Right and she will automatically take her weight on to that foot and be ready to commence with her Left foot.

Here are a few more hints for men:

Don't hold your partner with a vice-like grip; you will interfere with her balance.

Don't hold your partner so loosely that she cannot feel your lead. A constant and even pressure is required.

Don't take very long steps if your partner is physically incapable of doing so. Adapt your stride to the normal length of your partner's.

Don't try intricate steps in a crowded ballroom.

## ABBREVIATIONS

used in this book and in Ballroom Dancing Descriptions.

| | | | |
|---|---|---|---|
| S | A slow step | NFR | No foot rise |
| Q | A quick step | CBM | Contrary Body Movement |
| R | Right | CBMP | Contrary Body Movement Position |
| L | Left | LOD | Line of Dance |
| RF | Right foot | PP | Promenade Position |
| LF | Left foot | OP | Outside partner |
| B | Ball of foot | PO | Partner outside |
| H | Heel | Diag. | Diagonal(ly) |
| T | Toe(s) | IE | Inside edge |

*Note.* Descriptions of many of these terms are included in "Definitions of Technical Terms," which follows.

## DEFINITIONS OF TECHNICAL TERMS

**Alignment.** This word has several meanings in dancing. It may refer to the position of the feet in a forward or backward step, when the feet should be perfectly in line, turned neither in nor out, and with the inside edge of each foot touching an imaginary line drawn through the middle of the body. It is also used to refer to the directional line of some part of a figure.

Its technical meaning for examination work is described on page 26.

**Amalgamation.**[*] A combination of two or more figures.

**Balance.** The correct distribution of the weight of the body when dancing.

**Basic Figure.** A figure that is considered to form a part of the basis of a particular dance.

**Brush.** When the moving foot is being taken from one open position to another open position, the word Brush is used to indicate that this foot must first close up to the foot supporting the weight of the body, but without the weight being changed.

**Chassé.** A figure of three steps in which the feet are closed on the 2nd step.

**Chassé Turn or Closed Turn.** A turn that is danced with a Chassé or with the feet closing on the 2nd or 3rd step.

**Contrary Body Movement.** The action of the body in turning figures. See pages 15–17.

**Contrary Body Movement Position.** A term used when the body is not turned, but the leg placed across the front or back of the body, so giving an appearance of Contrary Body Movement. See page 17.

**Fallaway Position.** A position used in advanced variations in which the man and lady move backwards in Promenade Position.

**Figure.**[*] A completed set of steps.

**Footwork.** This is dealt with on pages 17–20.

**Heel Pivot.** A turn on the heel of one foot only, in which no change of weight occurs. The Heel Pivot might be termed a "compact Chassé," and is used instead of a Chassé in the last part of the Quarter Turn to Left in the Quickstep. A full description is:

[*] See note on page 33.

After stepping back with the RF, turning the body to L (S), move LF towards RF, at the same time turning on the heel of RF (QQ), then close LF to RF without weight, LF is brought back with first the heel and then the ball of the foot skimming the floor. When the feet are closed, the ball of LF should be touching the floor with heel very slightly raised. The feet must be kept parallel throughout the turn with the LF slightly in advance.

The following step must be taken forward with the LF (S).

**Heel Turn.** A turn on the heel of the stepping foot the closing foot being kept parallel to it throughout The weight is transferred to the closing foot at the end of the turn. It should be noted that, although the major part of the turn is on the heel, it is actually commenced on the ball of the foot. This will occur naturally and is shown in the charts.

A Heel Turn is the backward part of an Open Turn.

**Heel Pull.** This is a type of Heel Turn used by the man in some backward Natural Turns. The feet may be kept apart instead of closed, and the weight is more forward than in a Heel Turn.

**Hesitation.** A figure or part of a figure in which progression is temporarily suspended, and the weight retained on one foot for more than one count.

**Hover.** A part of a figure in which the moving or turning of the body is checked, while the feet remain almost stationary.

**Line of Dance.** The normal line of forward progression along each of the four sides of the room.

**Natural Turn.** A turn to the R.

**Open Turn.** A turn in which the third step passes the second step instead of closing. The lady's counterpart to a man's Open Turn is usually a Heel Turn.

**Outside Partner.** This indicates a step taken forward by the lady or man that does not follow the partner's opposite foot but is taken to the R of both his (or her) feet. In such steps the bodies must keep close contact, the outside movement being achieved by stepping rather across the front of the body. The partner's step would be described "Partner Outside," and must be taken across the body at the back. Thus all such steps are placed in CBMP. In some advanced variations the outside step is taken on the Left side of the partner.

**Partner in Line,**
**Partner Square,**
**Square to Partner.**
$\left\{\vphantom{\begin{array}{c}a\\a\\a\\a\\a\end{array}}\right.$
Terms used to indicate that the couple are standing in the normal dance position, i.e. facing each other and with the man's and lady's feet approximately opposite each other.

**Pivot.** A turn on the ball of one foot, the other foot being kept in front or behind in CBMP.

**Poise.** The position of the body in relation to the feet.

**Promenade Position.** The position in which the man's R side and the lady's L side are kept in close contact, and the opposite sides of the bodies turned out to form a "V" shape. The feet are usually turned to the same direction as the body.

**Quick.** A term used in timing steps. A quick step always occupies half the time of a slow step.

**Reverse Turn.** A turn to the L.

**Rhythm.** The word "Rhythm" is used in a broad sense, and usually refers to the accented beats of the music which recur regularly and give character to the music. Rhythm, however, is something much more subtle than this. It might be likened to colour. There are basic colours from which the expert can produce an infinite variety of beautiful shades. Similarly we have basic rhythms in all our dance music. The expert musician will produce numerous subsidiary rhythms from these, thus giving the music an entirely different character, which the expert dancer will endeavour to express in his dancing.

**Rise and Fall.** This is dealt with on pages 20–24.

**Step.**[*] This usually refers to one movement of the foot, although from a "time value" point of view this is incorrect. In the case of a walk forward or backward, for instance, the time value of the step is not completed until the moving foot is drawn up to the foot supporting the weight, ready to commence another step. Thus, when instructed to rise at the end of a step the dancer should not commence to rise until the moving foot is passing the foot supporting the weight of the body.

**Sway.** This is dealt with on pages 27–28.

**Swivel.** A turn on the ball of one foot.

**Tempo.** This indicates the speed of the music. The approved speeds for the standard dances are:

Waltz    30 bars a minute    Quickstep  50 bars a minute
Foxtrot  30 bars a minute    Tango       33 bars a minute

**Time.** The number of beats in each bar of music.

**Variation.** A varied and more advanced figure, additional to the basic figures.

## HOW TO READ THE CHARTS

The diagrams will be found to be of great assistance to readers if the following points are understood:

The squares on which the feet are placed represent a size of 2 ft by 2 ft for each square. The feet have been drawn to the same scale.

The distances between the steps have been made as far as possible mathematically correct, so that the exact length of a step can be gauged. The distances shown represent an average step. When the dancer is proficient, the steps can be lengthened considerably, but only to a length that is consistent with ease of movement.

---

[*] The following analogy provides an easy method of remembering the meaning of the terms "step," "figure," and "amalgamation". Think of a step as a "syllable," a figure as a "word," and an amalgamation as a "sentence". A complete dance could be compared to a paragraph.

*Each figure was drawn in the first place with both the man's and the lady's steps on the same chart, so that if a chart is drawn to scale on the floor it should be possible for a couple to dance together using the exact positions shown in this book.*

The LOD is shown by an arrow on each chart. The right-hand edge of the page will represent the wall of the side of the room along which the dancer is moving.

When using the charts always hold the book so that the *toe* of each step you are looking at is pointing *away from you*. If a turn is made, turn the book also.

The RF is shown in black; the LF is outlined only. They are also marked "R" and "L".

When a foot is shown in dotted outline, this indicates a swivel on the ball or the heel of the foot to which it is connected, and shows the finishing position of that foot when that part of the turn has been made. Where only a slight swivel has been made this has been omitted.

It will be noted that in Heel Turns two dotted outlines are shown, indicating that the turn commences on the ball of the foot and continues on the heel of the same foot. No attempt should be made to commence the turn on the ball of the foot; this will occur naturally when dancing. It was necessary to include this to make the charts correspond with actual practice.

The lines connecting the feet give some idea of the path of the foot when moving to the next step.

## Special Notes

*Alignment.* The keen student of dancing should note that, technically, the leading step of any turning figure should be taken either straight forward or straight backward from the body, but in practice this is not quite possible in the case of *backward* turning steps, which tend to move *very slightly* outwards. The 4th step of the man's Natural Turn (Waltz) is an example.

In drawing the man's and lady's steps on one chart it was found necessary to show this slight loss of alignment; it was not possible to place the feet correctly without doing so.

The dancer should, however, take great care to keep such steps in alignment when possible.

*Parallel Positions.* Students are also warned that in the standard technique the 2nd step of some turns is described as being in a *parallel position.*

In practice, this parallel position of the feet is not possible when the feet are apart, as in the 2nd and 5th steps of the Natural and Reverse Turns in the Waltz. On most side steps the feet are turned slightly outwards, and any attempt to keep them parallel would seriously restrict the ease and flow of the turn.

It is also most important to remember that when taking a step to the side no attempt must be made to turn *on* the preceding step. To make an actual foot swivel on the first step would impede the movement.

The body should swing forward over the first step, and this will result in the heel leaving the floor quite naturally. It will then turn *as* the second step moves to the side.

## THE DESCRIPTIONS

The descriptions of each figure have been written in the simplest possible manner for the novice to understand them, and this happens to be a good way for the candidate to give an oral description of the figures in a professional examination if requested.

Details of the Contrary Body Movement, Rise and Fall, the amount of turn used, and useful hints regarding guiding and amalgamations are given afterwards.

It should be noted that in all turning figures the turn should be gradual. It is only in Pivots that the full amount of turn is completed on one step.

A number of positional and directional terms are used in the descriptions, and it is essential for the reader to commit these to memory. They are shown in the accompanying diagrams.

It is most important to remember that the positions of the steps in Diagram 1 are in relation to the body only. This means that such steps always move in the same direction from the body, irrespective of the position of the dancer in the room.

Diagram 2 indicates the various positions of the body and the directions of the steps *in relation to the room*.

Thus, the description "RF forward, diag. to wall" would mean a step taken straight forward from the body, and in a direction diagonally to the wall.

# Position of Steps in Relation to the Body

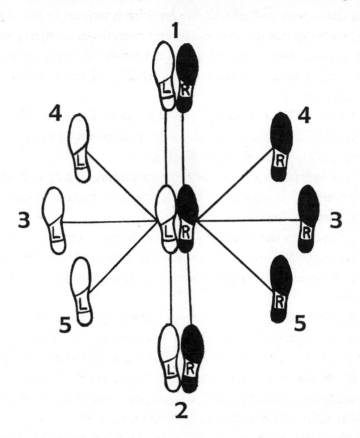

**DIAGRAM 1**
1. RF or LF forward
2. RF or LF back
3. RF or LF to side
4. RF or LF diagonally forward
5. RF or LF diagonally back

# Directions of Steps or Positions of Body in Relation to the Room

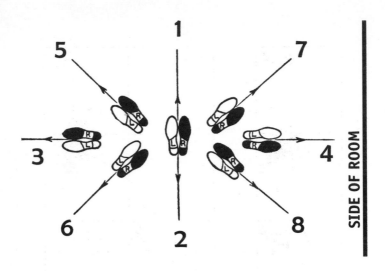

**DIAGRAM 2**

*Positions of Body in the Room*
1. Facing LOD
3. Facing Centre
4. Facing Wall
5. Facing Centre Diagonally
7. Facing Wall Diagonally

*Directions of Steps*
1. Down the LOD
2. Against the LOD
3. To Centre
5. Diagonally to the Centre
6. Diagonally to the Centre against the LOD
7. Diagonally to the Wall
8. Diagonally to the Wall against the LOD

**"Across the LOD".** Another term that has been used is "across the LOD". This term can easily be understood by referring to the diagram on page 39.

# Illustration of the Term
## "Across the Line of Dance"

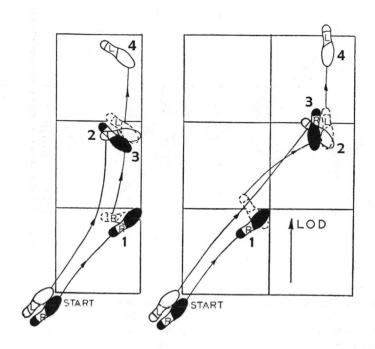

**Quarter Turn to Right (Man)**
The second step has been taken to the side on the same LOD as the first step

**Natural Turn (Man)**
The second step has been taken "across the LOD" of the first step

**"Centre."** Note that the "centre," as used in such expressions as "diagonally to the centre," is not the actual centre point of the room, but that part of the room which is on the man's L when he is facing the LOD.

# SECTION I

# THE QUICKSTEP

This dance might be termed the "joy" dance of modern dancing. Whilst the basic figures are quite simple, the tempo of the music and the whole character of the dance seem to invite a care-free interpretation of its bright rhythm. The beginner will find the basic steps easy to learn and easy to fit to music. The advanced dancer will discover that the music lends itself to an infinite variety of steps.

In most sports and pastimes, a sound knowledge of the basic work is necessary before the "frills" can be indulged in with any degree of pleasure. The dancer who masters the fundamentals of the Quickstep will have command of a dance that can never grow stale, a dance that is unquestionably the most attractive expression of rhythm the world has ever known.

## GENERAL NOTES

*Time.* 4/4. Four beats in a bar. The 1st and 3rd beats are accented.

*Tempo.* Music should be played at 50 bars a minute, although a slight latitude is permitted for Amateur tests.

*Basic Rhythms.* The figures consist of various combinations of "Slows" and "Quicks". Each "Slow" has 2 beats of music. The "Quicks" have 1 beat each.

## For the Beginner

The foundation of the Quickstep is the Walk and the Chassé, this latter figure usually being included as a part of the basic figures. The following suggestion regarding the order in which to learn the basic figures should prove useful to the beginner.

After the Walk:

*Quarter Turns.* These should be learned first.

*Natural Turn.* This is excellent groundwork for other figures and should be learnt in preference to the Natural Pivot Turn, which is the alternative turn to use at corners.

*Progressive Chassé and Forward Lock Step.* These two figures follow the above in popularity and it is advisable to learn them next.

*Reverse Turns.* The Chassé Reverse Turn is the most useful Reverse Turn; it is compact and easier to dance in a crowded room.

Further details of how to amalgamate these figures and to introduce other figures are given after the descriptions.

## THE WALK, FORWARD AND BACKWARD

A full description of the Walk is given on pages 9–15, and, although the ultimate aim of the dancer should be to construct the dance so that the Walk as a separate figure is eliminated, it is most essential to learn this first.

When the basic principles of the Walk have been mastered, put on the music at a fairly slow tempo – about 40 bars per minute – and gradually increase the speed as confidence is acquired.

The Walk should be practised alone, and then with a partner until it can be danced with ease and comfort in a forward and backward direction.

Special points to note in the Quickstep Walk are:

1. The steps will be slightly shorter than in the Foxtrot, owing to the quicker music.

2. For the same reason the knees will not relax quite so much as in the slower tempo.

Whilst practising the Walk pay careful attention to the Hold and the Poise of the body. If they are wrong now, they will most likely get worse when the more difficult figures are attempted.

## QUARTER TURNS TO RIGHT AND LEFT – MAN

The Quarter Turns are progressive movements and are important basic figures.

They consist of a Chassé Turn, making a quarter turn to the R, followed by a compact type of turn to the L known as a Heel Pivot. The Heel Pivot is rather too difficult for beginners, but the method of turning described below is similar to a Heel Pivot, and is better than substituting a Chassé Turn, which was formerly considered to be the only alternative open to a novice. A full description of the Heel Pivot is given on page 31.

The Quarter Turn to Right is normally commenced facing diagonally to the wall, although it may be commenced facing the LOD when preceded by a figure ending in that direction.

## QUARTER TURN TO RIGHT

### Man

1. RF forward, diag. to wall, turning body to R.          S
2. LF to side, on same LOD, body facing wall.             Q
3. Continue turning slightly and close RF to LF.          Q
4. LF to side and slightly back. Body now backing
   diag. to centre.                                       S

*Contrary Body Movement.* CBM on 1.

*Rise and Fall (Body).* Commence to rise at end of 1; continue to rise on 2 and 3; up on 4. Lower at end of 4. (Note the gradual rise).

*Body Sway.* Sway to R on 2 and 3; level on 4.

*Amount of Turn.* A quarter turn to R when commenced facing diagonally to the wall, or three-eighths when commenced facing the LOD.

*Footwork.* 1 H T. 2 T. 3 T. 4 T H.

*General Note.* It should be noted that the fourth step (LF) moves in a sideways direction along the LOD. Its actual position in relation to the body, however, will be side and slightly back.

## QUARTER TURN TO LEFT

### Man

1. RF back, diag. to centre, body turning to L.                S
2. Bring LF back to RF, heels together, L toe
   pointing diag. to wall.                                    Q
3. With slight pressure on ball of LF, close RF
   parallel to LF, turning on R heel.                        Q
4. LF forward, diag. to wall.                                 S

Steps 2 and 3 are a simplified way of dancing a Heel Pivot (described on page 31).

*Contrary Body Movement.* CBM on 1. Slight CBM on 4.

*Rise and Fall (Body).* Slight rise between 2 and 3 (NFR).

*Body Sway.* Sway to R on 2 and 3.

*Amount of Turn.* A quarter turn to left when commenced backing diagonally to the centre and ended facing diagonally to the wall. Three-eighths when ended facing the LOD. Three-eighths when commenced backing the LOD (following the Chassé Reverse Turn or the Quick Open Reverse) and ended facing diagonally to the wall.

*Footwork.* 1 T H. 2 H. 3 H (RF) pressure on T of LF. 4 H.

*General Note.* The Quarter Turn to Right and the Quarter Turn to Left are shown together in the diagram as this is their popular use.

## QUARTER TURNS TO RIGHT AND LEFT – LADY

The Quarter Turns are a progressive figure, turning alternately
to R and L by means of Chassé Turns.

## QUARTER TURN TO RIGHT

### Lady

1. LF back, diag. to wall, with body turning to R.     S
2. RF to side, on same LOD, body backing to wall.     Q
3. Close LF to RF (face diag. to centre).     Q
4. RF diag. forward.     S

*Contrary Body Movement.* CBM on 1.

*Rise and Fall (Body).* Commence to rise at end of 1 (NFR); continue
to rise on 2 and 3; up on 4. Lower at end of 4. (Note the gradual rise).

*Body Sway.* Sway to L on 2 and 3. Level on 4.

*Amount of Turn.* A quarter turn to R when commenced backing
diagonally to the wall, or three-eighths when commenced backing the
LOD.

*Footwork.* 1 T H. 2 T. 3 T. 4 T H.

*General Note.* It will be noticed that the lady's 4th step differs
slightly from the man's. The lady should tend to step "in" towards the
man on this step, so that it ends slightly between his feet.

## QUARTER TURN TO LEFT

### Lady

1. LF forward, diag. to centre, turning body to L.     S
2. RF to side, body backing towards wall.     Q
3. Continue turning and close LF to RF.     Q
4. RF back, diag. to wall.     S

*Contrary Body Movement.* CBM on 1.

*Rise and Fall (Body).* Rise at end of 1; up on 2 and 3. Lower at end
of 3.

*Body Sway.* Sway to L on 2 and 3.

*Amount of Turn.* A quarter turn to left when commenced facing diagonally to the centre and ended backing diagonally to the wall. Three-eighths when ended backing the LOD. Three-eighths when

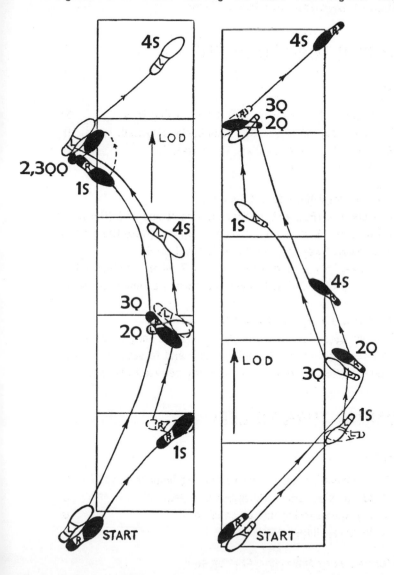

**Quarter Turns to Right and Left**
**Left: Man Right: Lady**

commenced facing the LOD (following the Chassé Reverse Turn or the Quick Open Reverse) and ended backing diagonally to the wall.

*Footwork.* 1 H T. 2 T. 3 T H. 4 T.

*General Note.* The Quarter Turn to Right and Quarter Turn to Left are shown together in the diagram as this is their popular use.

# PROGRESSIVE CHASSÉ

## Man

The Progressive Chassé finish to the Quarter Turn to Right is one of the most attractive movements in the Quickstep, however, the Quarter Turn to Left, with its small compact heel pivot type of turn, is always used when following with a reverse figure such as the Double Reverse Spin. The Progressive Chassé will be found more suitable when the Quarter Turn to Right is to be followed by a natural figure, or a variation that is commenced with the RF outside partner.

Commence facing diagonally to the wall, and then dance the Quarter Turn to R. SQQS. Continue:

1. RF back, diag. to centre, with body turning to L.     S
2. LF to side, along the LOD, body facing wall.     Q
3. Close RF to LF.     Q
4. LF to side, and slightly forward.     S
5. RF forward, outside partner, diag. to wall.     S

*Contrary Body Movement.* CBM on 1 and 5. The 5th step is placed in CBMP.

*Rise and Fall (Body).* Commence to rise at end of 1 (NFR); continue to rise on 2 and 3; up on 4. Lower at end of 4. Note the gradual rise which is completed only on the 3rd step.

*Body Sway.* There is no sway.

*Amount of Turn.* Make a quarter turn to the L.

*Footwork.* 1. T H. 2. T. 3. T. 4. T. H- 5. H.

*General Notes.* Care should be taken not to turn too much when dancing the wide Chassé (Steps 2, 3, 4). Keep the body practically square to the wall the whole time, otherwise the bodies will become out of alignment on the outside step.

The Progressive Chassé could be danced after the Natural Spin Turn, a Chassé Reverse Turn, or 1, 2, 3 of the Quick Open Reverse.

Follow the Progressive Chassé with:

1. Use the 5th step as the 1st step of a Natural Turn, or any natural figure.
2. Forward Lock. This is described on pages 62–63.
3. Any more advanced variation, such as the Fish Tail.

## PROGRESSIVE CHASSÉ

### Lady

The Progressive Chassé finish to the Quarter Turn to Right is one of the most attractive movements in the Quickstep. It is usually danced when the man wishes to follow the Quarter Turn with a figure that commences with a turn to the R. The Quarter Turn to Left is always used when a reverse figure is to follow.

Commence with the back diagonally to the wall, and then dance steps of the Quarter Turn to R. Finish facing diagonally to the centre. SQQS. Continue:

1. LF forward, diag. to centre, body turning to L.          S
2. RF to side, along the LOD, body facing centre.          Q
3. Close LF to RF                                          Q
4. RF to side, and slightly back.                          S
5. LF back, partner outside, diag. to wall.                S

*Contrary Body Movement.* CBM on 1 and 5. The 5th step is placed in CBMP.

*Rise and Fall (Body).* Commence to rise at end of 1; continue to rise on 2 and 3; up on 4. Lower at end of 4. Note the gradual rise.

*Body Sway.* There is no sway.

*Amount of Turn.* Make a quarter turn to the L.

*Footwork.* 1 H T. 2 T. 3 T. 4 T H. 5 T.

*General Notes.* The lady should have no difficulty in knowing which ending to the Quarter Turn is being used. When using the Progressive Chassé, the man's body will not turn so much to the L on the first step as when a Heel Pivot is employed.

## NATURAL TURN

### Man

The most useful figure to use at corners. It is sometimes more difficult to master than the Natural Pivot Turn (described later), but is excellent groundwork for similar figures in other dances.

It consists of a Chassé turn and a type of Heel Turn called a Heel Pull.

Commence facing the LOD or diagonally to the wall, the latter being the more comfortable position.

| | | |
|---|---|---|
| 1. | RF forward, turning body to R. | S |
| 2. | LF to side, across the LOD. | Q |
| 3. | Continue turning on ball of LF and close RF to LF. | Q |
| 4. | LF back, down the LOD and turning body to R. | S |
| 5. | Pull RF firmly back, at the same time turning to R on L heel. Finish with RF at the side of LF, feet parallel and slightly apart. Transfer weight to RF at end of step. | S |
| 6. | LF forward. | S |

*Contrary Body Movement.* CBM on 1 and 4; slight on 6.

*Rise and Fall (Body).* Rise at end of 1; Up for 2 and 3; lower at end of 3.

*Body Sway.* Sway to the R on 2 and 3.

*Amount of Turn.* When commenced diagonally to the wall near a corner, make three-eighths of a turn on the first three steps. On the Pull Step (4, 5, and 6) make either a quarter turn to face the new LOD or three-eighths to face diagonally to the wall of the new LOD.

*Footwork.* 1 H T. 2 T. 3 T H. 4 T H. 5 H, IE of foot, whole foot. 6 H.

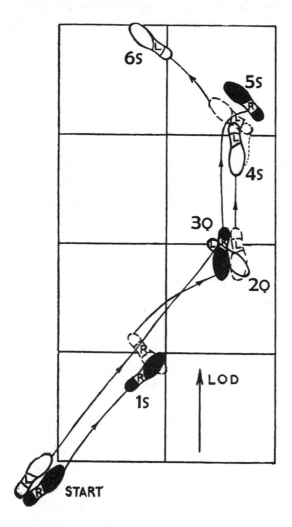

**Natural Turn (Man)**

*General Notes.* If the Natural Turn is used along the side of the room, the 5th step is wider, and then close LF to RF without weight. Count "S" (This is known as the Natural Turn with Hesitation and is similar to the Hesitation Change described fully in the Waltz section). Follow with the Chassé Reverse Turn or a Progressive Chassé to R.

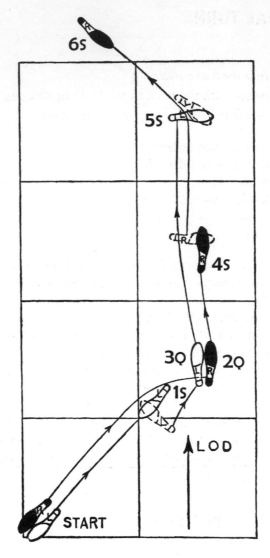

**Natural Turn (Lady)**

# NATURAL TURN

## Lady

This figure is used at corners.

Commence with the back to the LOD or diagonally to wall, the latter being the more comfortable position.

1. LF back, turning body to R.                        S
2. RF to side, across the LOD.                        Q
3. Close LF to RF.                                    Q
4. RF forward down LOD, turning body to R.            S
5. LF to side.                                        S
6. RF back.                                           S

*Contrary Body Movement.* CBM on 1 and 4; slight on 6.

*Rise and Fall (Body).* Rise at end of 1 (NFR); up on 2 and 3. Lower at end of 3.

*Body Sway.* Sway to the L on 2 and 3.

Amount of Turn. When commenced diagonally to the wall near a corner, make three-eighths of a turn on the first three steps. On steps 4, 5, and 6 make either a quarter turn to back the new LOD or three-eighths to back diagonally to the wall of the new LOD.

*Footwork.* 1 T H. 2 T. 3 T H. 4 H T. 5 T H. 6 T.

*General Notes.* If the Natural Turn is used along the side of the room the 5th step is wider. Close RF to LF without weight on step 6, count "S" (This is known as the Natural Turn with Hesitation. Please refer to man's General Notes.)

# NATURAL PIVOT TURN

## Man

This is an alternative right turn which is best when used at a corner. It consists of 1, 2, and 3 of the Natural Turn, followed by a Pivot. Although difficult to dance well, a beginner will sometimes find this figure easier to lead than the Natural Turn. It can be used by experienced dancers to progress along the sides of the room.

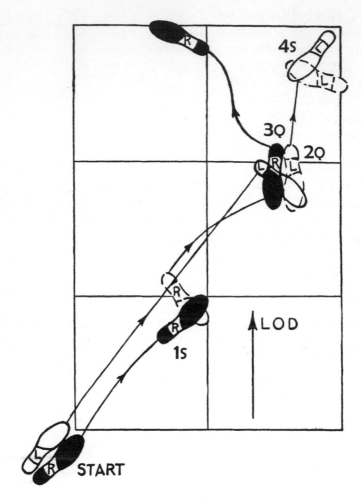

**Natural Pivot Turn (Man)**

The Natural Spin Turn is a better figure to employ for forward progression along the sides of the room.

Commence facing the LOD or facing diagonally to the wall, the latter being the better position.

1. RF forward, turning body to R.                                    S
2. LF to side, across the LOD.                                       Q
3. Continue turning on ball of LF and close RF to LF.                Q
4. Step back with the LF with toe turned in, and
   pivot three-eighths of a turn to R on the ball of LF.
   Keep RF in front.                                                 S

To continue, step forward on to RF diag. to wall of the new LOD and go into the Quarter Turn to R.

*Contrary Body Movement.* CBM on 1 and 4. As the pivot is made, the RF is held in CBMP.

*Rise and Fall (Body).* Rise at end of 1; up on 2 and 3. Lower at end of 3.

*Body Sway.* Sway to the R on 2 and 3.

*Amount of Turn.* From a diagonal position make three-eighths turn on the first three steps. The 4th step is made with the back to the LOD. Make three-eighths of a turn on the pivot. To continue along the same LOD, pivot a half-turn.

*Footwork.* 1. H T. 2 T. 3 T H. 4 T H T. Note: although footwork of step 4 is given as T H T the turn is made on the ball of the foot and with the heel in contact with the floor.

*General Notes.* The 4th step of the Pivot Turn is shorter than the 4th step of the Natural Turn and the knees are more relaxed. Beginners will find the Pivot quite easy to lead, by making the step back on the LF quite small, not letting the heel touch the floor, and keeping the weight forward. As this step is taken the man guides the lady with his R hand, so that her forward impetus is received on his R side. He will then turn quite easily to the R on the ball of the LF, and if the RF is kept forward, it will be ready to commence the Quarter Turn to R. Advanced dancers, with more control on the actual Pivot, will be able to get a slight forward thrust on the RF to swing into the Quarter Turn.

# NATURAL PIVOT TURN

## Lady

This is an alternative right-hand turn which should be used at a corner. It consists of 1, 2, and 3 of the Natural Turn, followed by a Pivoting action.

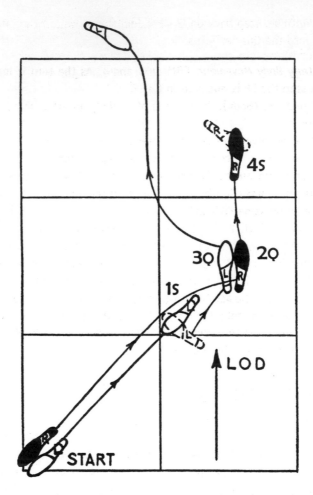

**Natural Pivot Turn (Lady)**

Commence with the back to the LOD or diagonally to the wall, the latter position being the more comfortable.

1. LF back, turning body to R.                                        S
2. RF to side, across the LOD.                                        Q
3. Close LF to RF.                                                    Q
4. RF forward and turn three-eighths of a turn to R
   with a **Pivoting** action.                                       S

To continue, step back on to LF diagonally to wall of the new LOD and go into the Quarter Turns.

*Contrary Body Movement.* CBM on 1 and 4. As the turn is made on the 4th step the LF is not held in CBMP.

*Rise and Fall (Body).* Rise at end of 1 (NFR); up on 2 and 3. Lower at end of 3.

*Body Sway.* Sway to the L on 2 and 3.

*Amount of Turn.* If commenced from a diagonal position make three-eighths of a turn on the first three steps. The 4th step is taken down the LOD and three-eighths of a turn is made on the 4th step. To continue along same LOD make a half-turn.

*Footwork.* 1 T H. 2 T. 3 T H. 4 H T H. Note: the turn on step 4 is made on the ball of RF with the heel in close contact with the floor.

*General Notes.* The man's fourth step will tend to move slightly leftwards and the lady should endeavour to step forward with her RF between his feet. The action on this step is like a pivot, but no attempt must be made to hold the LF in CBMP. The LF will move slightly leftwards during the turn, but should move backwards, with CBM for the first step of the following figure.

## NATURAL SPIN TURN

### Man

The Natural Spin Turn is in some respects a continuation of the Natural Pivot Turn. It is also used in the Waltz. A chart and fuller notes are inclued in the description of the figure in that dance.

Commence facing diagonally to the wall.

1, 2, 3. First three steps of Natural Turn.
   Finish with back to LOD.                                           SQQ
4. LF back (medium-length step with toe turned in)
   and pivot half a turn to R on the ball
   of the LF. Keep RF in front in CBM position.                          S
5. RF forward, down LOD, body still turning to R.                        S
6. LF to side and slightly back. Finish with back to
   centre diagonally.                                                    S

To continue, step back with RF into the Quarter Turn to L, the Progressive Chassé or Reverse Pivot.

*Contrary Body Movement.* CBM on 1, 4, and 5. The 5th step is in CBMP.

*Rise and Fall (Body).* Rise at end of 1; up on 2 and 3. Lower at end of 3. Rise at end of 5; up on 6. Lower at end of 6.

*Body Sway.* Sway to the R on 2 and 3. No sway on actual spin.

*Amount of Turn.* On steps 1 to 3 make three-eighths of a turn, a half-turn on 4, and three-eighths of a turn between steps 5 and 6. When taken at a corner make three-eighths turn on the Pivot (step 4) and a quarter between 5 and 6, to end backing diag. to centre of the new LOD. This smaller amount of turn is easier. Beginners should attempt this first.

*Footwork.* 1 H T. 2 T. 3 T H. 4 T H T. 5 H T. 6 T H.

The turn is made on the ball of foot on step 4, with the heel in contact with the floor.

*General Notes.* In leading the spin remember not to let the weight go too far back on 4.

## NATURAL SPIN TURN

### Lady

Commence backing diagonally to the wall.

| | |
|---|---|
| 1, 2, 3. First three steps of Natural Turn. | SQQ |
| 4. RF forward, and turn about half a turn to R on the ball of RF with a pivoting action. | S |
| 5. Still turning, move the LF back and slightly to side, down the LOD. | S |
| 6. Continue turning on ball of LF and take a small step diagonally forward with RF. Body facing diag. to centre. | S |

To continue, step forward with LF into the Quarter Turn to L or into the Progressive Chassé or Reverse Pivot.

*Contrary Body Movement.* CBM on 1 and 4.

*Rise and Fall (Body).* Rise at end of 1 (NFR); up on 2 and 3. Lower at end of 3. Rise at end of 5; up on 6. Lower at end of 6. The rise is taken from the ball of LF on 5.

*Body Sway.* Sway to L on 2 and 3.

*Amount of Turn.* On steps 1 to 3 make three-eighths of a turn. Make a half a turn on step 4 and three-eighths of a turn between 5 and 6.

*Footwork.* 1 T H. 2 T. 3 T H. 4 H T. 5 T. 6 T H.

*Note.* The moving of the LF sideways at the end of the pivoting action will result in the R heel leaving the floor and this heel will not lower again as it does when a back step, with CBM, is to follow.

*General Notes.* On the 6th step, the RF should brush lightly up to the LF before stepping diagonally forward.

# CHASSÉ REVERSE TURN

## Man

The Chassé Reverse Turn is a forward Chassé turn and is normally followed by the Quarter Turn to L, a Progressive Chassé or the Reverse Pivot.

Commence facing diagonally to the centre. Finish backing LOD.

1. LF forward, turning body to L.                    S
2. RF to side, across the LOD.                       Q
3. Continue turning on ball of RF and close LF to RF.   Q

*Contrary Body Movement.* CBM on 1.

*Rise and Fall (Body).* Rise at end of 1; up on 2 and 3. Lower at end of 3.

*Body Sway.* Sway to the L on 2 and 3.

*Amount of Turn.* Make three-eighths of a turn.

*Footwork.* 1 H T. 2 T. 3 T H.

*General Notes.* The best entry is the Natural Turn with Hesitation. (See notes on Natural Turn on pages 48-9.)

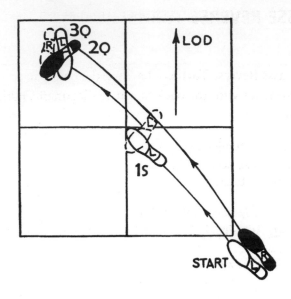

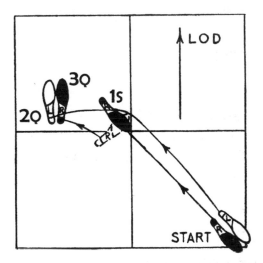

**Chassé Reverse Turn**
**Top: Man   Bottom: Lady**

# CHASSÉ REVERSE TURN

## Lady

The Chassé Reverse Turn is a backward Chassé turn.

Commence with the back to centre diagonally. Finish facing the LOD.

| | | |
|---|---|---|
| 1. | RF back, turning body to L. | S |
| 2. | LF to side, across LOD. | Q |
| 3. | Close RF to LF. | Q |

*Contrary Body Movement.* CBM on 1.

*Rise and Fall (Body).* Rise at end of 1 (NFR); up on 2 and 3. Lower at end of 3.

*Body Sway.* Sway to R on 2 and 3.

*Amount of Turn.* Make three-eighths of a turn.

*Footwork.* 1 T H. 2 T. 3 T H.

*General Notes.* Please refer to the notes on the man's steps.

# CROSS CHASSÉ

## Man

The Cross Chassé is a popular figure consisting of a Chassé taken to the man's R side and finishing forward outside the lady.

It is normally commenced and finished facing diagonally to the wall.

| | | |
|---|---|---|
| 1. | LF forward. | S |
| 2. | RF to side. | Q |
| 3. | Close LF to RF. | Q |
| 4. | RF forward, outside partner. | S |

*Contrary Body Movement.* Slight CBM on 1. CBM on 4 when using this step as the first step of a turning figure. The 4th step is taken well across the body in CBMP.

*Rise and Fall (Body).* Rise at end of 1; up on 2 and 3. Lower at end of 3.

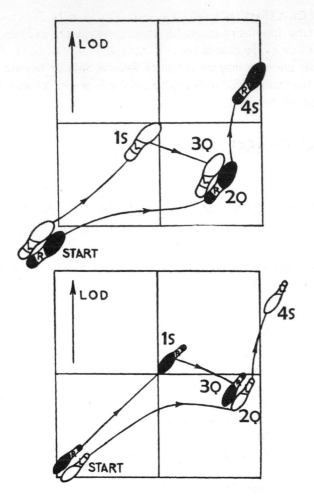

**Cross Chassé**
**Top: Man  Bottom: Lady**

*Body Sway.* Sway to the L on 2 and 3.

*Amount of Turn.* Normally there is no turn in this figure. A turn to the L is sometimes made in advanced variations.

*Footwork.* 1 H T. 2 5. 3 T H. 4 H.

*General Notes.* Care should be taken to keep contact with the partner when the RF is taken outside the lady on the 4th step.

The Cross Chassé is usually preceded by the Quarter Turn to L. End the Quarter Turn facing diagonally to wall and use the last step of the Quarter Turn as the first of the Cross Chassé.

Other precedes may be a Double Reverse Spin or Reverse Pivot. Follow the Cross Chassé with any Natural figure or with a Forward Lock, described on page 62.

# CROSS CHASSÉ

## Lady

An easy and popular figure in which the lady does a Chassé to her L, finishing with a step back on the LF with the partner's RF outside.

Normally commenced and finished with the back diagonally to the wall.

| | |
|---|---|
| 1. RF back. | S |
| 2. LF to side. | Q |
| 3. Close RF to LF. | Q |
| 4. LF back, with partner outside. | S |

*Contrary Body Movement.* Slight CBM on 1. CBM on 4 when following the Cross Chassé with a turning figure. The 4th step is taken well across the body in CBMP.

*Rise and Fall (Body).* Rise at end of 1 (NFR); up on 2 and 3. Lower at end of 3.

*Body Sway.* Sway to the R on 2 and 3.

*Amount of Turn.* Normally there is no turn in this figure. A turn to the L may be made in advanced variations, but this should never be done by beginners.

*Footwork.* 1 T H. 2 T. 3 T H. 4 T.

*General Notes.* The lady should make sure that her 4th step is taken well across the body, otherwise an ugly hip movement will result when the man steps outside. Keep the hips well forward as this step is taken.

# FORWARD LOCK

## Man

The Lock Step is a very popular figure.

It consists of a forward Chassé in which the feet are crossed on the second quick step.

It commences with a step forward on the RF, which must be taken outside the partner. The last step of the Progressive Chassé or Cross Chassé would form excellent entries to this figure.

The Forward Lock is normally commenced and finished facing diagonally to the wall.

| | | |
|---|---|---|
| 1. | RF forward, outside partner, diagonally to wall. | S |
| 2. | LF diag. forward. | Q |
| 3. | Cross RF behind LF. | Q |
| 4. | LF diag. forward. | S |
| 5. | RF forward, outside partner, diag. to wall. | S |

*Contrary Body Movement.* Slight CBM on 1. Steps 1 and 5 will be placed in CBMP. Use CBM on the 5th step of the Lock when following with a turn to R.

*Rise and Fall (Body).* Commence to rise at end of 1; continue to rise on 2 and 3. Up on 4. Lower at end of 4. Note the gradual rise.

*Body Sway.* There is no sway.

*Footwork.* 1 H T. 2 T. 3 T. 4 T H. 5 H.

*General Notes.* Although the figure travels diagonally to wall the body should be facing between the wall and diagonally to wall so that contact with partner is kept. The Lock is often danced backwards by the man after the Progressive Chassé to R. (Also see Zig Zag, Back Lock and Running Finish on page 67.) It would be followed with a Heel Pull or a Running Finish. Following the Progressive Chassé to R, the complete rhythm would be SQQSSQQSQQSS or SQQSSQQSSQQS. Either rhythm for the Running Finish is correct. It is a matter of personal expression. The description of a Lock taken backwards would be the same as given in the lady's Lock. Please also refer to page 67.

# LOCK STEP

## Lady

The Lock consists of a backward Chassé in which the feet are crossed on the second quick step.

It is danced when the man is dancing a Forward Lock. The last step of the Progressive Chassé or the Cross Chassé forms an excellent entry to this figure.

Normally commenced backing diagonally to the wall, in which position the above figures are ended.

| | | |
|---|---|---|
| 1. | LF back, diag. to wall, partner outside. | S |
| 2. | RF back. | Q |
| 3. | Cross LF in front of RF. | Q |
| 4. | RF diag. back. | S |
| 5. | LF back diag. to wall, partner outside. | S |

*Contrary Body Movement.* Slight CBM on 1. Steps 1 and 5 will be placed back in CBMP. Use CBM on the 5th step of the Lock Step when following with a turn to R.

*Rise and Fall (Body).* Commence to rise at end of 1 (NFR); continue to rise on 2 and 3; up on 4. Lower at end of 4. Note the gradual rise.

*Body Sway.* There is no sway.

*Footwork.* 1 T H. 2 T. 3 T. 4 T H. 5 T.

*General Notes.* Although the rise commences at the end of 1 there is no foot rise, and care should be taken to have the L heel in contact with the floor when this foot commences to move back to cross in front of RF on the third step.

The lady may dance a Forward Lock after a Progressive Chassé to R, when the description would be the same as given in the man's steps of the Lock. (Also see Zig Zag, Back Lock and Running Finish on page 67.)

## REVERSE PIVOT

### Man

This is a most useful and attractive figure of only one step and is used in place of a Heel Pivot to make a quick turn to the left. Notes on its uses are given below. See also the diagram on page 87.

Commence backing the LOD.

1. Slip RF back, under the body (small step) in a direction diag. to centre, with the toe turned in. Now pivot to L on ball of RF, holding LF forward in CBMP.                                                                S

*Contrary Body Movement.* CBM on 1. This step is also placed in CBMP and the LF is held forward in CBMP.

*Rise and Fall (Body).* There is no rise.

*Body Sway.* There is no sway.

*Amount of Turn.* An eighth of a turn to L is made between the preceding step and the pivot and up to a further three-eighths of a turn on the RF.

*Footwork.* 1. THT (but RF is kept practically flat).

*General Notes.* It is important to remember that the body commences to turn to L as the RF moves back, and this results in the RF moving in a direction diag. to centre and ending well under the body in CBMP. The weight should be kept forward. If the Pivot is commenced backing diag. to centre after a Natural Spin Turn or the Quarter Turn to R, the RF will move back in a direction to centre on the pivot. In some amalgamations the Reverse Pivot can be counted Q or "&".

The Reverse Pivot could be preceded by the Quarter Turn to R, the Natural Spin Turn, or Quick Open Reverse Turn, etc. Figures that could follow the pivot are:

(a) If ended facing diag. to wall. Cross Chassé or Cross Swivel.

(b) If ended facing LOD. The best endings are the Double Reverse Spin, a Quick Open Reverse or a Progressive Chassé to R.

## Lady

Commence facing the LOD.

1. Slip the LF forward (small step), in a direction
   diag. to centre, with body turning to L. Now pivot
   to L on ball of LF holding the RF at back in CBMP.     S

*Contrary Body Movement.* CBM on 1. The LF is also placed in CBMP
and the RF held in CBMP.

*Rise and Fall (Body).* There is no rise.

*Body Sway.* There is no sway.

*Amount of Turn.* An eighth of a turn to L is made between the
preceding step and the pivot and up to a further three-eighths of a
turn on the LF.

*Footwork.* 1 T H. (Turn is made on the ball of foot with the foot
practically flat.)

*General Notes.* The man should hold the lady firmly as he
commences the pivot and she will then feel his body turn to the L. The
lady will then automatically follow the direction of his RF with her LF.
Amalgamations are given under the man's steps.

# PROGRESSIVE CHASSÉ TO RIGHT

## Man

This is a delightful and most useful figure. It is similar to the
Progressive Chassé described on page 46 but danced moving to
the right instead of to the left, the man dancing the lady's steps
of a Progressive Chassé. It can be taken after a Natural Turn
with Hesitation, the Reverse Pivot or a Double Reverse Spin.

Commence facing diagonally to centre.

1. LF forward, diag. to centre, turning to L.                S
2. RF to side, with body backing towards wall.               Q
3. Close LF to RF, now backing diag., to wall.               Q
4. RF to side and slightly back, still moving
   sideways along LOD.                                       S
5. LF back, diag. to wall, partner outside.                  S

*Contrary Body Movement.* CBM on 1 and 5. The 5th step is placed in CBMP.

*Rise and Fall (Body).* Commence to rise at end of 1; continue to rise on 2 and 3; up on 4. Lower at end of 4.

*Body Sway.* There is no sway.

*Amount of Turn.* Make a quarter turn to L.

*Footwork.* 1 H T. 2 T. 3 T. 4 T H. 5 T.

*General Notes.* Although a quarter turn to L is made with the feet it is better to turn the body slightly less so that the body is backing between wall and diag. to wall on steps 3 to 5. Note the gradual rise which is most important. The Progressive Chassé to R may be commenced facing the LOD following the Quarter Turn to L, Reverse Pivot or Double Reverse Spin ended in this alignment, in which case a three-eighths turn is made on the Progressive Chassé to R. Good amalgamations are:

(a) Natural turn with Hesitation (see page 48), Progressive Chassé to R, Back Lock and Running Finish

(b) Natural Spin Turn and Reverse Pivot (ended facing diag. to centre or LOD), Progressive Chassé to R, the Tipple Chassé to R commenced backing diag. to wall

(c) Making a half turn to L on the Progressive Chassé to R to end backing diag. to centre "SQQSS", then bring lady in line and step RF back into 2 and 3 of the Outside Change (see Waltz section, pages 111-114) "QQ". Now step RF forward, outside partner, into a Forward Lock (or Fish Tail with no turn).

## PROGRESSIVE CHASSÉ TO RIGHT

### Lady

Commence backing diagonally to centre. The lady is dancing the man's steps of the Progressive Chassé.

| | | |
|---|---|---|
| 1. | RF back, diag. to centre, turning to L. | S |
| 2. | LF to side, along LOD, body facing wall. | Q |
| 3. | Close RF to LF. | Q |
| 4. | LF to side and slightly forward. | S |
| 5. | RF forward, diag. to wall, outside partner. | S |

*Contrary Body Movement.* CBM on 1 and 5. The 5th step is placed in CBMP.

*Rise and Fall (Body).* Commence to rise at end of 1 (NFR); continue to rise on 2 and 3; up on 4; Lower at end of 4

*Body Sway.* There is no sway.

*Amount of Turn.* Make a quarter turn to L.

*Footwork.* 1 T H. 2 T. 3 T. 4 T H. 5 H.

*General Notes.* On step 2 the LF will be pointing diag. to wall but when the RF closes, the body should be held between the wall and diag. to wall to ensure good contact with partner. The Progressive Chassé to R may be commenced backing the LOD, in which case three-eighths turn is made. Refer to man's General Notes for amalgamations.

# ZIG ZAG, BACK LOCK AND RUNNING FINISH

## Man

The figure originated from the Running Zig Zag, now seldom danced. It consists of the first part of the Zig Zag followed by a Back Lock, ending with a Running Finish. It is an important figure for the keen dancer to master as parts of it recur in more advanced variations.

Commence facing the LOD.

| | | |
|---|---|---|
| 1. | LF forward, turning body to L. | S |
| 2. | RF to side, on same LOD, back parallel to wall. | S |
| 3. | Continue turning slightly to L, and step back LF, partner outside, diag. to wall. | S |
| 4. | RF back. | Q |
| 5. | Cross LF in front of RF. | Q |
| 6. | RF diag back, still moving back diag. to wall. | S |
| | Now into the Running Finish: | |
| 7. | LF back, partner outside, turning body to R. | Q |
| 8. | RF to side and slightly forward with body almost facing the LOD. | Q |
| 9. | LF forward, preparing to step outside partner, L side leading. | S |
| 10. | RF forward, outside partner. | S |

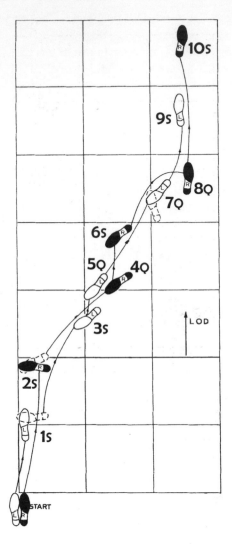

**Zig Zag, Back Lock and Running Finish (Man)**

*Contrary Body Movement.* CBM on 1, 3 (slight), 7 and 10. Steps 3, 7 and 10 are placed in CBMP.

*Rise and Fall (Body).* There is no rise on steps 1 and 2. Commence to rise at end of 3 (NFR) continue to rise on 4 and 5; up on 6; lower at end of 6. Rise at end of 7; up on 8 and 9; lower at end of 9. Note

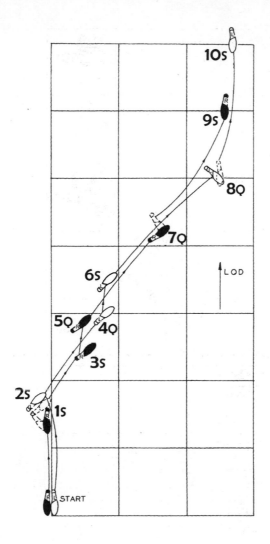

**Zig Zag, Back Lock and Running Finish (Lady)**

that the rise is taken from the ball of foot on step 7. The L heel does not lower to the floor.

*Body Sway*. Sway to L on 8 and 9.

*Amount of Turn*. There is a quarter turn to L between steps 1 and 2 and a slight turn to L between 2 and 3. Make three-eighths turn to R

**Promenade Position**

between 7 and 8. The body will turn slightly less and will complete the turn between steps 8 and 9.

*Footwork.* 1 H T. 2 T H. 3 T H. 4 T. 5 T. 6 T H. 7 T. 8 T. 9 T H. 10 H.

*General Notes.* Although step 3 moves back diag. to wall the body should be backing between wall and diag. to wall. This will ensure better contact with partner. Steps 7 to 10, the Running Finish, can be counted QQSS or SQQS. Both are correct. Try to use an upward stretch of the body on step 7 which will help the man to move freely and lightly on these steps. Step 10 will become the first step of any Natural figure.

## ZIG ZAG, LOCK AND RUNNING FINISH

### Lady

This is a very popular figure, consisting of the first part of the Zig Zag, a Forward Lock Step ending with a Running Finish. Commence backing the LOD.

| | | |
|---|---|---|
| 1. | RF back, turning body to L. | S |
| 2. | Close LF to RF turning on R heel and making a heel turn to face diag. to wall. | S |
| 3. | RF forward, outside partner, diag. to wall. | S |
| 4. | LF diag. forward. | Q |
| 5. | Cross RF behind LF. | Q |
| 6. | LF diag. forward, still moving diag. to wall. Now into the Running Finish: | S |
| 7. | RF forward, outside partner, turning body to R. | Q |
| 8. | LF to side, body backing diag. to centre. | Q |
| 9. | Still turning to R, step back RF, R side leading. Now moving back down LOD. | S |
| 10. | LF back, partner outside. | S |

*Contrary Body Movement.* CBM on 1, 3 (slight), 7 and 10. Steps 3, 7 and 10 are placed in CBMP.

*Rise and Fall (Body).* Commence to rise at end of 3: continue to rise on 4 and 5; up on 6; lower at end of 6. Rise at end of 7; up on 8 and 9; lower at end of 9.

*Body Sway.* Sway to R on 8 and 9.

*Amount of Turn.* Turn three-eighths to L between steps 1 and 2, the body turning slightly less, thus ensuring good contact when stepping outside on step 3. Turn a quarter to R between 7 and 8 and an eighth between 8 and 9.

*Footwork.* 1 T H. 2 H. 3 H T. 4 T. 5 T. 6 T H. 7 H T. 8 T. 9 T H. 10 T.

*General Notes.* When taking step 7 swing the body well forward into the step. This will help the man to dance the Running Finish with a free and flowing movement.

## TIPPLE CHASSÉ TO RIGHT

### Man

The Tipple Chassé to Right is a good ending to the first three steps of the Natural Turn and is a free moving figure to use at corners.

After 1, 2, 3 of a Natural Turn approaching a corner, dance the Tipple Chassé to Right, ended with steps 2 to 5 of a Forward Lock moving diag. to wall of the new LOD.

Commence backing the LOD near a corner.

| | | |
|---|---|---|
| 1. | LF back, down the LOD and turning body to R. | S |
| 2. | RF to side, now facing new LOD. | Q |
| 3. | Close LF to RF. | Q |
| 4. | Turning slightly to R, RF to side and slightly forward. | S |
| 5. | LF diag. forward, L side leading and moving diag. to wall. | Q |
| 6. | Cross RF behind LF. | Q |
| 7. | LF diag. forward, preparing to step outside partner. | S |
| 8. | RF forward, outside partner, diag. to wall. | S |

*Contrary Body Movement.* CBM on 1 and 8. Step 8 is placed in CBMP.

*Rise and Fall (Body).* Commence to rise at end of 1 (NFR); continue to rise on 2 and 3; up on 4 (see note); up on 5, 6 and 7; lower at end of 7.

*Note.* A slight flexing of the knees may be used on step 4, straightening as step 5 is taken. The R heel should not lower to the floor.

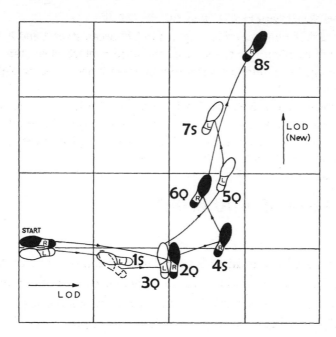

**Tipple Chassé to Right (Man)**

*Body Sway.* There is no sway.

*Amount of Turn.* Make a quarter to R between steps 1 and 2 and an eighth between steps 3 and 4.

*Footwork.* 1  T H. 2 T. 3 T. 4 T. 5 T. 6 T. 7 T H. 8 H.

*General Notes.* The body will turn a little quicker than usual between steps 1 and 2 to completely face the new LOD. After turning slightly to R as step 4 is taken, remember to soften the knee slightly before moving diag. forward into the Forward Lock. An alternative method of dancing the figure is given below.

Tipple Chassé to R with R Sway. Precede with steps 1, 2, 3 of the Natural Turn as usual. When dancing steps 1 to 4, turn only a quarter turn to R to end facing the new LOD. Step 4 will be taken to side – not side and slightly forward. Turn the head to the R for steps 2, 3, 4 and sway to the R. The rise will be: slight rise on 2 and 3. Lower on 4. Rise for the following Forward Lock, which will be danced diag. to centre of the new LOD: Commence to rise at end of 4; continue to rise on 5 and 6; up on 7. Lower at end of 7.

Footwork on step 4 will be: T H of RF and IE of T of LF.

The Tipple Chassé to R can be danced after 4 steps of a Natural Turn along the side of the room, when three-eighths turn will be made on the Chassé. It can also be danced after a Back Lock.

## TIPPLE CHASSÉ TO RIGHT

### Lady

The Tipple Chassé to Right is normally used after three steps of a Natural Turn.

Commence facing the LOD near a corner.

1. RF forward, down LOD turning body to R.                    S
2. LF to side, now backing new LOD.                          Q
3. Close RF to LF.                                           Q
4. Turning slightly to R, step to side and slightly
   back with LF.                                             S

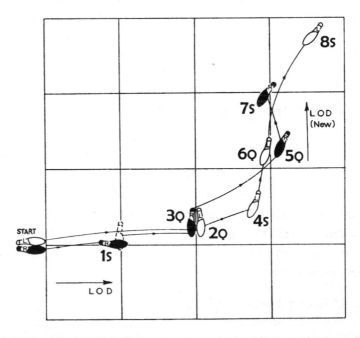

**Tipple Chassé to Right (Lady)**

5. RF back, R side leading and moving diag. to wall.     Q
6. Cross LF in front of RF.                              Q
7. RF diag. back.                                        S
8. LF back, partner outside, diag. to wall.              S

*Contrary Body Movement.* CBM on 1 and 8. The 8th step is placed in CBMP.

*Rise and Fall (Body).* Commence to rise at end of 1; continue to rise on 2 and 3, up on 4 (see note); up on 5, 6 and 7. Lower at end of 7.

*Body Sway.* There is no sway.

*Amount of Turn.* Make a quarter turn between steps 1 and 2 and an eighth between steps 3 and 4.

*Footwork.* 1 H T. 2 T. 3 T. 4 T. 5 T. 6 T. 7 T H. 8 T.

*General Notes.* If the man uses the slight flexing of the knees on step 4, the lady will soften her L knee, straightening again as the RF moves back for the Lock. The L heel should not lower to the floor.

When the man underturns the Tipple Chassé, as explained below the description of the man's steps, the lady will turn her head more to her L and sway to the L on steps 2, 3, 4. She will use only a slight rise on steps 2 and 3 and will lower on 4. Rise for the following Back Lock will be: commence to rise at end of 4; continue to rise on 5 and 6; up on 7. Lower at end of 7. Footwork on step 4 will be: T H  of LF and IE of T of RF.

# DOUBLE REVERSE SPIN

## Man

Originally a Waltz variation, this figure is now much used in the Quickstep. The name is rather misleading as there is no double spin, neither is it danced twice as its name might imply.

Commence facing the LOD. Finish facing diagonally to the wall, or down the LOD if wishing to continue into another reverse movement.

1. LF forward, turning body to L.                        S
2. RF to side, across LOD.                               S
3. 4. Continue turning on ball of RF and close
   LF to RF without weight (toe pivot).                  QQ

Then step forward with LF diag. to wall into the next figure.

*Contrary Body Movement.* CBM on 1.

*Rise and Fall (Body).* Rise at end of 1; up on 2, 3, and 4. Lower at end of 4.

*Body Sway.* There is no sway.

*Amount of Turn.* Make a complete turn or slightly less on the whole figure. The turn must be gradual. Do not force the turn on the 1st step. Most of the "swing" of the turn should be felt as the LF is closing. Three-eighths of a turn should be made on the first 2 steps.

*Footwork.* 1 H T. 2 T. 3 T (both feet). 4 T H (RF).

*General Notes.* The Double Reverse Spin is usually preceded by the Quarter Turn to L or a Reverse Pivot, which should be turned to face the LOD. Follow with a Cross Chassé or Cross Swivel. If the figure is turned to finish on the LOD go into any Reverse Figure.

A chart of this figure appears in the Waltz Section.

# DOUBLE REVERSE SPIN

## Lady

Commence backing the LOD.

1. RF back, turning body to L.                                    S
2. Close LF to RF, turning on R heel (Heel Turn).
   Finish facing LOD.                                            S
3. Continue turning on ball of LF and take a small
   step to the side and slightly back with RF.                   Q
4. Still turning slightly, cross LF in front of RF.              Q
   Then step back RF, diag. to wall into the next figure.

*Contrary Body Movement.* CBM on 1.

*Rise and Fall (Body).* Rise slightly at end of 1 (NFR); continue to rise on 2; up on 3 and 4. Lower at end of 4.

*Body Sway.* There is no sway.

*Amount of Turn.* Make a complete turn or slightly less on the whole figure. A half turn is made on the first 2 steps.

*Footwork.* 1 T H. 2 H T. 3 T. 4 T H.

A chart and further notes appear in the Waltz Section.

# CROSS SWIVEL

## Man

A delightful variation for experienced dancers only. The steps are easy, but the figure requires good balance to dance effectively. A diagram appears on page 79.

Commence facing diagonally to the wall. Finish facing diagonally to the centre.

1. LF forward turning body to L.                                      S
2. Swivelling to L on ball of LF, close
   (or nearly close) RF to LF without weight.            S
3. Forward RF outside partner.                                  S

*Contrary Body Movement.* CBM on 1 and 3. The 3rd step is placed in CBMP.

*Rise and Fall (Body).* There is no rise.

*Body Sway.* Sway to L on 2.

*Amount of Turn.* Normally a quarter turn is made. It is possible to make up to half a turn.

*Footwork.* 1 H. 2 Pressure on T of LF with foot flat, pressure on IE of T of RF 3 H.

*General Notes.* A good Cross Swivel depends on the first step. This should be long and bold, with a confident swing to the L. LF should be kept quite flat, and when RF closes, balance will be assisted if it is kept slightly back and a few inches apart at the end of the turn. The pressure on the inside edge of RF will also assist the balance. Precede with the Quarter Turn to L, the Double Reverse Spin, or the Reverse Pivot. Follow with:

(a) The Running Finish. Replace the weight back to the LF with a slight turn to the R, making this the first step of the Running Finish, counting SQQS or QQSS. See page 67.

(b) The Fish Tail. This is described on page 78.

# CROSS SWIVEL

## Lady

Commence backing diagonally to wall.

| | | |
|---|---|---|
| 1. | RF back, turning body to L. | S |
| 2. | Swivelling a quarter turn to L on ball of RF, close LF to RF without weight. | S |
| 3. | LF back, partner outside. | S |

*Contrary Body Movement.* CBM on 1 and 3. The 3rd step is placed in CBMP.

*Rise and Fall (Body).* There is no rise.

*Body Sway.* Sway to R on 2.

*Amount of Turn.* The same as in the man's steps.

*Footwork.* 1 T H. 2 H, then IE of T of LF. 3 T. Note that the heel of RF on step 1 does not lower until the turn is completed.

*General Notes.* If the LF closes to RF slightly forward, balance will be assisted and it will help to avoid hurrying into the 3rd step.

# FISH TAIL

## Man

The Fish Tail is one of the most popular standard variations in the Quickstep.

The most attractive position to commence it is diagonally to the centre (after a Cross Swivel). Finish facing diagonally to the wall. Another amalgamation is given in the general notes below. When taken from a Cross Swivel, the last step of the Cross Swivel becomes the first step of the Fish Tail.

Dance 1, 2 of the Cross Swivel. Finish facing diagonally to the centre and continue as follows:

| | | |
|---|---|---|
| 1. | RF forward, outside partner, diag. to centre. | S |
| 2. | Move the LF slightly forward so that it is crossed behind the RF. Body commences to turn to R. | Q |

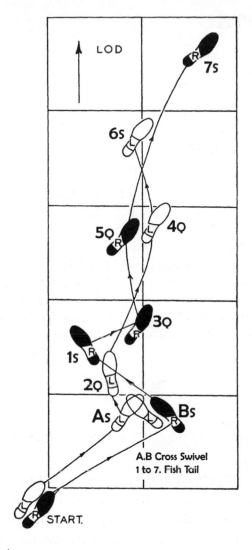

**Fish Tail (Man)**

3. Move the RF forward and slightly to the side. Body now facing diag. to wall. Small step outside partner.                Q
4. LF diag., forward, L side leading.                Q
5. Cross RF behind LF.                Q

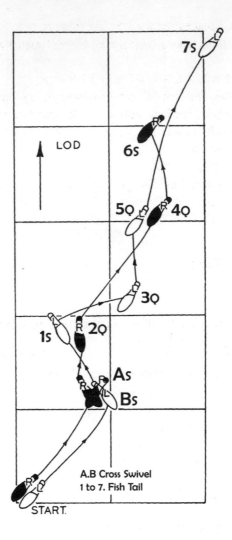

**Fish Tail (Lady)**

6. LF diag. forward.                                                    S

7. RF forward, outside partner. Diag. to wall.           S

Continue into any Natural figure.

*Contrary Body Movement.* CBM on 1 and 7. Both of these steps are placed in CBMP.

*Rise and Fall (Body).* Rise at end of 1; remain up for steps 2 to 6. Lower at end of 6.

*Body Sway.* Sway to the R on 2.

*Amount of Turn.* Make a quarter turn to R between 1 and 3. No more turn.

*Footwork.* 1 H T. 2 T. 3 T. 4 T. 5 T. 6 T H. 7 H.

*General Notes.* The Fish Tail can be danced at any time the man has taken a step outside the lady with his RF. It should be noted that if he is facing diagonally to wall on this step, no turn will be made on steps 1 to 3 of the Fish Tail.

Good amalgamations are:

(a) Quarter Turns, Cross Swivel, Fish Tail.

(b) Natural Spin Turn, Progressive Chassé, Fish Tail.

(c) Natural Spin Turn, Reverse Pivot, Cross Swivel, Fish Tail.

# THE FISH TAIL

## Lady

Dance 1, 2 of the Cross Swivel. Finish backing diagonally to the centre. Continue as follows:

| | | |
|---|---|---|
| 1. | LF back, partner outside. Diag. to centre. | S |
| 2. | Cross RF in front of LF. Turn body to the R. | Q |
| 3. | LF back, and slightly to side (small step) now backing diag. to wall. | Q |
| 4. | RF diag. back, R side leading. | Q |
| 5. | Cross LF in front of RF. | Q |
| 6. | RF diag. back. | S |
| 7. | LF back, diag. to wall. Partner outside. | S |

*Contrary Body Movement.* CBM on 1 and 7. Both are also placed in CBMP.

*Rise and Fall (Body).* Rise at end of 1; remain up for Steps 2 to 6. Lower at end 6.

*Body Sway.* Sway to the L on 2.

*Amount of Turn.* Make a quarter turn to R between 1 and 3.

*Footwork.* 1 T. 2 T. 3 T. 4 T. 5 T. 6 T H. 7 T.

*General Notes.* Please refer to the amalgamations given in the man's notes.

# RUNNING RIGHT TURN

## Man

The Running Right Turn is a composite figure, embracing the Natural Pivot Turn, followed by 1, 2, and 3 of a Foxtrot Natural Turn (danced SSS rhythm), and ended with the Running Finish.

This figure is best taken near a corner. The notes on pages 83-4 should be read carefully.

Commence facing diagonally to the wall.

| | |
|---|---|
| 1, 2, 3, 4. Do the Natural Pivot Turn, Finish facing the LOD. (This amount of turn can be modified.) | SQQS |
| 5. RF forward, in CBMP, turning body to R. | S |
| 6. LF to side, across the LOD. | S |
| 7. Continue turning on the ball of LF and step back with RF, R side leading. | S |
| Now follow with the Running Finish: | |
| 8. LF back, turning body to the R, partner outside. | Q |
| 9. Small step to side and slightly forward with RF, facing the new LOD. | Q |
| 10. LF forward, preparing to step outside partner, L shoulder leading. | S |
| 11. RF forward, outside partner. | S |

*Contrary Body Movement.* CBM on 1, 4, 5, 8, and 11. Steps 5, 8, and 11 are placed in CBMP.

*Rise and Fall (Body).* Rise at end of 1; up on 2 and 3. Lower at end of 3. Rise at end of 5; up on 6 and 7. Lower at end of 7. Rise at end of 8; up on 9 and 10. Lower at end of 10.

*Body Sway.* Sway to the R on 2 and 3; to the R on 6 and 7; to the L on 9 and 10.

*Footwork.* 1 H T. 2 T. 3 T H. 4 T H T. 5 H T. 6 T. 7 T H. 8 T. 9 T. 10 T H. 11 H.

*Amount of Turn.* 1¾ turns to R or less. Fuller details are given below.

There are four main alignments of the Running Right Turn, when the amount of turn used is as follows:

1. Approaching a corner. Make a half turn on the pivot; half turn on the Natural Turn; a quarter on the Running Finish to end down the new LOD (or three-eighths to face diag. wall).

2. Across a corner. Make three-eighths turn on the pivot; half turn on the Natural Turn to cut across the corner; three-eighths on the Running Finish to end down the new LOD.

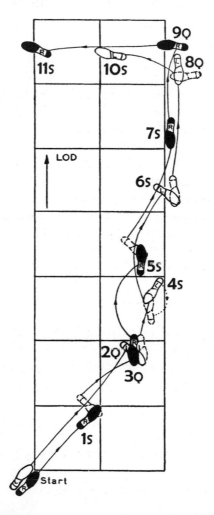

**Running Right Turn (Man)**

3. Round two corners in a narrow room. Make three-eighths turn on the pivot; three-eighths on the Natural Turn to end backing the new LOD; a quarter on the Running Finish to end down the 3rd LOD (or three-eighths to face diag. wall).

4. Along side of room. Make a half turn on the pivot; a half turn on the Natural Turn; three-eighths turn on the Running Finish to end facing diagonally to centre. Follow, in this case, with a Fish Tail or a Quick Open Reverse.

*General Notes.* When dancing alignments 1, 2 or 3 the last step becomes the first step of any Natural figure. An alternative timing for the Running Right Turn could be 'SQQSSQQSQQS'.

## RUNNING RIGHT TURN

### Lady

The Running Right Turn is a composite figure embracing the Natural Pivot Turn, followed by 1, 2, and 3 of a Foxtrot Natural Turn (danced SSS rhythm), and ended with the Running Finish.

This figure is best taken near a corner.

Commence with the back diagonally to the wall.

| | |
|---|---|
| 1, 2, 3, 4. Do the Natural Pivot Turn. Finish with back to LOD. | SQQS |
| 5. LF back, down LOD, turning body to the R. | S |
| 6. Close RF to LF, turning on L heel (Heel Turn). | S |
| 7. LF forward down LOD, preparing to step outside partner, L side leading. | S |
| 8. RF forward, outside partner, turning body to R. | Q |
| 9. LF to side. | Q |
| 10. RF back, down new LOD, R side leading. | S |
| 11. LF back, down new LOD, partner outside. | S |

*Contrary Body Movement.* CBM on 1, 4, 5, 8, and 11. Steps 8 and 11 are placed in CBMP.

*Rise and Fall (Body).* Rise at end of 1 (NFR); up on 2 and 3. Lower at end of 3. Rise slightly at end of 5 (NFR); continue to rise on 6; up on 7. Lower at end of 7. Rise at end of 8; up on 9 and 10. Lower at end of 10.

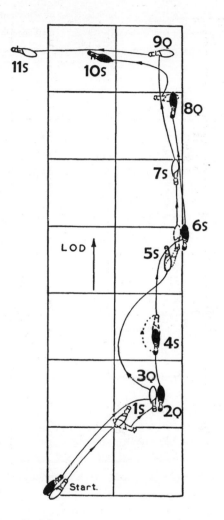

**Running Right Turn (Lady)**

*Body Sway.* Sway to the L on 2 and 3; to the L on 6 and 7; to the R on 9 and 10.

*Amount of Turn.* 1¾ turns to R or less. Full details are given following the description of the man's steps.

*Footwork.* 1 T H. 2 T. 3 T H. 4 H T H. 5 T H. 6 H T. 7 T H. 8 H T. 9 T. 10 T H. 11 T.

*General Notes.* The lady will use a "pivoting action" on the 4th step and step back with CBM on step 5. An alternative timing could be 'SQQSSQQSQQS'. For other alignments see under man's steps.

## QUICK OPEN REVERSE

### Man

This is a standard variation that is most attractive to dance, but it looks very untidy if it is danced badly. The man's steps are similar to the first 4 steps of a Foxtrot Reverse Turn, but danced in a quicker rhythm and with the lady outside on the 3rd step.

Suggested entries and endings are given in the general notes.

Commence facing the LOD.

| | | |
|---|---|---|
| 1. | LF forward, turning body to L. | S |
| 2. | RF to side, across the LOD. | Q |
| 3. | Continue turning on the ball of RF and step back with LF, partner outside. | Q |
| 4. | RF back, down the LOD. (See notes below.) | S |

*Contrary Body Movement.* CBM on 1 and 4. The 3rd step is placed in CBMP.

*Rise and Fall (Body).* Rise at end of 1; up on 2 and 3. Lower at end of 3.

*Body Sway.* Sway to L on 2 and 3.

*Amount of Turn.* A half turn is made on the first three steps.

*Footwork.* 1 H T. 2 T. 3 T H. 4 T.

*General Notes.* In leading into this figure a strong swing forward on the first step (LF) should be used. This will result in an early rise and give that lightness which is necessary for the speed of the figure. The 3rd step should be rather "cut under" the body in CBM Position, and this will accentuate the sway.

*Amalgamations.* The figure may be danced after a Heel Pivot, after a Reverse Pivot and after a Double Reverse Spin. It can also be danced

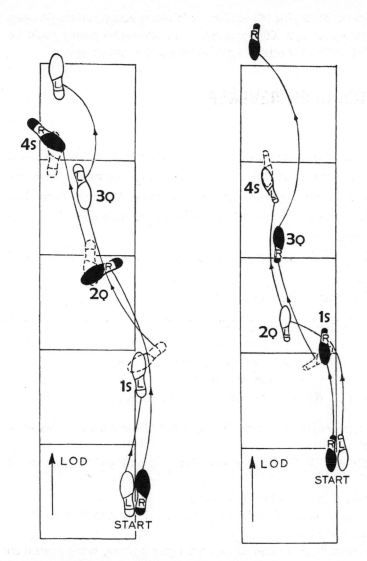

**Quick Open Reverse Turn ending with a Reverse Pivot**
**Left: Man   Right: Lady**

after a step forward on RF outside partner. A good amalgamation would be: Closed Impetus (or underturn a Spin Turn to end backing diagonally to centre against the LOD), Progressive Chassé, ending with RF forward, outside partner and moving diagonally to centre; Quick Open Reverse.

*Endings:*

(a) The Progressive Chassé. The last step of the Quick Open Reverse will be the first step of the Progressive Chassé.

(b) A Four Quick Run. (See page 89.)

(c) Use a Reverse Pivot on the 4th step. Turn three-eighths on the pivot and follow with the Cross Swivel. Turn a half on the pivot and follow with another Quick Open Reverse or any Reverse figure.

## QUICK OPEN REVERSE

### Lady

This is a most attractive standard variation.

For suitable entries and endings please refer to the amalgamations given in the notes on the man's steps.

Commence backing the LOD.

| | | |
|---|---|---|
| 1. | RF back, turning body to L. | S |
| 2. | Small step to side and slightly forward with LF. | Q |
| 3. | RF forward, down the LOD. Outside partner. | Q |
| 4. | LF forward, in line with man. | S |

*Contrary Body Movement.* CBM on 1 and 4. The 3rd step is placed in CBMP.

*Rise and Fall (Body).* Rise at end of (NFR); up on 2 and 3. Lower at end of 3.

*Body Sway.* Sway to R on 2 and 3.

*Amount of Turn.* A half turn is made on the first 3 steps.

*Footwork.* 1 T H. 2 T. 3 T H. 4 H.

*General Notes.* Please refer to the amalgamations given in the man's notes.

# FOUR QUICK RUN

## Man

This is one of the most popular and useful variations in the Quickstep. It is used when stepping back on RF, and the Quick Open Reverse is one of the best entries. Commence backing the LOD.

| | | |
|---|---|---|
| 1. | RF back, turning to the L. | S |
| 2. | Step to side and slightly forward, along the LOD with LF. Body facing wall. | Q |
| 3. | Small step forward with RF outside partner. Diag. to wall. | Q |
| 4. | LF diag. forward. | Q |
| 5. | Cross RF behind LF. | Q |
| 6. | LF diag. forward. | S |
| 7. | RF forward, outside partner, diag. to wall. | S |

*Contrary Body Movement.* CBM on 1 and 7. The 3rd and 7th steps are placed in CBMP.

*Rise and Fall (Body).* Rise at the end of 1, remain up for steps 2 to 6. Lower at end of 6.

*Body Sway.* There is no sway.

*Amount of Turn.* Make three-eighths of a turn to L between 1 and 2.

*Footwork.* 1 T H T. 2 T. 3 T. 4 T. 5 T. 6 T H. 7 H.

*General Notes.* On steps 2 to 7 the feet are pointing diagonally to wall, but the figure will tend to travel more sideways, along the LOD, with the body facing between the wall and diagonally to wall.

*Best Amalgamations.*

(a) Quick Open Reverse into Four Quick Run.

(b) Chassé Reverse Turn into Four Quick Run (for average dancers).

## FOUR QUICK RUN

### Lady

Commence facing the LOD.

| | | |
|---|---|---|
| 1. | LF forward, turning to L. | S |
| 2. | Step to side RF with back towards wall. | Q |
| 3. | Still turning slightly, step back LF (small step) partner outside. Diag. to wall. | Q |
| 4. | RF diag. back. | Q |
| 5. | Cross LF in front of RF. | Q |
| 6. | RF diag. back. | S |
| 7. | LF back, diag. to wall, partner outside. | S |

*Contrary Body Movement.* CBM on 1 and 7. The 3rd and 7th steps are placed in CBMP.

*Rise and Fall (Body).* Rise at the end of 1. Remain up for steps 2 to 6. Lower at end of 6.

*Body Sway.* There is no sway.

*Amount of Turn.* Three-eighths turn to L between 1 and 3.

*Footwork.* 1 H T. 2 T. 3 T 4 T. 5 T. 6 T H. 7 T.

*General Notes.* See notes under man's steps.

## THE V-SIX

### Man

This is an attractive and popular standard variation. As the name suggests, it makes the shape of the letter 'V'. and there are six steps each side of the 'V'.

The standard entry is steps 1 to 3 of the Natural Turn ended backing diag. to centre. The V-Six consists of a Back Lock commenced with lady in line moving diagonally centre, steps 2 and 3 of the Outside Change (See Waltz section), and a Forward Lock diagonally to wall.

Commence backing diagonally to the centre and move diagonally to centre on steps 1 to 6.

1. LF back, turning body to R.   S
2. RF back, R side leading.   Q
3. Cross LF in of RF.   Q
4. RF back, R side still leading.   S
5. LF back, partner outside.   S
6. RF back, turning body to L lady in line.   Q
7. LF to side and slightly forward, along the LOD.
   Body facing wall. L toe pointing diag. to wall.   Q
8-12. RF forward, outside partner, to continue with the
   Forward Lock, moving diag. to wall.   SQQSS

*Contrary Body Movement.* CBM on 1, 6, 8 (slight), and 12. The 5th, 8th and 12th steps are placed in CBMP.

*Rise and Fall (Body).* Commence to rise at end of 1 (NFR); continue to rise on 2 and 3; up on 4. Lower at end of 4. Commence to rise at end of 5 (NFR); continue to rise on 6; up on 7. Lower at end of 7. Commence to rise at end of 8; continue to rise on 9 and 10; up on 11. Lower at end of 11.

*Body Sway.* There is no sway.

*Amount of Turn.* Make a quarter turn to L between steps 6 and 7.

*Footwork.* 1. T. H 2. T 3. T 4. T. H 5 T. H 6. T 7. T. H 8. H. T 9. T 10. T 11. T. H 12. H.

*General Notes.* The V-Six may also be danced following the Natural Spin Turn ended backing diag. to centre, in which case it would commence with step 2. It is important to lower as usual at the end of the Natural Spin Turn. Another good entry is from any figure ended with RF forward outside partner, when near a corner. The first step of the V-Six is placed in CBMP with partner outside, and the Back Lock will move diag. to centre of the new LOD.

# THE V-SIX

## Lady

This is a most attractive standard variation in the pattern of the 'V' and is commenced facing diagonally to centre having danced steps 1-3 of the Natural Turn ended in this alignment. The lady will dance a Forward Lock commenced in line with partner, steps 2 and 3 of the Outside Change (see Waltz section), and a Back Lock.

Commence facing diagonally to the centre and move diagonally to centre on steps 1 to 6.

| | | |
|---|---|---|
| 1. | RF forward, turning body to R. | S |
| 2. | LF forward, L side leading. | Q |
| 3. | Cross RF behind LF. | Q |
| 4. | LF forward, L. side still leading. | S |
| 5. | RF forward, outside partner. | S |
| 6. | LF forward in line with partner, turning body to L. | Q |
| 7. | RF to side and slightly back, along the LOD. | Q |
| 8-12. | LF back, partner outside, to continue with the Back Lock, moving diag. to wall. | SQQSS |

*Contrary Body Movement.* CBM on 1, 6, 8 (slight), and 12. The 5th, 8th and 12th steps are placed in CBMP.

*Rise and Fall (Body).* Commence to rise at end of 1; continue to rise on 2 and 3; up on 4. Lower at end of 4. Commence to rise at end of 5; continue to rise on 6; up on 7. Lower at end of 7. Commence to rise at end of 8 (NFR); continue to rise on 9 and 10; up on 11. Lower at end of 11.

*Body Sway.* There is no sway.

*Amount of Turn.* Make a quarter turn to L between steps 6 and 7.

*Footwork.* 1. H. T 2. T 3. T 4. T. H 5. H. T 6. T. 7. T. H 8. T. H 9. T 10. T. H 11. T. H 12. T.

*General Notes.* Please refer to the amalgamation given in the man's notes.

## CLOSED TELEMARK, OPEN TELEMARK, CLOSED IMPETUS AND OPEN IMPETUS

These four figures are frequently used in Quickstep, Waltz, and Foxtrot. The method of dancing them is the same in each dance, but the rhythm is changed to suit the tempo of the music.

Descriptions are given in the section of the book to which the figure originally belonged. In the following notes, the alternative rhythms are given, together with notes on the best way of amalgamating them into each dance.

## Closed Telemark

This was originally a Foxtrot variation, and a description will be found on page 183.

*Rhythm.* When danced in the Quickstep the Rhythm is SSSS. It can be danced SQQS, but it is not advisable for beginners to attempt this quicker rhythm. When danced in the Waltz, each step has one beat. Other technical details are unaltered.

*Amalgamation (Quickstep).* The Telemark is usually danced when the man is stepping outside the lady on her left side. If it is used directly following the Quarter Turn to L, the lady may mistake the lead for that of a Double Reverse Spin. A good amalgamation is – 1 to 3 of Natural Turn, Open Impetus, Wing (see Waltz section), Closed Telemark, Fish Tail. Complete rhythm would be: SQQSSS SQQ SSSS QQQQSS. A good Waltz amalgamation would be – Open Telemark, Wing, Telemark (see Waltz Section).

## Open Telemark

This is more popular in Waltz and Foxtrot, and descriptions will be found on pages 138 and 186-7. A diagram is given on page 141.

*Rhythm.* When danced in Quickstep the rhythm is SSSS. The quicker rhythm of SQQS could be used by advanced dancers. Other technical details are unaltered.

*Amalgamation.* Open Telemark, Open Natural Turn, ending with a Closed Impetus or Running Finish. Complete rhythm for the latter amalgamation would be: SSS SQQ SQQS.

## Closed Impetus

This was originally a Foxtrot variation, and a description will be found in the Foxtrot Section on page 180.

*Rhythm*. When danced in the Quickstep the rhythm, including the first 3 steps of the Natural Turn, would be: SQQSSSS. When danced in the Waltz, each step has one beat. Other technical details remain unaltered.

*Amalgamation*. The Closed Impetus can be used in place of the Natural Spin Turn in both the Quickstep and Waltz. Many good dancers prefer this figure to the Natural Spin Turn, especially in the Waltz. It should be noted, however, that only five-eighths of a turn is made on the Impetus Turn so that if it is danced along the sides of the room, the last step will be taken diagonally to centre against the LOD. A Progressive Chassé into a Quick Open Reverse Turn could follow.

## Open Impetus

This was originally a Waltz variation, and a description will be found in the Waltz Section on page 144.

*Rhythm*. When danced in the Foxtrot the rhythm is SQQS. When danced in the Quickstep the rhythm, including the first 3 steps of the Natural Turn, would be: SQQSSSS. A good amalgamation is included in the notes on the Telemark on the preceding page. Other technical details remain unaltered.

*Amalgamation*. Foxtrot. Dance 1, 2, 3 of Natural Turn. SQQ. Follow with the Open Impetus finishing in Promenade Position moving diag. to the centre. SQQS. Turn the lady square and go into steps 2, 3, 4 of a Feather Ending taken diag. to centre. QQS. Follow with a Reverse figure.

# SUGGESTED QUICKSTEP AMALGAMATIONS

1. Quarter Turn to R–Quarter Turn to L–Cross Chassé–Forward Lock–1-3 of Natural Turn at corner, continuing into the Tipple Chassé to R, ended diag. wall of the new LOD.

2. Quarter Turn to R–Progressive Chassé–Forward Lock–Natural Spin Turn.

3. Natural Turn with Hesitation–Chassé Reverse Turn–Progressive Chassé–Fish tail (without turn).

4. Natural Spin Turn–Quarter Turn to L ended facing the LOD–Zig Zag, Back Lock, Running Finish.

5. Natural Turn with Hesitation–Progressive Chassé to R–Back Lock–Running Finish, ended diag. to centre–Fish Tail.

6. Quarter Turn to R or Natural Spin Turn–Quarter Turn to L and Reverse Pivot, ended facing the LOD–Double Reverse Spin–Cross Swivel–Fish Tail.

7. Natural Spin Turn (underturning to face diag. to wall) RF back into a Progressive Chassé, moving towards centre and ended facing diag. to centre–Quick Open Reverse–Four Quick Run–Running Right Turn.

8. Progressive Chassé approaching a corner–check back into the V-Six, moving diag. to centre of the new LOD–Running Right Turn.

# SECTION II
# THE WALTZ

The steps of the modern Waltz are probably the easiest of the present-day dances to learn. Steps, however, are by no means the most important factor in modern dancing, and the dancer must pay very careful attention to several other details before the delightful rhythmic swing and lilt of the dance can be captured. The correct use of Contrary Body Movement resulting in an easy swing of the body into the turns, the correct relaxing and straightening of the knees, in conjunction with the Rises, and the controlled use of Body Sways, all play their part in producing a dance that is continuously flowing with a rhythmic, lilting movement. These points are dealt with under their respective headings and should be studied after the basic principles are understood.

## GENERAL NOTES

*Time.* 3/4. Three beats in a bar.

*Tempo.* Music should be played at 30 bars a minute.

*Basic Rhythm.* There are no "Slows" and "Quicks" in the Waltz. Count 1, 2, 3. The first beat is accented.

*Figures.* Closed Changes, Natural Turn, Reverse Turn, Hesitation Change, Outside Change, Natural Spin Turn, Whisk, Chassé from Promenade Position, Reverse Corté, Back

Whisk, Double Reverse Spin, Progressive Chassé to Right, Open Telemark (with Cross Hesitation finish), Wing, Drag Hesitation and Back Lock, Outside Spin, Turning Lock, Weave from Promenade Position.

For the novice there are but three basic figures in the Waltz, and the normal construction of the Waltz is made from these figures only. It must be understood that a complete circle in six steps is never danced, the construction being based on diagonal lines which require only three-eighths of a turn to be made on each three steps. Normally no turn is made on a Closed Change step, this figure being used to change the dancer from a Natural Turn to a Reverse Turn or *vice versa*.

The following method of practising is described for a man dancer. A lady should use the steps and directions that are the normal opposite.

The beginner should learn the Closed Change step first, commencing it first with the RF and then the LF, and dancing it continuously in a straight line down the room. It is advisable, even at this early stage, to acquire some knowledge of the Rise and Fall, and even the Body Sway, as these details are easy to remember and will prove helpful when the turns are attempted.

Learn the Natural Turn next, and practise the two figures in this way:

Dance the Closed Change Steps when moving down the sides of the room. When near a corner, dance a full Natural Turn (six steps), finishing facing the next Line of Dance. Continue with the Change Steps to the next corner.

This, of course, is based on the assumption that the room is not very large. In a very large room it would be advisable to use one part of the room only, as it is only possible to regain the Line of Dance after a Natural Turn by departing from the normal lines of the dance.

The Reverse Turn should be learned next, and then an attempt should be made to amalgamate the three figures in the following manner.

Commence facing diagonally to the wall.

Step forward with the RF and dance 1, 2, 3 of the Natural Turn. Finish with the back to the LOD.

Step backward with the LF and dance 4, 5, 6 of the Natural Turn. Finish facing diagonally to the centre.

Step forward with the RF and dance the Closed Change, making no turn.

Step forward with the LF diagonally to the centre and dance 1, 2, 3 of the Reverse Turn. Finish with the back to the LOD.

Step backward with the RF and dance 4, 5, 6 of the Reverse Turn. Finish facing diagonally to the wall.

Step forward with the LF and dance the Closed Change, making no turn, and still facing diagonally to the wall.

This is the same as the commencing position and the amalgamation can be repeated.

Remember that only a Natural Turn is danced round a corner. If the corner is acute, two complete turns could be danced. Care must be taken to adjust the amount of turn on each part so that the new LOD is faced from a diagonal position. If this has not been done, a slight turn on a Closed Change will give the diagonal position from which all turns should be commenced. Remember, however, that a Closed Change commencing with the LF may only be turned to the L, and a RF Closed Change only turned to the R.

Naturally, an experienced dancer, with the use of variations, will not have to bother too much about the diagonal positions, but the beginner will be advised to pay careful attention to this point in the early stages.

Further details of how to amalgamate the basic figures with standard variations are given with the descriptions of the latter. The following notes should be very carefully read.

## Special Notes

*Contrary Body Movement.* The Contrary Body Movement on the first step of each turn must not be exaggerated. On the forward part of any turning figure it is much more important to feel a *forward swing*, rather than a conscious twist of the body on the first step. It should be remembered that the first step is the *strong* step, and from the swing of this step it should be possible to take a wide second step without further effort. The closing of the feet on the third step must be controlled by keeping the inside of the toes of the closing foot pressed firmly to the floor. It should never be lifted and allowed to close quickly.

*Knees.* When taking the weight on the first step of any turn or Closed Change allow the knee to relax slightly. This will prevent any jar or stop in the movement of the body, and also tend to make the subsequent rise softer.

*Sway.* The Sway is quite pronounced in turning figures in the Waltz.

## Footwork and Rises

In the Waltz, as in other dances, there is no foot rise on the backward half of any turn or in a Closed Change when danced backward. Any attempt to rise early with the feet or body would seriously impede the flow of the movement. The rise must be gradual and felt throughout the turns, the full extent of the rise not being reached until the feet are closed on the third step. The notes on Rise and Fall given in the early part of the book should be studied with care.

The correct footwork on the backward turns is also of great importance. The first step of a turn is taken back on to the toe, gradually lowering to the heel as the second step moves to the side. When the second step is in position – to the side – the heel of the first step is released from the floor and even then it must not be raised abruptly.

A common fault with more advanced dancers is found in the movement of the foot when it commences to close for the third step. In the Natural Turn (lady) when the LF commences to close for the third step it is most important that the Left toe, or inside edge of the toe, should be pressed firmly to the floor. Many advanced dancers allow the toe to leave the floor when the second step is in position, which results in the LF leaving the floor before closing for the third step. Much control is lost in this way and the result will be ugly footwork and very often the closing foot will pass the supporting foot instead of closing firmly to it.

Another important point should be observed when the feet are closed in the Closed Changes and the Natural and Reverse Turns. If a *forward* step is to follow, the normal footwork is for the heel of the foot supporting the weight to lower to the floor and then come up again as the forward step is taken. To do this, however, will often result in the weight being dropped back just at the moment when a good forward swing is required. The heel of the supporting foot should *always lower lightly* and be raised again immediately; it should never drop heavily, as this retards the swing into the following step. To step forward without lowering the supporting heel at all would, of course, be equally bad.

## RIGHT FOOT CLOSED CHANGE
### (From Natural Turn to Reverse Turn)

#### Man
In the normal construction of the Waltz the Closed Change is taken either diagonally to the centre or diagonally to the wall. There is, however, no reason at all why it cannot be danced straight down the LOD for the purpose of practice.

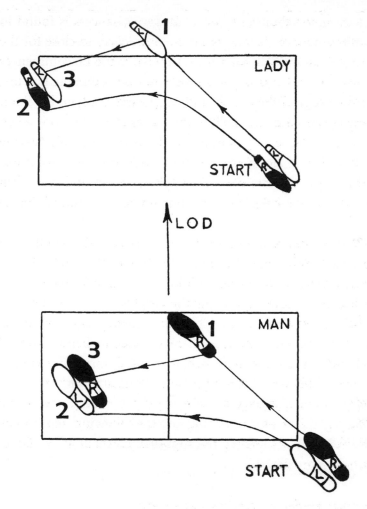

**Right Foot Closed Change (From Natural to Reverse Turn)**

The Natural Turn finishes facing diagonally to the centre. Commence the Closed Change from this position.

1. RF forward.
2. LF to side and slightly forward.
3. Close RF to LF.

Then go forward with LF into a Reverse Turn.

*Contrary Body Movement.* Slight CBM on 1.

*Rise and Fall (Body).* Commence to rise at end of 1; continue to rise on 2 and 3. Lower at end of 3.

*Body Sway.* Sway to R on 2 and 3.

*Footwork.* 1. H T. 2. T. 3. T H.

*General Notes.* The beginner should endeavour to place the 2nd step to the side, as the swing on the first step will result in the correct position being achieved quite naturally. Care must be taken not to allow this step to move too much forward, otherwise alignment will be lost and the following turn made more difficult.

It is permissible to make a slight turn to R on this figure.

## Lady

1. LF back.
2. RF to side and slightly back.
3. Close LF to RF.

Then go back with RF into a Reverse Turn.

*Contrary Body Movement.* Slight CBM on 1.

*Rise and Fall (Body).* Commence to rise at end of 1 (NFR); continue to rise on 2 and 3. Lower at end of 3.

*Footwork.* 1. T H. 2. T. 3. T H.

*Body Sway.* Sway to L on 2 and 3.

# LEFT FOOT CLOSED CHANGE
## (From Reverse Turn to Natural Turn)

### Man

This figure is similar to the Closed Change from Natural to Reverse Turns, described and illustrated on pages 100–102.

The Reverse Turn finishes facing diagonally to the wall. Commence the Closed Change from this position.

1. LF forward.
2. RF to side and slightly forward
3. Close LF to RF.

Then go forward with RF into a Natural Turn.

*Contrary Body Movement.* Slight CBM on 1.

*Rise and Fall (Body).* Commence to rise at end of 1; continue to rise on 2 and 3. Lower at end of 3.

*Body Sway.* Sway to L on 2 and 3.

*Footwork.* 1. H T. 2. T. 3. T H.

*General Notes.* The action for this Closed Change is the same as for a Closed Change from Natural Turn to Reverse Turn, and the general notes thereon apply also to this figure. A slight turn to the Left may be made.

## Lady

1. RF back.
2. LF to side and slightly back.
3. Close RF to LF.

Then go back with LF into a Natural Turn.

*Contrary Body Movement.* Slight CBM on 1.

*Rise and Fail (Body).* Commence to rise at end of 1 (NFR); continue to rise on 2 and 3. Lower at end of 3.

*Body Sway.* Sway to R on 2 and 3.

*Footwork.* 1. T H. 2. T. 3. T H.

# NATURAL TURN

## Man

This figure is described as it is used in the normal construction of the Waltz. Beginners should read carefully the introductory notes on this dance.

Commence facing diagonally to the wall. Finish facing diagonally to the centre.

1. RF forward, turning body to R.
2. Long step to side with LF across the LOD.
3. Continue turning on ball of LF and close RF to LF. (Back now to LOD.)

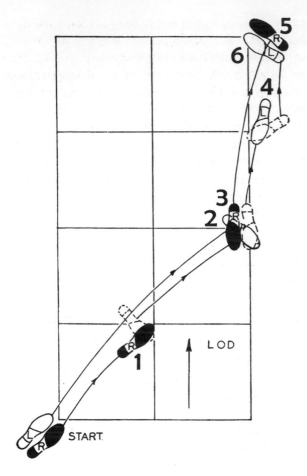

**Natural Turn (Man)**

4. LF back, turning body to R.
5. RF to side, on the same LOD.
6. Close LF to RF.

*Contrary Body Movement.* CBM on 1 and 4.

*Rise and Fall (Body).* Commence to rise at end of 1; continue to rise on 2 and 3. Lower at end of 3. Commence to rise at the end of 4 (NFR); continue to rise on 5 and 6. Lower at end of 6. Remember to relax the knee slightly on steps 1 and 4. This will soften the movement considerably.

*Body Sway.* Sway to R on 2 and 3. Sway to L on 5 and 6.

*Footwork.* 1. H T. 2. T. 3. T H. 4. T H. 5. T. 6. T H.

*Amount of Turn.* Make three-eighths of a turn on each three steps.

*General Notes.* It will be noticed in the description and in the diagram that the 2nd step of the forward turn is longer than the 2nd step (step No. 5) of the backward turn. This is owing to the fact that the person on the outside of a circle will necessarily have a longer distance to travel. For the same reason, there is a continuation of the turn on the ball of the foot on the 2nd step of the forward turn. On the backward turn the 5th step is placed with the R foot turned outwards – pointing in the finishing direction. There will be only a slight body turn as the L foot closes on 6.

# NATURAL TURN

## Lady

This figure is described as it is used in the normal construction of the Waltz. Beginners should read carefully the introductory notes on this dance.

Commence with the back diagonally to the wall. Finish with the back diagonally to the centre.

1. LF back, turning body to R.
2. RF to side, across the LOD.
3. Close LF to RF, body now facing LOD.
4. RF forward, turning body to R.
5. Long step to side with LF on the same LOD.
6. Continue turning on ball of LF and close RF to LF.

*Contrary Body Movement.* CBM on 1 and 4.

*Rise and Fall (Body).* Commence to rise at end of 1 (NFR); continue to rise on 2 and 3. Lower at end of 3. Commence to rise at end of 4; continue to rise on 5 and 6. Lower at end of 6. Remember to relax the knee slightly on steps 1 and 4. This will soften the movement considerably.

*Body Sway.* Sway to L on 2 and 3; sway to R on 5 and 6.

*Amount of Turn.* Make three-eighths of a turn on each three steps.

*Footwork.* 1. T H. 2. T. 3. T H. 4. H T. 5. T. 6. T H.

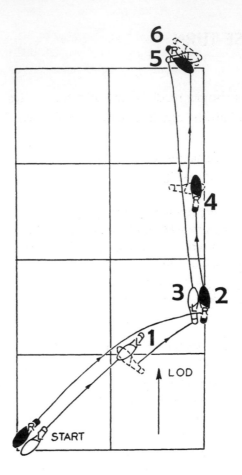

**Natural Turn (Lady)**

*General Notes.* It will be noticed in the description and in the diagram that the 2nd step of the forward part of the turn is longer than the 2nd step of the backward part of the turn. This is owing to the fact that the person on the outside of a circle will necessarily have a longer distance to travel. For the same reason there is a continuation of the turn on the ball of the foot on the 2nd step of the forward turn. On the backward half the 2nd step is placed with R foot turned outwards, pointing down the LOD. There will only be a slight body turn as the L foot closes on 3. Note also that the lady should use a good forward swing on the 4th step to assist the turn.

# REVERSE TURN

## Man

Beginners should read the introductory notes on this dance. These explain the amalgamation of steps which lead into this figure.

Commence facing diagonally to the centre. Finish facing diagonally to the wall.

1. LF forward, turning body to L.
2. Long step to side with RF, across the LOD.
3. Continue turning on ball of RF and close LF to RF. (Back now to LOD.)
4. RF back, turning body to L.
5. LF to side, on the same LOD.
6. Close RF to LF.

*Contrary Body Movement.* CBM on 1 and 4.

*Rise and Fall (Body).* Commence to rise at end of 1; continue to rise on 2 and 3. Lower at end of 3. Commence to rise at end of 4 (NFR); continue to rise on 5 and 6. Lower at end of 6.

*Body Sway.* Sway to L on 2 and 3; sway to R on 5 and 6.

*Amount of Turn.* Make three-eighths of a turn on each three steps.

*Footwork.* 1. H T. 2. T. 3. T H. 4. T H. 5. T. 6. T H.

*General Notes.* The notes at the foot of the description of the Natural Turn, regarding the length of the 2nd step of each part of the turn, and the continuation of the turn on the ball of the foot, apply also to the Reverse Turn. (See diagram overleaf.)

# REVERSE TURN

## Lady

Commence with the back diagonally to the centre. Finish with the back diagonally to the wall.

1. RF back, turning body to L.

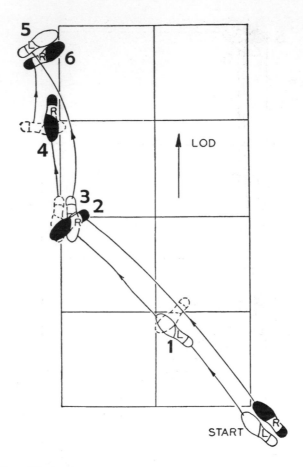

**Reverse Turn (Man)**

2. LF to side, across the LOD.
3. Close RF to LF. (Body now facing LOD.)
4. LF forward, turning body to L.
5. Long step to side with RF, on the same LOD.
6. Continue turning on ball of RF and close LF to RF.

*Contrary Body Movement.* CBM on 1 and 4.

*Rise and Fall (Body).* Commence to rise at end of 1 (NFR); continue to rise on 2 and 3. Lower at end of 3. Commence to rise at end of 4; continue to rise on 5 and 6. Lower at end of 6.

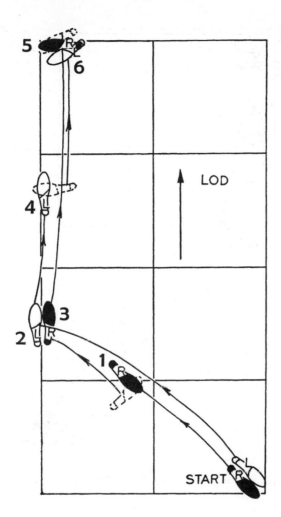

**Reverse Turn (Lady)**

*Body Sway.* Sway to R on 2 and 3; sway to L on 5 and 6.

*Amount of Turn.* Make three-eighths of a turn on each three steps.

*Footwork.* 1. T H. 2. T. 3. T H. 4. H T. 5. T. 6. T H.

*General Notes.* The notes at the foot of the description of the Natural Turn, regarding the length of the 2nd step of each part of the turn, and the continuation of the turn on the ball of the foot, apply also to the Reverse Turn.

## HESITATION CHANGE

### Man

A most useful and attractive variation which is used as a link between 1, 2, and 3 of the Natural Turn, and 1, 2, and 3 of the Reverse Turn.

Commence facing diagonally to the wall and dance 1, 2, and 3 of the Natural Turn. Finish with the feet together, and with the back to the LOD. Continue with:

4. LF back, turning body to R.
5. Pull RF back firmly, at the same time turning on L heel. Finish with RF at the side of LF, feet parallel and about 15cm (6 inches) apart, facing diag. centre.
6. Hesitate, and slowly close LF to RF without weight.

Then go forward with LF into a Reverse Turn.

*Contrary Body Movement.* CBM on 1 and 4.

*Rise and Fall (Body).* Normal rise is used on steps 1, 2, 3 of the Natural Turn. There is no rise on steps 4, 5, 6.

*Body Sway.* Sway to R on 2 and 3; sway to L on 5 and 6.

*Amount of Turn.* Three-eighths of a turn on 1, 2, and 3. Three-eighths of a turn on 4, 5, and 6. Less turn may be made at a corner.

*Footwork.* 1. H T. 2. T. 3. T H. 4. T H. 5. H, IE of foot, whole foot. 6. IE of T of LF.

*General Notes.* Care should be taken to "Pull" the RF back firmly on step 5, with pressure first on the heel and then on the inside edge of the R foot. Advanced dancers will add greatly to the attraction of the figure by pulling the R foot back very slowly, so that it takes nearly two beats to assume its position at the side of the LF. As the LF brushes to RF the body will commence to turn to the L, thus maintaining a continuous movement of the body in spite of the hesitation effect of the figure. Both ways are correct. It is a matter of personal expression. This figure is also danced in the Quickstep and is known as the Natural Turn with Hesitation. It is counted "S Q Q S S S".

# HESITATION CHANGE

## Lady

This figure forms a useful link between 1, 2, and 3 of the Natural Turn, and 1, 2, and 3 of the Reverse Turn.

Commence with the back diagonally to the wall and dance 1, 2, and 3 of the Natural Turn. Finish with the feet together, facing the LOD.

4. RF forward, turning body to R.
5. LF to side, across the LOD.
6. Hesitate, and slowly close LF to RF without weight.
Then step back on RF and go into the Reverse Turn.

*Contrary Body Movement*. CBM on 1 and 4.

*Rise and Fall (Body)*. Normal rise is used on steps 1, 2, 3 of the Natural Turn. There is no rise on steps 4, 5, and 6 although the 5th step is taken on the ball of LF before lowering the heel.

*Body Sway*. Sway to L on 2 and 3. Sway to R on 5 and 6.

*Amount of Turn*. Three-eighths of a turn on 1, 2, and 3; three-eighths of a turn on 4, 5, and 6. Less turn may be made at a corner.

*Footwork*. 1. T H. 2. T. 3. T H. 4. H T. 5. T H. 6. IE of T (RF).

*General Notes*. It should be noted that the 5th step is taken well across the LOD with no continuation of the turn on the ball of LF as the RF brushes. The action of the man's Heel Pull brings this foot across the LOD instead of in the position shown for the 5th step of a Natural Turn (on the same LOD).

# OUTSIDE CHANGE

## Man

The Outside Change is one of the most useful figures in the Waltz especially in a crowded room. When it has been found impossible to complete the full amount of turn on the first part of the Natural Turn so that these 3 steps end backing diag-

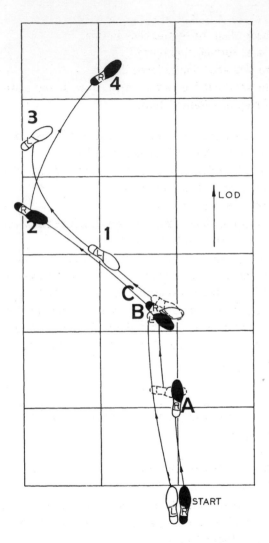

**Outside Change (following 1 to 3 of Natural Turn) (Man)**

onally to centre, the Outside Change is easily the best figure to employ.

Dance steps 1, 2, 3 of a Natural Turn and end backing diagonally to centre, then:

1. LF back, diag. to centre. Lady in line.
2. RF back, turning slightly to L.
3. LF to side and slightly forward.
4. RF forward, outside partner, diag. to wall, and make this the first step of a Natural Turn.

*Contrary Body Movement.* CBM on 2 and 4 (the first step of the next Natural Turn). The 4th step is placed in CBMP.

Rise and Fall (Body). Commence to rise. at end of 1 (NFR); continue to rise on 2; up on 3. Lower at end of 3.

*Body Sway.* There is no sway.

*Amount of Turn.* Make a quarter turn to L between 2 and 3.

*Footwork.* 1. T H. 2. T. 3. T H. 4. H.

*General Notes.* Steps 1, 2 and 3 of the Natural Turn are shown in the diagram. The gradual rise between steps 1 and 3 makes the figure far more attractive to dance. Remember to draw the LF back with the heel in contact with the floor as it moves back for the 3rd step. On step 3 the LF will point diag. to wall but the body should be facing between wall and diag. to wall. The LF may be taken to side in Promenade Position on step 4.

## Lady

Commence facing diagonally to centre after steps 1, 2, 3 of a Natural Turn. Then:

1. RF forward, in line with man.
2. LF forward, turning slightly to L.
3. RF to side and slightly back, now backing diag. to wall.
4. LF back, diag. to wall, partner outside, and make this the first step of a Natural Turn.

*Contrary Body Movement.* CBM on 2 and 4. The 4th step is placed in CBMP.

*Rise and Fall (Body).* Commence to rise at end of 1; continue to rise on 2; up on 3. Lower at end of 3.

*Body Sway.* There is no sway.

*Amount of Turn.* Make a quarter turn to L between 2 and 3.

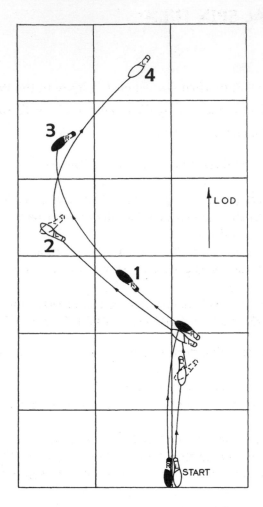

**Outside Change (following 1 to 3 of Natural Turn) (Lady)**

*Footwork.* 1. H T. 2. T. 3. T H. 4. T.

*General Notes.* Steps 1, 2 and 3 of the Natural Turn are shown in the diagram. Although the feet are backing diag. to wall on step 3 the body should be backing between wall and diag. to wall. Step 4 may be taken in Promenade Position.

# NATURAL SPIN TURN

## Man

The Natural Spin Turn is a delightful figure in the Waltz rhythm. Commence facing diagonally to the wall. Finish with the back diagonally to the centre.

1, 2, 3. First three steps of the Natural Turn, Finish with back to LOD.
4. LF back (medium-length step with the toe turned in), and pivot half a turn to R on the ball of the LF. Keep RF in front in CBMP whilst pivoting.
5. RF forward, down LOD, body still turning to R.
6. LF to side and slightly back, Finish with back to centre diagonally.

To continue, step back RF into 4, 5, 6 of Reverse Turn, making only a quarter of a turn. Finish facing diag. to wall.

*Contrary Body Movement.* CBM on 1, 4, and 5. The 5th step is held in CBMP.

*Rise and Fall (Body).* Commence to rise at end of 1; continue to rise on 2 and 3. Lower at end of 3. Rise at end of 5; up on 6. Lower at end of 6.

*Body Sway.* Sway to R on 2 and 3. No sway on actual spin.

*Amount of Turn.* On steps 1 to 3 make three-eighths of a turn, half a turn on 4, and three-eighths of a turn between steps 5 and 6.

*Footwork.* 1. H T. 2. T. 3. T H. 4. T H T. 5. H T. 6. T H

*Note:* Although the footwork on 4 is given as T H T the turn is made on the ball of LF with the heel in contact with the floor.

*General Notes.* The Natural Spin Turn should be used by beginners at the corners of the room, when three-eighths of a turn is made on 4 and a quarter, turn between 5 and 6.

The Natural Spin Turn is a convenient step to use preceding a Double Reverse Spin or an Open Telemark. When the man commences the 4, 5 and 6 of the Reverse Turn, his back is diagonally to the centre instead of down the LOD. Thus he can end this turn facing the LOD, which is the most attractive position to commence the Double Reverse Spin.

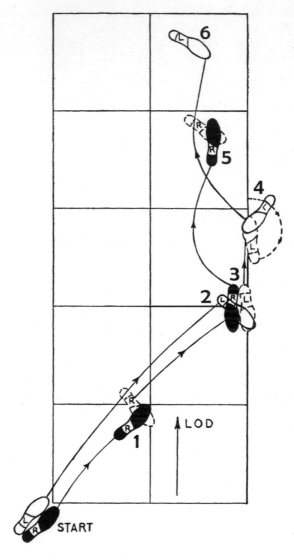

**Natural Spin Turn (Man)**

Two good amalgamations are:

(a) Natural Spin Turn followed by 4, 5, and 6 of the Reverse Turn. Finish facing the LOD. Double Reverse Spin; finish facing diagonally to the wall. LF Closed Change, followed by a Natural Turn.

(b) Natural Spin Turn, followed by 4, 5, and 6 of the Reverse Turn. Finish facing the LOD. Double Reverse Spin. Finish facing the LOD. Follow with an advanced figure such as the Open Telemark or Drag Hesitation.

(c) The Turning Lock may follow the Spin Turn.

## NATURAL SPIN TURN

### Lady

The Spin Turn is one of the most popular variations in the Waltz.

Commence with the back diagonally to the wall. Finish facing the centre diagonally.

1, 2, 3. First three steps of the Natural Turn. Finish facing the LOD.
4. RF forward, turning half a turn to R with a pivoting action. The L leg is not held in CBMP.
5. Still turning, move the LF back and slightly to side, down the LOD.
6. Continue turning on the ball of LF, and take a small step diagonally forward with RF, body facing centre diagonally. To continue, step forward with LF into 4, 5, 6 of Reverse Turn.

*Contrary Body Movement.* CBM on 1 and 4.

*Rise and Fall (Body).* Commence to rise at end of 1 (NFR); continue to rise on 2 and 3. Lower at end of 3. Rise at the end of 5; up on 6. Lower at end of 6. The rise is taken from the ball of LF on 5. The L heel does not lower.

*Body Sway.* Sway to L on 2 and 3. No sway on actual spin.

*Amount of Turn.* On steps 1 to 3 make three-eighths of a turn. Make half a turn on 4 and three-eighths of a turn between 5 and 6.

*Footwork.* 1. T H. 2. T. 3. T H. 4. H T. 5. T. 6 T H. Note the footwork on 4. Turn is made on the ball of RF and the heel does not lower as the 5th step is taken.

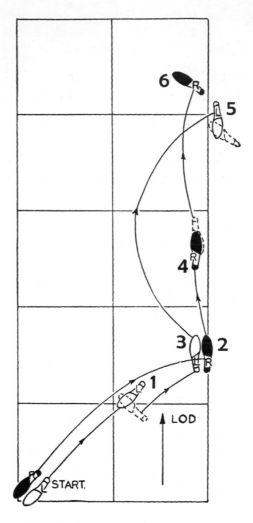

**Natural Spin Turn (Lady)**

*General Notes.* On the 6th step, the RF should brush lightly up to the LF before stepping diagonally forward.

It is important to remember that the lady does not use a true pivot on step 4. The "pivoting action" indicates that the weight is held over the RF slightly longer than in a normal turn, but the LF is not held in CBMP during the turn. To do so is, in fact, impossible.

# WHISK

## Man

The Whisk is a delightful figure to dance, and it has the advantage that it is quite easy to lead. It introduces another position to ballroom dancing, a position that is now known as "Whisk Position".

It is usually danced after a complete Reverse Turn.

Commence and finish the Whisk facing diagonally to the wall.

1. LF forward, diag. to wall.
2. RF to the side and slightly forward, commencing to turn lady to PP.
3. Cross LF behind and a few inches to the R of RF, now in PP, facing diag. to wall.

Endings to this figure are given below.

*Contrary Body Movement.* Slight CBM on 1.

*Rise and Fall (Body).* Commence to rise at end of 1; continue to rise on 2; up on 3. Lower at end of 3.

*Body Sway.* Sway to the L on 2, 3.

*Amount of Turn.* There is no turn for the man.

*Footwork.* 1. H T. 2. T. 3. T H.

*General Notes.* As the 1st step is taken the man must apply pressure with his R hand on the lady's L side to turn her to PP.

Care must be taken not to let the weight fall back on the 3rd step. When the 3rd step is in position the body should be inclined to the L, and it is this L sway of the body while the foot is crossed behind that makes the figure so attractive. The L heel will lower lightly as the RF moves forward into the following figure, which is usually the Chassé from PP, as shown in the diagram.

The Whisk may be used at a corner. If commenced facing diag. to wall near a corner the man will make a quarter turn to L on the Whisk and the lady will make no turn. When danced in this way the man's 2nd step will be "RF diag. forward, R side leading" and the lady's 2nd step will be "LF back, L side leading". Man will be facing LOD on 2 and facing

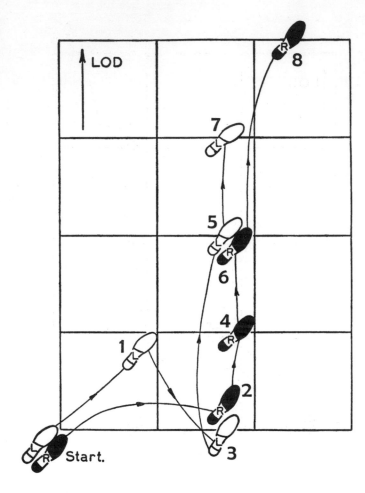

**Whisk and Chassé from Promenade Position (Man)**
**Steps 1,2,3 are The Whisk**
**Steps 4 to 8 are The Chassé from Promenade Position**

diag. to wall of the new LOD on 3. This amount of turn may be used on the side of the room to follow with the Weave from PP or a Wing.

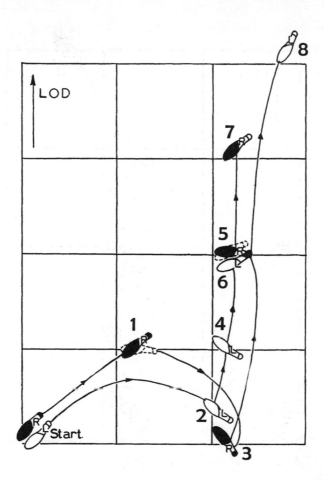

**Whisk and Chassé from Promenade Position (Lady)**
Steps 1,2,3 are The Whisk
Steps 4 to 8 are The Chassé from Promenade Position

# WHISK

## Lady

This is a delightful variation and the lady can help to make it look most attractive. The notes on page 122 and also those given with the man's description should be studied.

It is usually danced after a complete Reverse Turn.
Commence backing diagonally to the wall.

1. RF back, diag. to wall.
2. LF diagonally back, commencing to turn to PP.
3. Turning into PP, cross the RF behind and a few inches to the L of LF. Finish facing diag. to centre.

The two nicest endings to this figure are given in the man's description, and notes on these will be found below.

*Contrary Body Movement.* Lady has no CBM as she is turning to the R.

*Rise and Fall (Body).* Commence to rise at end of 1 (NFR); continue to rise on 2; up on 3. Lower at end of 3.

*Body Sway.* Sway to the R on 2, 3.

*Amount of Turn.* The lady's feet will make a quarter turn between steps 1 and 2 but her body turns slightly less. Her body will complete the turn on 3.

*Footwork.* 1. T H. 2. T. 3. T H.

*General Notes.* As the lady takes her first step back the man will apply pressure on her L side, to indicate the Whisk. This will result in her second step being placed diagonally back, but the body should not complete the turn into PP until the RF is crossing behind on 3. Care should be taken not to let the weight fall back on the 3rd step. When the 3rd step is in position the body should be inclined to the R. The R heel will lower lightly as the LF moves forward into the following figure. Now please refer to the man's General Notes.

## CHASSÉ FROM PROMENADE POSITION

### Man

This is the most popular ending to the Whisk or Back Whisk. It is similar to the Progressive Chassé used in the Quickstep and may follow any figure that has ended in Promenade Position. The Whisk and Chassé from Promenade Position are shown together in the diagram.

Commence in Promenade Position, facing diagonally to wall, with LF crossed behind RF in the "Whisk" position.

1. RF forward across the body in PP moving
   along the LOD. (1)
2. LF to side and slightly forward along the LOD,
   turning lady to her left ($^1/_2$ beat). (2)
3. Close RF to LF. Lady square. ($^1/_2$ beat). (and)
4. LF to side and slightly forward, on the same LOD. (3)
5. RF forward outside partner, diag. to wall, and make
   this the first step of a Natural Turn. (1)

The Chassé is counted 1, 2, "and" 3, denoting that there is only a half beat on each of the 2nd and 3rd steps.

*Contrary Body Movement.* CBM on 1 (slight) and 5. These two steps are also placed in CBMP.
*Rise and Fall (Body).* Commence to rise at end of 1; continue to rise on 2 and 3; up on 4. Lower at end of 4.
*Body Sway.* There is no sway.
*Amount of Turn.* There is no turn for the man.
*Footwork.* 1. H T. 2. T. 3. T. 4. T H. 5. H.
*General Notes.* The slight CBM on 1 will ensure that the body is practically square to the wall the whole time, thus keeping the bodies in a good alignment on step 5, the outside step.

# CHASSÉ FROM PROMENADE POSITION

## Lady

This is shown in the diagram following the Whisk and is by far the most popular ending to this figure. The steps are similar to those of the Progressive Chassé in Quickstep, apart from the first step which is taken in Promenade position.

Commence in Promenade Position, facing diagonally to centre, with RF crossed behind LF in the "Whisk" position.

1. LF forward across the body in PP, moving along
   the LOD and turning body to L. (1)

2. RF to side along the LOD, body facing centre
   ($^1/_2$ beat). (2)
3. Close LF to RF, feet now backing diag. wall.
   ($^1/_2$ beat). (and)
4. RF to side and slightly back. (3)
5. LF back, partner outside, diagonally to wall. (1)

The Chassé is counted 1, 2 "and" 3, denoting that there is only a half beat on each of the 2nd and 3rd steps.

*Contrary Body Movement.* CBM on 1 and 5. These two steps are also placed in CBMP.

*Rise and Fall (Body).* Commence to rise at end of 1; continue to rise on 2 and 3; up on 4; lower at end of 4.

*Body Sway.* There is no sway.

*Amount of Turn.* Make a quarter turn to the L.

*Footwork.* 1. H T. 2. T. 3. T. 4. T H. 5. T.

*General Notes.* Although the feet will back diag. to wall on steps 3 and 4 the body is practically square to the wall to ensure a good alignment as the man steps outside on 5. (This becomes the first step of the following Natural Turn.)

## REVERSE CORTÉ

### Man

The steps of man and lady differ in this figure, the man making a hesitation movement whilst the lady turns with two extra steps. The Reverse Corté itself has only three steps but in the description and diagram the following 4, 5 and 6 of the Natural Turn is given as this differs slightly to the normal Natural Turn. The Reverse Corté can be made much more attractive by departing from the orthodox amount of turn. Particulars of this are given under the general notes.

Commence facing diagonally to the centre and dance 1, 2, and 3 of the Reverse Turn. Finish with the back to the LOD.

1. RF back, body turning to L.
2. Turning on the ball or heel of the RF, close LF to RF. Finish with back diag. to centre against the LOD, weight on RF.
3. Hesitate.
4. LF back, diag. to centre against LOD (partner outside).
5. RF to side (no turn) getting into line with lady.
6. Close LF to RF.

Then go forward with RF, diag. to wall, into a Natural Turn.

*Contrary Body Movement.* CBM on 1, slight CBM on 4. The 4th step is taken back in CBMP.

*Rise and Fall (Body).* Rise on 2; up on 3. Lower at end of 3. Commence to rise at end of 4 (NFR); continue to rise on 5 and 6. Lower at end of 6.

*Body Sway.* Sway to R on 2 and 3. Sway to L on 5 and 6.

*Amount of Turn.* Three-eighths of a turn on preceding Reverse Turn. Three-eighths of a turn on first three steps of Corté. No turn on 4, 5, and 6.

*Footwork.* 1. T H. 2. H (LF) then Toes (both feet). 3. T H (RF). 4. T H. 5. T. 6. T H.

*Note.* If the turn is made on the ball of RF on 2 the footwork of the first three steps will be: 1. T H T. 2. Toes of both feet. 3. T H (RF). Even when the turn is made on the ball of foot on 2, the feet should be kept flat, and the rise is taken on the 2nd beat in both cases, after the turn is completed.

*General Notes.* The amount of turn given above is sometimes the easiest way for the novice to dance this figure. A more general method is to make half a turn on 1, 2, and 3 of the Corté, and then turn about an eighth of a turn to the R on 4, 5, and 6 to regain the diagonal position necessary for the following Natural Turn.

Advanced dancers make this figure much more attractive by overturning the first three steps, making five-eighths of a turn, so that the 4th step is taken back diagonally to the wall against the LOD. A quarter turn must then be made on 4, 5, and 6 to regain the diagonal position necessary for the following Natural Turn. See page 129 for the Back Whisk ending.

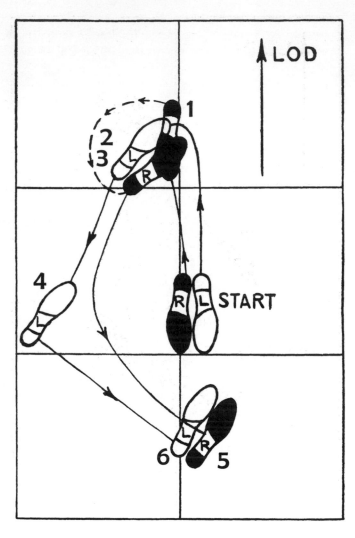

**Reverse Corté (Man)**
**(Followed by 4 to 6 of Natural Turn)**

# REVERSE CORTÉ

## Lady

The Reverse Corté is an attractive variation in which the lady

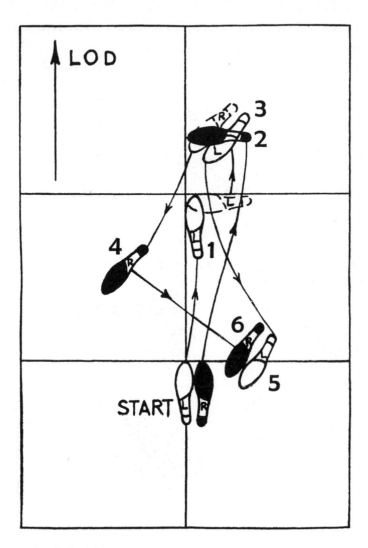

**Reverse Corté (Lady)**
**(Followed by 4 to 6 of Natural Turn)**

takes a step to the side and then closes whilst the man is hesitating. The Reverse Corté has only three steps. The following 4, 5 and 6 of the Natural Turn are given in the description and diagram.

Commence with the back diagonally to the centre and dance 1, 2, and 3 of the Reverse Turn. Finish facing the LOD.

1. LF forward turning body to L.
2. Small step to side with RF, on same LOD and still turning to L.
3. Close LF to RF. Finish facing diagonally to centre against the LOD.
4. RF forward, outside partner.
5. LF to side (no turn) partner getting into line.
6. Close RF to LF.
   Then go back with LF, diag. to wall, into a Natural Turn.

*Contrary Body Movement.* CBM on 1, slight CBM on 4. The 4th step is taken forward in CBMP.

*Rise and Fall (Body).* Commence to rise at end of 1; continue to rise on 2 and 3. Lower at end of 3. Commence to rise at end of 4; continue to rise on 5 and 6. Lower at end of 6. It should be noted that the lady rises slightly earlier than the man on this figure.

*Body Sway.* Sway to L on 2 and 3. Sway to R on 5 and 6.

*Amount of Turn.* Three-eighths of a turn is made on the preceding Reverse Turn. Three-eighths of a turn on first three steps of the Corté. No turn on 4, 5, and 6.

*Footwork.* 1. H T. 2. T. 3. T H. 4. H T. 5. T. 6. T H.

*General Notes.* When the man overturns the first three steps of the Reverse Corté (described in notes on man's steps) the lady must take her 2nd step slightly across the LOD, and continue to turn as the 3rd step closes.

## BACK WHISK
### (From a Reverse Corté)
### Man

The Back Whisk is a very popular ending to the first three steps of the Reverse Corté and is described from this position. Other entries to the Back Whisk are given in the General Notes on page 130.

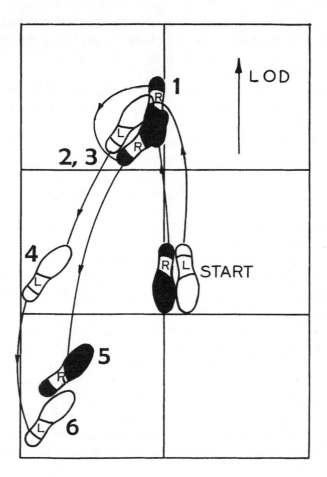

**Back Whisk (Man)**
**(From a Reverse Corté)**

Commence facing diagonally to centre and dance 1, 2, and 3 of a Reverse Turn. Finish backing the LOD.

1, 2, 3. Dance a Reverse Corté. Finish backing diag. to centre against the LOD.

4. LF back, partner outside.

5. RF diag. back. Commence to turn the lady to PP at the end of the step.

6. Cross LF behind RF. Man and lady now in PP.

Now step forward RF, along the LOD in PP and follow with the Chassé from Promenade Position page 122.

*Contrary Body Movement.* CBM on 1 and 4 (slight). Step 4 is placed in CBMP.

*Rise and Fall (Body).* Rise on 2; up on 3. Lower at end of 3. Commence to rise at end of 4 (NFR); continue to rise on 5; up on 6. Lower at end of 6.

*Body Sway.* Sway to R on 2 and 3. Sway to L on 5 and 6.

*Amount of Turn.* Make three-eighths turn to L on steps 1, 2, 3 of the Reverse Corté. No turn on the Back Whisk.

*Footwork.* 1, 2, 3 (See notes on Reverse Corté footwork). 4. T H. 5. T. 6. T H.

*General Notes.* It is advisable to use the Footwork of T H on step 1 of the Reverse Corté, making the turn on the heel of the RF. Do not drop backwards too quickly on the Back Whisk. Lower the L heel softly on step 6 and release it again as the RF moves forward in PP for the following Chassé, details of which will be found on page 122.

The Back Whisk can be danced after steps 1, 2, 3 of a Natural Turn, when the man will turn his body up to three-eighths of a turn to R between steps 4 and 5. When turn is used, step 5 (RF) will be placed to side and slightly back instead of diag. back. The lady will be in line with the man on step 4.

## BACK WHISK
### (From a Reverse Corté)
#### Lady

The Back Whisk is of course a Forward Whisk for the lady and is often used after steps 1, 2, 3 of a Reverse Corté.

Commence backing diagonally to centre and dance 1, 2, and 3 of a Reverse Turn. Finish facing the LOD.

1, 2, 3 Dance a Reverse Corté; Finish facing diag. to centre against the LOD.

4. RF forward, outside partner, turning body to R.

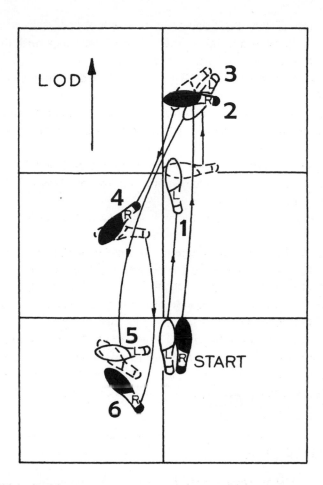

**Back Whisk (Lady)**
**(From a Reverse Corté)**

5. LF to side, with body facing centre and commencing to turn
   to PP.
6. Cross RF behind LF. Now in PP facing diag. to centre.
Now step forward LF, along the LOD in PP and follow with the
Chassé from Promenade Position, turning square to man. See page
123.

*Contrary Body Movement.* CBM on 1 and 4. Step 4 is placed in CBMP.

*Rise and Fall (Body)*. Commence to rise at end of 1; continue to rise on 2 and 3; lower at end of 3. Commence to rise at end of 4; continue to rise on 5; up on 6; lower at end of 6.

*Body Sway*. Sway to L on 2 and 3. Sway to R on 5 and 6.

*Amount of Turn*. Make three-eighths of a turn to L on steps 1, 2, 3 of the Reverse Corté. Make an eighth turn to R between steps 4 and 5 and an eighth between 5 and 6.

*Footwork*. 1. H T. 2. T. 3. T H. 4. H T. 5. T. 6. T H.

*General Notes*. When dancing steps 4, 5, 6 of The Back Whisk, it is better style to tend to underturn the body, thus avoiding the tendency to turn outwards too much on step 6. The head may turn to the R on step 6.

The Back Whisk can be danced after steps 1, 2, 3 of a Natural Turn, when the lady will usually have to turn more between steps 4 and 6. Please see notes following the man's steps.

The normal ending to the Back Whisk is the Chassé from Promenade Position with the lady turning square to the man. This is described on page 124.

The Wing and the Weave from Promenade Position are two attractive but more advanced endings.

## DOUBLE REVERSE SPIN

### Man

This figure is rather misnamed as it is not a spin, nor is it necessary to dance it twice. The man does two steps and a "toe pivot" whilst the lady does four steps. It should only be attempted by advanced dancers.

The commencing position and the amount of turn depend on the preceding figure. It is described below as a complete turn. Commence facing the LOD.

|  |  | Beats |
|---|---|---|
| 1. | LF forward, turning body to L. | 1 |
| 2. | RF to side, across the LOD. | $1/2$ |
|  | "and" Continue turning on ball of RF and close |  |

LF to RF. Keep weight on RF and finish facing
approximately to outside wall.
3. Continue turning on ball of RF to face the LOD.          1
Then step forward with LF into next figure.

*Note.* Although the man has actually only two steps and a pivot on
the R toe, the exact timing of each part of the turn has been given, as
it is necessary for the man to accelerate the closing of the LF to assist
the lady's turn. Advanced dancers may prefer to delay the speed of the
turn, counting "1, 2, 3 and".

*Contrary Body Movement.* CBM on 1.

*Rise and Fall (Body).* Rise at end of 1; up on 2 and 3. Lower at end
of 3.

*Body Sway.* There is no sway.

*Amount of Turn.* Three-quarters, seven-eighths or a complete turn
may be made.

*Footwork.* 1. H T. 2. T. 3. T (LF) then T H (RF).

*General Notes.* Positions from which this figure can be taken and the
amount of turn used are:

(a) The Easiest Amalgamation. With RF do a Closed Change to centre
diagonally. Double Reverse Spin, making only three-quarters of a turn
to finish facing the wall diagonally. Forward with LF into a Closed
Change or the Whisk.

(b) Closed Change commencing with RF as above.

Double Reverse Spin finishing facing LOD. Follow with another
Double Reverse Spin to face diagonally to wall and so into the Whisk.

(c) The Best Amalgamation. Do the Natural Spin Turn, 1 to 6. Finish
with back diagonally to centre.

Now do 4, 5 and 6 of Reverse Turn, making three-eighths of a turn
to finish facing LOD.

Double Reverse Spin, making a complete turn. Follow with:
Progressive Chassé to R or the Drag Hesitation and Back Lock.

# DOUBLE REVERSE SPIN

## Lady

Commence with the back to the LOD. (See notes on the man's
steps.)

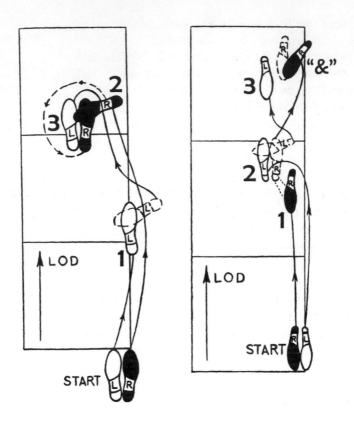

**Double Reverse Spin**
**Left: Man   Right: Lady**

|  | Beats |
|---|---|
| 1. RF back, turning body to L. | 1 |
| 2. Close LF to RF, turning on R heel. Finish facing LOD. Weight on LF. | 1/2 |

|  | Beats |
|---|---|
| "and" Continue turning on ball of LF as RF is moved to the side and slightly back. Finish with back diagonally to wall. | 1/2 |
| 3. Still turning, cross LF in front of RF. Finish with back to LOD. | 1 |

Then step back with RF into next figure.

*Contrary Body Movement.* CBM on 1.

*Rise and Fall (Body).* Rise slightly at end of 1 (NFR); continue to rise on 2; up on 3 and 4. Lower at end of 4.

*Body Sway.* There is no sway.

*Amount of Turn.* Please see notes at the foot of the description of the man's steps.

*Footwork.* 1. T H. 2. H T. 3. T. 4. T H.

*General Notes.* The lady will notice that she has four steps to dance in three beats of music. It is most important for her to get the acceleration on the 2nd step (Heel Turn) so that the 2nd and 3rd steps are the quick ones. The 4th step must be firm and, controlled, with the balance kept well over it, to enable the following step to be taken with ease.

Some advanced men dancers delay the speed of the turn. The lady will then use the rhythm of 1, 2, 3 "and", or one beat, one beat, half beat, half beat.

When the Double Reverse Spin is ended diagonally to wall, the lady should be backing towards wall on the 3rd step.

# OUTSIDE SPIN

## Man

This is a difficult variation, but is both useful and attractive. The man's steps are similar to those of 4, 5 and 6 of the Natural Spin Turn, but he leads his partner outside him on 1. It is usually danced after the hesitation on the 3rd step of the Reverse Corté.

The commencing position depends on the preceding figure. It is described below as following the 3rd step of the Reverse Corté, so that the commencing position will be facing diagonally to the wall.

1. Very small step back with LF, partner outside, with the toe turned in, and pivot three-eighths of a turn to R to face against the LOD.

2. RF forward, outside partner, still turning to the R.
3. Step to side LF with body facing diag. to centre, and then continue turning on ball of LF until body faces diag. to wall. The LF will then be directly behind the RF.
   To continue, step forward RF into a Natural Turn.

*Contrary Body Movement.* CBM on 1 and 2.
*Rise and Fall (Body).* Rise at end of 2; up on 3. Lower at end of 3.
*Body Sway.* There is no sway.
*Amount of Turn.* A complete turn is made between 1 and 3.
*Footwork.* 1. T H T. 2. H T. 3. T H.
*General Notes.* Care should be taken to make the 1st step very small and it is better to slip this foot into position with firm pressure on it. The weight should be kept well forward as the step is taken. The position of the 3rd step is also important. If too much turn is made between the 2nd and 3rd steps there will be a stop in the flow of the movement before entering the following Natural Turn.

The Outside Spin may be underturned, and this type of Outside Spin is usually taken after a Back Lock or Progressive Chassé to R. Three-quarters of a turn is made, and the 3rd step will be placed to the side and slightly back, with the body backing diag. to centre. The following step will be a step back with RF, into 4, 5, 6 of a Reverse Turn. The Turning Lock could follow this Outside Spin.

# OUTSIDE SPIN

## Lady

This is an advanced variation, and difficult for the lady to do neatly. The lady's steps of this figure are entirely different from the Natural Spin Turn. It is usually danced after the 3rd step of the Reverse Corté, and is described from this position.

Commence with the back diagonally to the wall.

1. RF forward, outside partner, body turning to R.
2. Turning on ball of RF, close LF to RF. (The weight should not be taken on to LF until body is facing the wall.)
3. Continue turning on ball of LF and take a small step forward on RF between partner's feet.

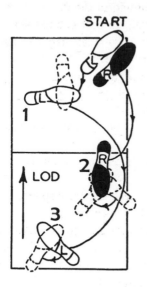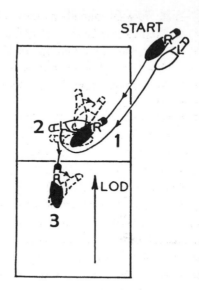

**Outside Spin**
**Left: Man   Right: Lady**

Note. As the RF (3) is moving forward, both man and lady are still turning. The weight is not taken on to the RF, until the lady's body is backing the LOD. She will continue to turn, so that by the time she is backing diagonally to the wall, her RF is forward and across the body in CBMP. To continue step back with the LF into a Natural Turn.

*Contrary Body Movement.* CBM on 1. The lady turns into CBMP on 3.
*Rise and Fall (Body).* Commence to rise at end of 1; continue to rise on 2; up on 3. Lower at end of 3.
*Body Sway.* There is no sway.
*Amount of Turn.* A complete turn is made between 1 and 3. See also notes on the man's steps. When the Outside Spin is underturned the lady's 3rd step will be diagonally forward as in the Natural Spin Turn (6th step). The following step will be a step forward with LF into 4, 5, 6 of the Reverse Turn.
*Footwork.* 1. H T. 2. T. 3. T H.
*General Notes.* The lady must be careful not to take the small step forward on RF (3rd step) too quickly, otherwise she will be obstructed by the man's R toe.

## OPEN TELEMARK
## (With Cross Hesitation finish)

### Man

The Open Telemark is adapted from the Closed Telemark, which is described in the Foxtrot Section. The term "Open" indicates that the figure is finished in Promenade Position. Many variations are taken from the Open Telemark. The Cross Hesitation finish is described below. The Open Telemark may be commenced when facing diagonally to centre or LOD.

Commence facing diagonally to the centre, which is the easiest position.

1. LF forward, diag. to centre, turning body to L.
2. RF to side, across the LOD.
3. Continue turning on ball of RF until body is facing towards outside wall, and step to side and slightly forward with LF. (Now in PP. See General Notes.)

Follow with Cross Hesitation:

1. RF forward, diag. to wall in PP, body still facing wall.
2. Close LF to RF without weight, turning body slightly to L.
3. Hesitate. (Body now facing diagonally to wall.) To continue, step back with LF diag. to centre against the LOD (partner outside) into 4, 5, and 6 of Natural Turn danced with no turn, as given following the Reverse Corté, or into a Back Whisk or Outside Spin.

*Contrary Body Movement.* CBM on 1 of Open Telemark. The 1st step of the Cross Hesitation is in CBMP.

*Rise and Fall (Body).* Open Telemark: rise at end of 1; up on 2 and 3. Lower at end of 3. Cross Hesitation: commence to rise at end of 1; continue to rise on 2 and 3. Lower at end of 3.

*Body Sway.* Open Telemark: Sway to L on 2. No sway on the Cross Hesitation.

*Amount of Turn.* Turn of man and lady differs in these figures. Open Telemark: man turns three-quarters of a turn, the body turning slightly less. Cross Hesitation: man turns an eighth of a turn with the body.

When the Open Telemark is commenced facing the LOD a little more turn is made.

*Footwork.* Open Telemark: 1. H T. 2. T. 3. T H. Cross Hesitation: 1. H T. 2. Toes (both feet). 3. T H (RF).

*General Notes.* As the man continues to turn on his second step of the Open Telemark, he must guide the lady by applying pressure with the base of his R hand on her L side. He must endeavour to indicate that he is turning to Promenade Position and that she is not to continue the turn with him. The man's LF should be pointing diagonally to wall on the 3rd step. His body is facing the wall. On the first step of the Cross Hesitation the RF is pointing diagonally to wall.

A more attractive way of dancing the Cross Hesitation is to make a quarter turn to the L on 1, 2, and 3, so that the following 4th step of the Natural Turn is commenced with the man stepping back with the LF diagonally to the wall against the LOD. He must then turn a quarter turn to the R on 4, 5, and 6 of the Natural Turn. A Back Whisk may follow the Cross Hesitation.

Note that when more turn is to be made on the Cross Hesitation, or if the Wing variation is to follow, the 3rd step of the Open Telemark should be placed to the side and slightly back.

Entries (a), (b), and (c) given in the notes on the Double Reverse Spin, may be used as entries to the Open Telemark.

The Cross Hesitation may be danced diagonally to centre after an Open Impetus. The Wing ending to the Open Telemark is described on page 140.

# OPEN TELEMARK
## (With Cross Hesitation finish)

### Lady

The Open Telemark can be commenced backing the LOD or backing diagonally to the centre. It is described from the latter position.

1. RF back, diag. to centre, turning body to L.
2. Close LF to RF, turning on R heel (Heel Turn). Finish facing the LOD.

3. RF diag. forward in PP, R side leading.

Follow with Cross Hesitation:

1. LF forward, across the body in PP, turning body to L.
2. RF to side, still turning to get square to partner.
3. Close LF to RF.

To continue, step forward with RF outside partner into 4, 5, and 6 of Natural Turn, etc. (See man's notes.)

*Contrary Body Movement.* CBM on 1 of Open Telemark. CBM and CBMP on the 1st step of Cross Hesitation.

*Rise and Fall (Body).* Open Telemark: rise slightly at end of 1 (NFR); continue to rise on 2; up on 3. Lower at end of 3. Cross Hesitation: commence to rise at end of 1; continue to rise on 2 and 3. Lower at end of 3.

*Body Sway.* Open Telemark: sway to R on 2. Cross Hesitation: sway to the L on 2, 3.

*Amount of Turn.* Turn of lady and man differs in this figure. Open Telemark: three-eighths of a turn between 1 and 2, with a slight body turn to L on 3. Cross Hesitation: three-eighths of a turn to L.

*Footwork.* Open Telemark: 1. T H. 2. H T. 3. T H. Cross Hesitation: 1. H T. 2. T. 3. T H.

*General Notes.* The R side lead on 3 of the Open Telemark will tend to keep the position compact, a desirable feature. On this step the lady may turn her head to the R to face the direction of the 3rd step, or may leave it in the normal position. It is a matter of personal taste.

The Wing ending to the Open Telemark is described on page 142.

# WING

## Man

This is a standard variation that is very popular. The steps for the man are similar to the Cross Hesitation, but no rise is made. The man makes a slight turn to the L, while the lady walks round him to his L side.

Dance 1, 2, and 3 of the Open Telemark, ending in Promenade Position. In this case, the 3rd step of the Open

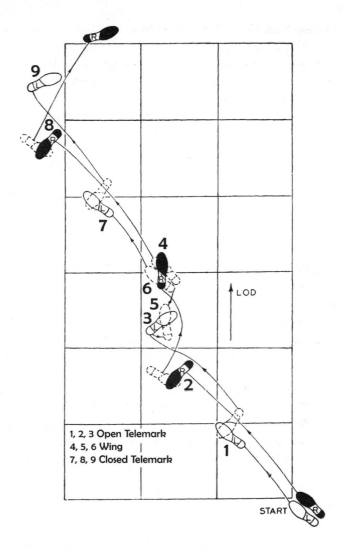

1, 2, 3 Open Telemark
4, 5, 6 Wing
7, 8, 9 Closed Telemark

LOD

START

**Open Telemark, Wing and Closed Telemark (Man)**

Telemark is to the side and slightly back across the LOD. Continue as follows:

1. RF forward and across the body in PP, with the body turning to the L. RF should be pointing down the LOD and body facing

between wall and diag. to wall.

2. With the weight on RF let body turn slightly to L to face the LOD and LF commences to close.
3. LF closes to RF without weight, and at the same time turn the RF and body to face diag. to centre.

Now step forward LF, outside the lady on her L side, into a Closed Telemark or Progressive Chassé to R.

*Contrary Body Movement.* The 1st step is taken in CBMP.

*Rise and Fall.* There is slight rise on 2 and 3 (NFR).

*Body Sway.* There is no sway.

*Amount of Turn.* Up to a quarter turn to L may be made.

*Footwork.* 1. H. 2. 3. Pressure on T of RF with foot flat and pressure on IE of T of LF.

*General Notes.* In leading this figure, the man must keep a slight pressure with his R hand on the lady's L side, and definitely lead her to his L side. The hold should be loosened slightly, but complete contact with partner should not be lost.

The man may end the Wing facing the LOD but the diag. to centre position will be found more natural.

The Wing is also danced after the Open Impetus Turn or the Whisk. A diagram appears on page 141.

# WING

## Lady

Dance 1, 2, and 3 of the Open Telemark. The position of the 3rd step will be forward and slightly to the R in PP, R side leading. Continue as follows:

1. LF forward in PP facing diag. to centre, turning to the L, and begin to walk round partner.
2. Small step forward with RF, facing centre. (Now in front of man but still slightly in PP.)
3. Small step forward with LF, facing against the LOD, and outside the man on his L side.

Step back with RF, with the man outside on the L, and go into

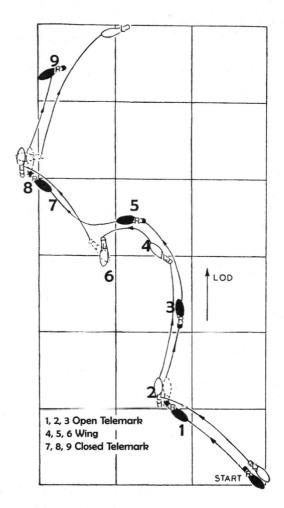

LOD

1, 2, 3 Open Telemark
4, 5, 6 Wing
7, 8, 9 Closed Telemark

START

**Open Telemark, Wing and Closed Telemark (Lady)**

any ending described in the notes on the man's steps.

*Contrary Body Movement.* The 1st and 3rd steps are taken in CBMP. CBM is used on 1.

*Rise and Fall (Body).* Commence to rise at end of 1; continue to rise on 2; up on 3. Lower at end of 3.

*Body Sway.* Sway to L on 2 and 3.

*Amount of Turn.* Up to a half turn to L may be made.

*Footwork.* 1. H T. 2. T. 3. T H.

*General Notes.* If the man ends facing diagonally to centre the lady will continue to turn another eighth to L as she steps back with the RF, but she should not actually swivel on her LF. The head may be turned to the L or R during the Wing. If turned to the L the position is more easily kept compact.

## OPEN IMPETUS
## (With Cross Hesitation finish)

### Man

This figure is similar to the Closed Impetus, but turning out to Promenade Position on the last step. It is normally preceded by the first half of the Natural Turn.

Dance 1, 2, and 3 of the Natural Turn. Finish with the back to LOD.

1. LF back, down LOD, turning body to the R.
2. Close RF to LF turning on the L heel (Heel Turn). Finish with weight on RF ready to step diag. to centre, and beginning to turn the lady to PP.
3. LF diag. forward in PP, L side leading. (LF is pointing diag. to centre, body facing the LOD.)

Continue with the Cross Hesitation as follows:

1. RF forward, in PP, diag. to centre.
2. Close LF to RF without weight, turning lady square.
3. Hesitate.

Continue by stepping back with LF (partner outside) diag. to wall against the LOD, and do 4, 5, and 6 of the Natural Turn or the Back Whisk, making a quarter turn to the R to finish facing diag. to wall.

*Contrary Body Movement.* CBM on 1 of the Open Impetus. The 1st step of the Cross Hesitation is placed in CBMP.

*Rise and Fall (Body).* Rise at end of 2; up on 3. Lower at end of 3. Cross Hesitation: Commence to rise at end of 1, continue to rise on 2 and 3. Lower at end of 3.

*Body Sway.* Sway to the L on 2. No sway on the Cross Hesitation.

*Amount of Turn.* Three-eighths on steps 1, 2 and a slight body turn to R on 3. There is a slight body turn only on the Cross Hesitation (to L).

*Footwork.* 1. T H. 2. H T. 3. T H. Cross Hesitation: 1. H T. 2. Toes (both feet). 3. T H (RF).

*General Notes.* After the Cross Hesitation the Outside Spin could be used, and followed by 1, 2, 3 of the Natural Turn, commenced diagonally to centre and ended backing centre. Follow with an Outside Change. The Wing or the Weave from PP could follow the Open Impetus.

# OPEN IMPETUS
## (With Cross Hesitation finish)
### Lady

This figure usually follows the first half of the Natural Turn. Finish facing LOD.

1. RF forward, turning body to the R.
2. LF to side, slightly across the LOD.
3. Continue turning on ball of LF and step to side with RF diag. to centre, having first brushed RF to LF and turned to PP (RF should point towards centre).

Continue with the Cross Hesitation as follows:

1. LF forward, across the body in PP turning body to l, moving diag. to centre.
2. RF to side (small step), still turning to get square to partner. Body backing LOD.
3. Close LF to RF. Now backing diag. to centre.

To continue, step forward with RF outside partner, diag. to wall against the LOD, and do 4, 5, and 6 of the Natural Turn, making a quarter turn to the R.

*Contrary Body Movement.* CBM on 1 of the Open Impetus. The 1st step of the Cross Hesitation is placed in CMBP, and CBM is also used to turn to the L.

*Rise and Fall (Body).* Rise at end of 2; up on 3. Lower at end of 3.

Cross Hesitation: Commence to rise at end of 1, continue to rise on 2 and 3. Lower at end of 3.

*Body Sway.* Sway to R on 2 of the Open Impetus. Cross Hesitation: sway to L on 2 and 3.

*Amount of Turn.* Make three-quarters of a turn on steps 1, 2, 3, the body turning slightly less to keep the position compact. There will be three-eighths of a turn to L on the Cross Hesitation.

*Footwork.* 1. H T. 2. T. 3. T H. Cross Hesitation: 1. H T. 2. T. 3. T H.

*General Notes.* When the Wing follows the Open Impetus Turn the lady will make an eighth of a turn on each step of the Wing to end backing diag. to centre.

## DRAG HESITATION AND BACK LOCK

### Man

Although these are two distinct variations and can be used separately, they are frequently danced as a complete amalgamation, and they are described as such below.

The Drag Hesitation can be commenced diagonally to the centre after a Closed Change on the RF, or down the LOD after the Double Reverse Spin. It is described from the latter position.

Commence facing the LOD.

### Drag Hesitation

1. LF forward, down the LOD turning body to L.
2. RF to side, on the same LOD. Body now facing centre. 3. Continue turning slightly to L and drag LF slowly to RF without putting the weight on to it.

Finish backing diag. to wall, preparing to pass partner outside.

### Back Lock

| | |
|---|---|
| 1. LF back, diag. to wall, partner outside. | (1) |
| 2. RF back. (1/2 beat). | (2) |
| 3. Cross LF in front of RF (1/2 beat). | (&) |
| 4. RF diag. back. | (3) |

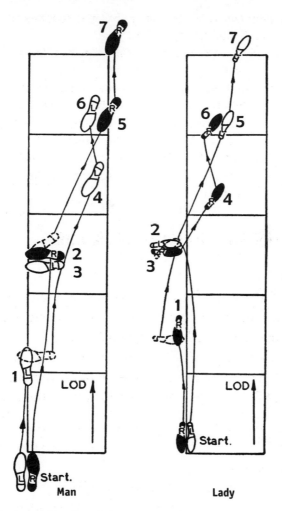

**Drag Hesitation and Back Lock (Man and Lady)**
**Steps 1, 2, 3 are the Drag Hesitation**
**Steps 4 to 7 are the Back Lock**

Continue by stepping back with LF diag. to wall and with partner outside, into 4, 5, 6 of a Natural Turn, or into Closed Impetus, Open Impetus, or a Back Whisk.

*Contrary Body Movement.* CBM on 1 of Drag Hesitation. CBM on 1 of Backward Lock. It is also placed in CBMP.

*Rise and Fall (Body).* Drag Hesitation: rise at end of 2; up on 3. Lower at end of 3. Back Lock: commence to rise at end of 1 (NFR); continue to rise on 2 and 3; up on 4. Lower at end of 4.

*Body Sway.* There is no sway on either figure.

*Amount of Turn.* Make three-eighths of a turn on the Drag Hesitation, or a quarter if commenced diag. to centre. No turn on the Back Lock.

*Footwork.* Drag Hesitation: 1. H T. 2. T. 3. Toes (both feet) then T H (RF). Backward Lock: 1. T H. 2. T. 3. T. 4. T H.

*General Notes.* It should be noted that the man rises at the end of 2 in the Drag Hesitation. If the man remembers to keep this step fairly wide and with no rise (although it is taken on the ball of the foot) and also to drag the LF slowly to RF, the lady will not mistake the lead for that of a Reverse Turn. It is easier to lead from a Double Reverse Spin than from a Closed Change.

After the Drag Hesitation, an underturned Outside Spin may be danced. Make three-quarters of a turn to the R on the Outside Spin, and follow it with a step back on RF, diag. to centre, into 4, 5, 6 of a Reverse Turn.

When 4, 5, 6 of the Natural Turn is used following the Back Lock, make a quarter turn to R to finish facing diag. to centre and follow with a Closed Change and a Reverse figure. If three-eighths of a turn is made, finish facing the LOD and follow with 1, 2, 3 of a Natural Turn and an Outside Change.

# DRAG HESITATION AND BACK LOCK

## Lady

Although these are two distinct variations and can be used separately, they are frequently danced as a complete amalgamation, and they are described as such below.

The Drag Hesitation can be commenced backing diagonally to the centre after a Closed Change on the LF or down the LOD after the Double Reverse Spin. It is described from the latter position.

Commence backing the LOD.

## Drag Hesitation

1. RF back, down the LOD turning body to L.
2. LF to side, on the same LOD.
3. Drag the RF slowly to LF without putting the weight on to it. Finish facing diag. to wall, preparing to step outside partner.

## Back Lock (Forward Lock for lady)

1. RF forward, diag. to wall, outside partner.    (1)
2. LF diag. forward (1/2 beat).    (2)
3. Cross RF behind LF (1/2 beat).    (&)
4. LF diag. forward.    (3)

Continue by stepping forward with RF, diag. to wall and outside partner into 4, 5, 6 of a Natural Turn, or into a Closed or Open Impetus Turn, or a Back Whisk.

*Contrary Body Movement.* CBM on 1 of Drag Hesitation. CBM on 1 of Back Lock. It is also placed in CBMP.

*Rise and Fall (Body).* Drag Hesitation: rise at end of 2; up on 3. Lower at end of 3. Back Lock: commence to rise at end of 1; continue to rise on 2 and 3; up on 4. Lower at end of 4.

*Body Sway.* There is no sway on either figure.

*Amount of Turn.* Make three-eighths of a turn or less on the Drag Hesitation. No turn on the Back Lock.

*Footwork.* Drag Hesitation: 1. T H. 2. T. 3. Toes (both feet) then T H (LF). Back Lock: 1. H T. 2. T. 3. T. 4. T H.

*General Notes.* The notes following the description of the man's steps should be studied.

# PROGRESSIVE CHASSÉ TO RIGHT

## Man

The Progressive Chassé to Right is a more recent addition in the Waltz but is very popular. The easiest entry is after a Hesitation Change which has ended diagonally to centre. More advanced entries are given in the General Notes. The man is dancing the lady's steps of the Progressive Chassé in Quickstep.

Commence facing diagonally to centre.

| | count |
|---|---|
| 1. LF forward, turning body to L. | 1 |
| 2. RF to side with body backing wall. | 2 |
| 3. Close LF to RF, turning slightly to L to back diag. to wall. | & |
| 4. RF to side and slightly back. | 3 |
| 5. Now step back LF, partner outside and continue with a Back Whisk or a Back Lock, etc. | 1 |

*Contrary Body Movement.* CBM on 1 and 5. Step 5 would be placed in CBMP.

*Rise and Fall (Body).* Commence to rise at end of 1; continue to rise on 2 and 3; up on 4; lower at end of 4.

*Body Sway.* No sway is used on this figure.

*Amount of Turn.* Make an eighth turn to L between 1 and 2 and an eighth between 2 and 3. The body should turn slightly less than the feet between 2 and 3.

*Footwork.* 1. H T. 2. T. 3. T. 4. T H. 5. T.

*General Notes.* The count of 1, 2, & 3 means that the 2nd and 3rd steps have a half beat only on each step. Other good entries are:

(a) Open Impetus or a Whisk followed by a Wing and ended facing diag. to centre. Now step forward LF outside lady on her L side, and continue with the Progressive Chassé to R.

(b) After the Wing, dance the Progressive Chassé to R making a half turn to L to end backing diag. to centre. Now step back LF with Lady outside, and continue with an Outside Change, lady getting in line on step 2. End facing diag. to wall and follow with a Natural figure.

## PROGRESSIVE CHASSÉ TO RIGHT

### Lady

The lady is dancing the man's steps of a Progressive Chassé as in quickstep. Commence backing diagonally to centre.

| | |
|---|---|
| 1. RF back, turning body to L. | 1 |
| 2. LF to side, along LOD, body facing wall. | 2 |
| 3. Close RF to LF. | & |

4. LF to side and slightly forward.                                    3
5. Now step forward RF, outside partner, diag. to wall
   and continue into a Back Whisk or a Forward Lock.    1

*Contrary Body Movement.* CBM on 1 and 5. Step 5 will be placed in CBMP.

*Rise and Fall (Body).* Commence to rise at end of 1 (NFR); continue to rise on 2 and 3; up on 4; lower at end of 4.

*Body Sway.* No sway is used on this figure.

*Amount of Turn.* Make a quarter turn to L between steps 1 and 3 but the body will turn slightly less.

*Footwork.* 1. T H. 2. T. 3. T. 4. T H. 5. H.

Please see the notes following the description of the man's steps.

# TURNING LOCK
## (After a Natural Spin Turn)

### Man

The Natural Spin Turn and Turning Lock has become one of the most popular variations in the Waltz. It consists of a Back Lock on which a turn is made to the left on the third step, allowing the dancer to continue into another Natural figure.

Dance a Natural Spin Turn and end backing diagonally to centre, with the LF to the side and slightly back in its normal position. Continue:

                                                                      Beats
1. RF back diag. to centre, with the R side leading.          1/2
2. Cross LF in front of RF.                                    1/2
3. RF back and slightly rightwards.                            1
4. With a slight body turn to L step to side and
   slightly forward LF.                                        1
5. The next step is taken forward with RF, diag. to
   wall outside partner, into a Natural Turn.

*Contrary Body Movement.* Although turn is made on step 3 CBM is not used.

*Rise and Fall (Body).* Commence to rise at end of 1; continue to rise on 2 and 3; up on 4. Lower at end of 4.

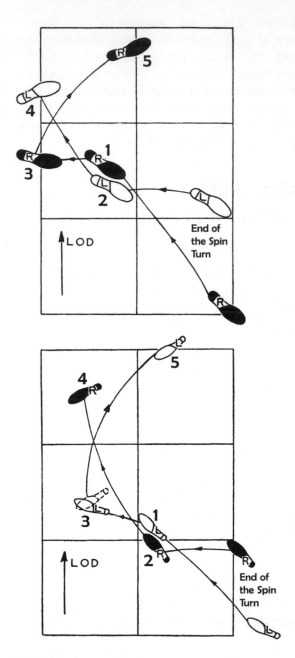

**Turning Lock Step After the Spin Turn**
**Top: Man   Bottom: Lady**

*Body Sway.* Sway to L on steps 1 and 2.

*Amount of Turn.* A quarter turn to L is made between 3 and 4.

*Footwork.* 1. T. 2. T. 3. T. 4. T H. 5. H.

*General Notes.* The R side lead and the sway to L on steps 1 and 2 are most important and enhance the beauty of the figure. The R side lead is lost as the RF moves back and rightwards on step 3. The continuance of the rise on step 3 is also important. Step 4 (LF) may be taken to the side in Promenade Position.

# TURNING LOCK
## (After a Natural Spin Turn)
### Lady

Commence facing diagonally to centre after a Natural Spin Turn. The weight will be on the RF which is placed diagonally forward. Lower the R heel lightly before moving forward into the first step of the Turning Lock.

| | | Beats |
|---|---|---|
| 1. | LF forward, diag. to centre, L side leading. | 1/2 |
| 2. | Cross RF behind LF. | 1/2 |
| 3. | LF forward and slightly leftwards, in line with partner. | 1 |
| 4. | With a slight body turn to L, step to side and slightly back with RF, backing diag. to wall. | 1 |
| 5. | The next step is taken back with LF, diag. to wall, with partner outside, into a Natural Turn. | |

*Contrary Body Movement.* CBM is not used when turning to L on step 3.

*Rise and Fall (Body).* Commence to rise at end of 1; continue to rise on 2 and 3; up on 4; lower at end of 4.

*Body Sway.* Sway. to R on steps 1 and 2.

*Amount of Turn.* A quarter turn to L is made between 3 and 4.

*Footwork.* 1. T. 2. T. 3. T. 4. T H. 5. T.

*General Notes.* Step 1 is taken on the ball of foot, rising higher throughout steps 2 and 3. Step 4 may be taken in PP.

# WEAVE FROM PROMENADE POSITION

## Man

The Weave was originally a Foxtrot variation and is described in the Foxtrot section of this book. The idea of commencing the Weave in Promenade Position was found to be so attractive that it is now used in both the Waltz and Foxtrot.

It is a beautiful figure with great rhythmic feeling and is not difficult to learn. When danced in the Waltz it can be taken after an Open Impetus or a Whisk. In the following description it is assumed that the man has danced the Whisk along the side of the room, ending in PP with his body facing diagonally to the centre. Notes on other entries are given below.

Commence in PP with man facing diagonally to centre and lady facing diagonally to centre against the LOD.

1. RF forward across the body in PP, moving towards centre and with RF pointing to centre.
2. Turning lady square, step forward LF, to centre.
3. Turning to L step to side and slightly back with RF, body backing the LOD.
4. Still turning slightly, step back LF, diag. to centre with the Lady outside.
5. RF back, diag. to centre, with Lady in line, and turning to the L.
6. LF to side and slightly forward.
7. The following step on RF is taken diag. to wall, outside partner, and is the first step of a Natural Turn.

*Contrary Body Movement*. CBM on 2, 5 and 7. The 1st, 4th and 7th steps are placed in CBMP.

*Rise and Fall (Body)*. Commence to rise at end of 1; continue to rise on 2; up on 3. Lower at end of 3. Commence to rise at end of 4 (NFR); continue to rise on 5; up on 6. Lower at end of 6.

*Body Sway*. No sway is used on this figure in the Waltz.

*Amount of Turn*. Make a half turn to L over 1 to 4 and a quarter turn to L between 5 and 6.

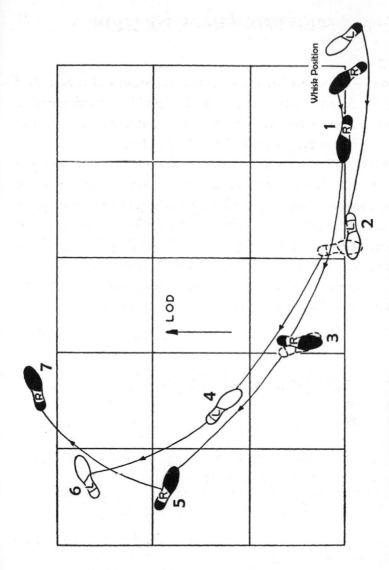

Whisk Position

LOD

Weave from Promenade Position Following the Whisk (Man)

*Footwork.* 1. H T. 2. T. 3. T H. 4. T H. 5. T. 6. T H. 7. H.

*General Notes.* Do not attempt to turn the lady square too abruptly at the end of step 1. The man should lead the lady to move more sideways on step 2 and she will then turn square gradually as the turn is continued on her RF. It is attractive to hurry the timing a little on steps 1, 2, so that a hover effect can be made before placing the 3rd step in position. The continuance of the rise on steps 2 and 5 enhances the rhythmic feeling of the figure.

Amalgamations. (a) Dance 1, 2, 3, of a Natural Turn and then a Back Whisk. End facing diag. to centre. Follow with the Weave.

(b) Dance an Open Impetus Turn, end moving towards centre in PP. Follow with the Weave.

(c) The Spin and Turning Lock could be ended in PP on step 4. Follow with the Weave, overturning the first 4 steps.

## WEAVE FROM PROMENADE POSITION

### Lady

The Weave from Promenade Position can be danced practically any time when the man and lady are in Promenade Position. It is described below after a Whisk danced along the side of the room, the lady facing diagonally to centre against the LOD.

Commence in PP as above, then:

1. LF forward in PP, facing diag. to centre against the LOD.
2. Turning to the L step to side and slightly back with RF, now backing diag. to centre and turning square to man.
3. Continue turning to L on ball of RF until facing the LOD and then step to side and slightly forward with LF with the L toe pointing diag. to centre. Now square.
4. RF forward, outside partner, diag. to centre.
5. LF forward, diag. to centre, in line with partner and turning to the L.
6. RF to side and slightly back, now backing diag. to wall.
7. The following step on LF is taken back diag. to wall with the partner outside, and is the first step of a Natural Turn.

*Contrary Body Movement.* CBM on 1, 5 and 7. The 1st, 4th and 7th steps are placed in CBMP.

*Rise and Fall (Body).* Commence to rise at end of 1; continue to rise on 2; up on 3. Lower at end of 3. Commence to rise at end of 4; continue to rise on 5; up on 6. Lower at end of 6.

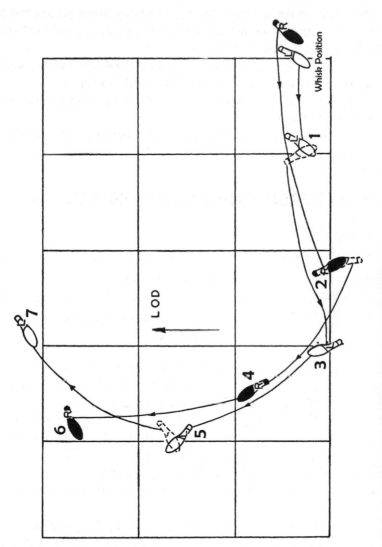

Whisk Position

LOD

Weave from Promenade Position Following the Whisk (lady)

*Body Sway.* No sway is used on this figure in the Waltz.

*Amount of Turn.* Make three-quarters of a turn to L between 1 and 4, and a quarter turn to L between 5 and 6.

*Footwork.* 1. H T. 2. T. 3. T H. 4. H T. 5 T. 6. T H. 7. T.

*General Notes.* Do not attempt to turn square too abruptly between steps 1 and 2. The 2nd step should move mainly side and the turn continue throughout steps 2 and 3.

It will be noted that the lady has much more turn to make than the man. The additional three-eighths of a turn is accounted for by the man making an eighth of a turn to L (with his RF) as his 1st step is taken, and the lady has an additional quarter turn to make to get square to the man. The head should be kept to the R on steps 1 and 2.

## SUGGESTED WALTZ AMALGAMATIONS

1. Natural Turn–RF Closed Change–Reverse Turn–LF Closed Change. Repeat.

2. Hesitation Change–1, 2, 3 of Reverse Turn–Reverse Corté and 4, 5, 6 of Natural Turn–Natural Spin Turn.

3. 1, 2, 3 of Natural Turn–Outside Change–Natural Spin Turn–Reverse Corté–Back Whisk–Chassé from PP.

4. Natural Spin Turn–4, 5, 6 of Reverse Turn, turning to LOD–Double Reverse Spin–Drag Hesitation–Back Lock. End with 4, 5, 6 of Natural Turn or: Open Impetus–Cross Hesitation–Back Whisk turning to face diag. to wall–Chassé from PP.

5. Reverse Turn–Whisk and Chassé from PP–Natural Spin Turn–Turning Lock.

6. Double Reverse Spin–Open Telemark–Wing–Closed Telemark.

7. Open Impetus–Wing–Overturned Progressive Chassé to R to end backing diag. to centre–Outside Change (Lady outside on the first step)–Natural Spin Turn.

8. Reverse Turn–Whisk, turning to Left to end facing the LOD or diag. to centre–Weave from PP.

9. Natural Spin Turn (underturned to end facing diag. to wall–4, 5, 6 of Reverse Turn ended facing diag. to centre–Open Telemark–Cross Hesitation–Outside Spin.

# SECTION III

# THE FOXTROT

The Foxtrot is characterized by long, gliding, and perfectly smooth steps, demanding ease of movement and control in order to give the dance a lazy and unhurried appearance.

The construction of the Foxtrot is such that it is only possible to dance it in a large and uncrowded ballroom. The keen dancer, who will doubtless practise and dance at one of the many excellent dance studios or public dance halls throughout the country, will find it of great assistance in acquiring balance and control.

Whilst the Foxtrot is the most delightful dance and most typical of English ballroom dancing, it is unfortunate that it is of little direct use to the social dancer. The social dancers, whose dancing activities are likely to be restricted to club, hotel and restaurant dances, would be well advised to learn to adapt the simple basic figures of the Quickstep to the slower tempo. This type of dancing is called "Rhythm Dancing" or "Social Foxtrot".

## GENERAL NOTES

*Time.* 4/4. 4 beats in a bar. The 1st and 3rd beats are accented, but not so definitely as in the Quickstep.

*Tempo.* Music should be played at 30 bars a minute.

*Basic Rhythms.* The figures consist of various combinations of "Slows" and "Quicks". Each "Slow" has 2 beats of music. The "Quicks" have 1 beat each.

*Figures.* Walks, Feather, Three Step, Natural Turn, Reverse Turn, Closed Impetus, Closed Telemark, Open Telemark, Change of Direction, Reverse Wave, Basic Weave, Natural Weave, Hover Feather, Natural Telemark, Hover Telemark, Outside Swivel, Weave from Promenade Position, Natural Twist Turn.

The first thing for the beginner to appreciate is that, whereas in the Quickstep the change to a quicker rhythm is made with a Chassé, in the Foxtrot this change is made with a figure called the Three Step, a description of which is given on pages 165 and 166.

The correct interpretation of the Three Step is of utmost importance, and the beginner would be well advised to prac- tise this, combined with the Walk, before attempting any other figure. Although the following amalgamation does not appear in the finished dance, it is by far the simplest method of acquiring the smooth and unhurried entry from the Walk to the Three Step which is the basis of the Foxtrot.

Face the Line of Dance

| | Count |
|---|---|
| Walk forward with RF | S |
| Walk forward with LF | S |
| Three Step (Right, Left, Right) | QQS |
| Walk forward with LF | S |
| Walk forward with RF | S |
| Three step (Left, Right, Left) | QQS |
| Repeat walk with RF, LF, etc. | |

This amalgamation should be practised with music, taking care that the entry to each Three Step is made without *obvious* effort. Careful attention to the footwork and rise and fall will help the dancer to attain a smooth and flowing movement.

Before learning the basic figures which comprise the Foxtrot, the novice should have some idea of its construction.

The Walk, as a separate figure, does not appear in the dance, all slow walking steps forming a part of a basic figure.

It should be noted that, in joining two figures such as the Three Step and the Natural Turn, the last step of the Three Step will also be the first step of the Natural Turn. Hints on amalgamation are given after the description of each figure, but, as a preliminary guide, the following amalgamation, which is the first to be attempted by the beginner, may be helpful.

### The Feather, Three Step and Natural Turn

Rhythm as separate figures:

| Feather | Three Step | Natural Turn |
|---------|------------|--------------|
| SQQS    | QQS        | SQQSSS       |

Rhythm when amalgamated:

| Feather | Three Step | Natural Turn |
|---------|------------|--------------|
| SQQS    | QQS        | QQSSS        |

Thus it will be noted that the last step of the Three Step (RF) has been used as the first of the Natural Turn.

## THE WALK – FORWARD AND BACKWARD

A full description of the Walk is given an pages 9–15, and unless this has been correctly mastered the pupil should not attempt the Foxtrot, which is the most difficult of all ballroom dances.

The Walk in the Foxtrot is practically the same as in the Quickstep, but the following special points should be noted.

1. The steps will be slightly longer than in the Quickstep owing to the slower music.

2. The slower music will result in the knees being slightly more relaxed than in the Quickstep.

This is especially noticeable when a slow step is to followed by a quick step. As the weight is taken on the slow step the knee will relax rather more than usual, and the gradual straightening of that knee will result in a "softer" entry into the following quick step.

# FEATHER

## Man

The Feather consists of a slow step followed by a type of Three Step in which the man steps outside the lady on the second quick step. The rise is also taken earlier.

It can be taken along the LOD, diagonally to the centre, or diagonally to the wall. In the first basic amalgamation it is taken along the LOD.

Commence and finish facing the LOD.

1. RF forward, turning body slightly to R.                    S
2. LF forward, preparing to step outside partner,
   L side leading                                              Q
3. RF forward, outside partner                                Q
4. LF forward, in line with partner                           S

*Contrary Body Movement.* CBM on 1 and 4. The 3rd step is placed in CBMP.

*Rise and Fall (Body).* Rise at end of 1; up on 2 and 3. Lower at end of 3.

*Body Sway.* Sway to R on 2 and 3.

*Amount of Turn.* There is no turn, except for the L side lead on steps 2 and 3.

*Footwork.* 1. H T. 2. T. 3. T H. 4. H.

*General Notes.* The stepping outside partner on the 3rd step needs great care, otherwise an ugly hip movement will result. The bodies must be kept square and together all the time. The L side lead on 2 will result in the man stepping forward in an "open" position, and this will enable him to step outside without losing contact with his partner. (See diagram on page 164.)

*Amalgamations.* (a) Feather down the LOD into the Three Step and Natural Turn.

(b) Feather diag. to centre, into any Reverse figure.

(c) Feather down the LOD into the Reverse Wave.

(d) Feather diag. to the wall or into a corner and followed by a Change of Direction step.

(e) A Three Step may follow a Feather or Feather movement that has been ended diag. to wall. It may be continued in a direction diag. to wall or curved to L to finish down the LOD.

# FEATHER

## Lady

The Feather consists of a slow step followed by a type of Three Step in which the man steps outside the lady on the 2nd quick step. The positions in which it is used will be found in the notes on the man's steps.

Commence with the back to the LOD. Finish with the back to the LOD.

1. LF back, turning body slightly to R.                       S
2. RF back, R side leading.                                   Q
3. LF back, partner outside.                                  Q
4. RF back, partner in line.                                  S

*Contrary Body Movement.* CBM on 1 and 4. The 3rd step is placed in CBMP.

*Rise and Fall (Body).* Rise at end of 1 (NFR); up on 2 and 3 (NFR). Lower at end of 3.

*Body Sway.* Sway to L on 2 and 3.

*Amount of Turn.* There is no actual turn.

*Footwork.* 1. T H. 2. T H. 3. T H. 4. T.

*General Notes.* Although the technical position of the 2nd step is RF back, the R side lead will result in this step being in an "open" position. If it is placed straight back, contact with partner may be lost. It is most important to remember that each step should move back from a forward position with the heel in contact with the floor and the

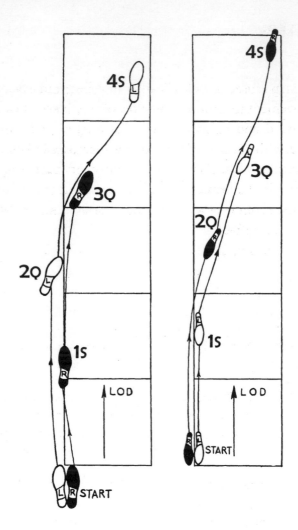

**The Feather**
**Left: Man   Right: Lady**

front toe released. If foot rise is used, the flow of the figure will be seriously restricted.

# THREE STEP

## Man

The Three Step is used to link a Feather movement to a Natural turning movement to maintain the flow of the dance. It can be danced forward and backward. As a basic figure it is always commenced with the RF when moving forward, and the LF when moving backward. When used as a part of another figure it is rhythmically the same, but the steps are altered in many cases. The description below is for moving forward, as when the figure is taken after a Feather.

Commence facing the LOD.

1. RF forward.
2. LF forward.
3. RF forward.

*Contrary Body Movement.* If danced as a separate figure for practise only, no CBM would be used. As an entry to the Natural Turn, CBM would be used on 3.

*Rise and Fall (Body).* Rise at end of 1; up on 2. Lower at end of 2.

*Body Sway.* Sway to L on 1 and 2.

*Amount of Turn.* Can be taken straight or may curve slightly to the L when taken after a Reverse Turn. The turn comes from the preceding slow step.

*Footwork.* 1. H T. 2. T H. 3. H.

*General Notes.* Avoid any effect of hurrying the two quick steps. Interpretation of the rhythm is largely a matter of personal expression. A good general hint is to be a little late with the second "Quick". All the steps must be long. The second will be very slightly shorter owing to the rise, whilst the third step, being an entry into the following Natural Turn, will be slightly longer, but avoid a forceful action. The CBM used on the last step of the preceding Feather results in the use of a slight R side lead on the first 2 steps.

## THREE STEP

### Lady

As a basic figure the Three Step is always commenced with the LF when moving backward and the RF when moving forward. The description below is for moving backward, as when the figure is taken after a Feather.

Commence backing the LOD.

| | | |
|---|---|---|
| 1. | LF back. | Q |
| 2. | RF back. | Q |
| 3. | LF back. | S |

*Contrary Body Movement.* If danced as a separate figure for practice, no CBM would be used. As an entry to the Natural Turn, CBM would be used on 3.

*Rise and Fall (Body).* Rise at end of 1 (NFR); up on 2 (NFR). Lower at end of 2.

*Body Sway.* Sway to R on 1 and 2.

*Amount of Turn.* The figure can be taken straight or may be curved slightly to the L after a Reverse Turn. The turn comes from the preceding slow step.

*Footwork.* 1. T H. 2. T H. 3. T.

*General Notes.* The man will use a R side lead on steps 1 and 2 and the lady should respond to this with a L side lead. Although rise will be felt in the body it is most important that when each step commences to move back from a forward position the heel is in contact with the floor with the front toe released. If the foot moves back with the toe in contact with the floor the movement will be seriously restricted.

## NATURAL TURN

### Man

The Natural Turn consists of an Open Turn and a type of Heel Turn called a Heel Pull.

The Natural Turn can be used either at a corner or when progressing along the sides of the room. It can be commenced facing the LOD or diagonally to the wall, the amount of turn on each part varying according to the commencing and finishing positions.

Commence facing the LOD. Finish facing diagonally to the centre or facing the new LOD.

1. RF forward, turning body to R.                                          S
2. LF to side, across the LOD.                                            Q
3. Continue turning on ball of LF and step RF back.     Q
4. LF back, down LOD turning body to R.                       S
5. Pull RF back firmly, at the same time turning on
   L heel. Finish with RF at the side of LF, feet parallel
   and about 25 cm (10 inches) apart. Weight on RF.     S
6. LF forward, body turning to the L.                             S

*Contrary Body Movement.* CBM on 1, 4 and 6.

*Rise and Fall (Body).* Rise at end of 1; up on 2 and 3. Lower at end of 3.

*Body Sway.* Sway to R on 2 and 3. Sway to L on 5.

*Footwork.* 1. H T. 2. T. 3. T H. 4. T H. 5. H, IE of foot, whole foot, then IE of LF. 6. H.

*Amount of Turn.* (a) When danced down the sides of the room. Make half a turn on 1, 2, 3; make three-eighths of a turn on 4, 5, 6 to finish facing diagonally to the centre and follow with a Feather into any Reverse figure.

When 4, 5, 6 are taken at a corner make a quarter turn to finish facing the new LOD and follow with a Feather, Three Step and Natural Turn, or a Feather and Reverse Wave. Alternatively, make an eighth of a turn on 4, 5, 6 and finish facing diagonally to the centre of the new LOD and follow with a Feather and any Reverse figure.

(b) When commenced very near a corner, make three-eighths of a turn on 1, 2, 3 so that steps 2, 3, 4 are taken moving across the corner. On 4, 5, 6 make a quarter turn to face diagonally to the new Centre or three-eighths of a turn to face the new LOD.

*General Notes.* Try to get the effect of "cutting" the RF under the body on the 3rd step. This will help the dancer feel the sway, Attempt to make the R toe just touch the L heel in passing.

When the RF is in position on 5, the body will cease to turn to the R, and will immediately commence to turn to the L as the LF starts to move forward. This gives a continuous and attractive movement of the body during a somewhat stationary part of the figure.

The first amalgamation to use is: Feather, Three Step, Natural Turn. Use the last step of the Three Step as the first of the Natural Turn.

A Closed Impetus may follow the 3rd step of the Natural Turn. The Hover Feather may follow the 5th step.

## NATURAL TURN

### Lady

The Natural Turn is used either at a corner or when progressing along the sides of the room.

It includes a Heel Turn and a Brush Step.

Commence with the back to the LOD. Finish with the back diagonally to the centre, or with the back to the new LOD. (See notes on man's steps.)

1. LF back, turning body to R.                                    S
2. Close RF to LF, turning on L heel (Heel Turn).
   Finish facing LOD, weight on RF.                          Q
3. LF forward.                                                        Q
4. RF forward, turning body to R.                            S
5. LF to side, across the LOD.                                 S
6. Brush RF up to LF, and then step back with RF, body
   turning to the L.                                                 S

*Contrary Body Movement.* CBM on 1, 4 and 6.

*Rise and Fall (Body).* Rise slightly at end of 1 (NFR); continue to rise on 2; up on 3. Lower at end of 3.

*Body Sway.* Sway to L on 2 and 3. Sway to R on 5.

*Amount of Turn.* Make half a turn between 1 and 3. Make three-eighths of a turn between 4 and 5, to finish with the back diagonally to the centre, or a quarter turn to finish backing the new

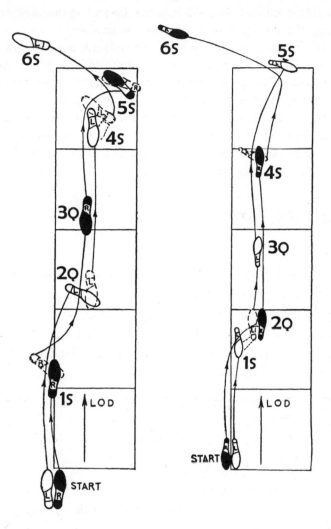

**Natural Turn**
**Left: Man   Right: Lady**

LOD if taken into a corner. (See also man's notes on the amount of turn.)

*Footwork.* 1. T H. 2. H T. 3. T H. 4. H T. 5. T H, then IE of T of RF. 6. T.

*General Notes.* Keep the hips well forward when taking the 3rd step. Relax the R knee well when taking the weight on to the 4th step, and then let the LF swing to the side across the front of the partner quite slowly on 5.

When brushing the RF to LF on the 6th step keep the knees well relaxed, and brush with the R toe about level with the L instep. It is not necessary for the toes of both feet to touch when brushing. Note that the body turns to the L as the RF moves back.

A Closed Impetus may follow the 3rd step of the Natural Turn. The Hover Feather may follow the 5th step.

## REVERSE TURN

### Man

The Reverse Turn consists of an Open Turn and a Feather Finish. It is a progressive figure, and cannot be used to turn a corner.

Commence facing diagonally to the centre and finish facing diagonally to the wall. The Reverse Turn should not be commenced from the LOD. The fact that the lady is always held slightly towards the man's R side makes it difficult to get good alignment on the backward steps if half a turn is attempted on the first part.

1. LF forward, turning body to L.                                S
2. RF to side, across the LOD.                                   Q
3. Continue turning on ball of RF and step LF back.              Q
4. RF back, down LOD, turning body to L.                         S
5. LF to side and slightly forward, body facing wall.            Q
6. RF forward, diag. to wall, outside partner.                   Q
7. LF forward, in line with partner.                             S

*Contrary Body Movement.* CBM on 1, 4, and 7. The 6th step is placed in CBMP.

*Rise and Fall (Body).* Rise at end of 1; up on 2 and 3. Lower at end of 3. Rise at end of 4; up on 5 and 6. Lower at end of 6.

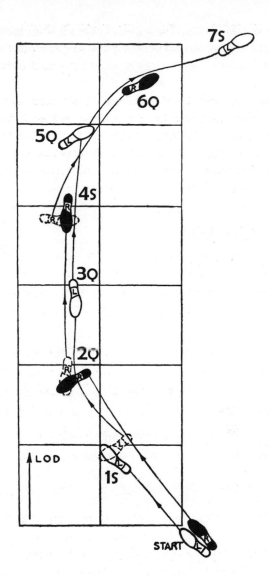

**Reverse Turn (Man)**

*Body Sway.* Sway to L on 2 and 3. Sway to R, on 5 and 6.

*Amount of Turn.* Make three-eighths of a turn between 1 and 3, and three-eighths of a turn between 4 and 7.

*Footwork.* 1. H T. 2. T. 3. T H. 4. T H . 5. T. 6. T H. 7. H.

*General Notes.* Do not let the 3rd step swing outwards. Keep it well behind the body. The 6th step should be placed slightly across the body in order to keep hip contact during the outside movement. The body should face the wall on 5, with the L side slightly forward.

Note that although the man is on the inside of the turn on the last part of the figure, he will get a foot rise on step 4. This exception to the usual rule is to enable him to get a good forward swing into the following Feather Finish.

The Reverse Turn should be preceded by a Feather taken diagonally to the centre, the last step of the Feather being used as the first of the Reverse Turn.

Follow with a Three Step, taken either diagonally to wall or curved to L to end down the LOD. Follow with the Natural Turn.

A Change of Direction or a Reverse Wave can also follow the Reverse Turn. (See diagram on page 171.)

## REVERSE TURN

### Lady

The Reverse Turn consists of a Heel Turn and a Feather Finish. It is preceded by a Feather.

Commence the Reverse Turn with the back diagonally to the centre. Finish with the back diagonally to the wall.

1. RF back, turning body to L.    S
2. Close LF to RF, turning on R heel (Heel Turn). Finish facing LOD, weight on LF.    Q
3. RF forward.    Q
4. LF forward, turning body to L.    S
5. RF to side, body backing the wall.    Q
6. Continue turning slightly, and step back with LF diag. to wall, partner outside.    Q
7. RF back, partner in line.    S

*Contrary Body Movement.* CBM on 1, 4, and 7. The 6th step is placed in CBMP.

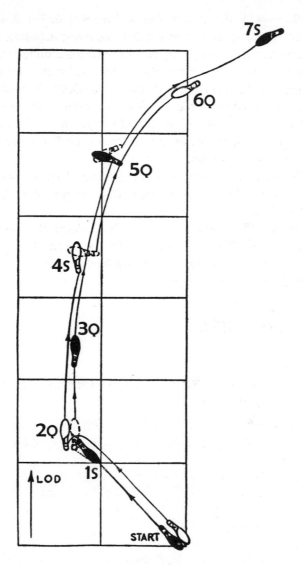

**Reverse Turn (Lady)**

*Rise and Fall (Body).* Rise slightly at end of 1 (NFR); continue to rise on 2; up on 3. Lower at end of 3. Rise at end of 4, up on 5; up on 6 (NFR). Lower at end of 6.

*Body Sway.* Sway to R on 2 and 3. Sway to L on 5 and 6.

*Amount of Turn.* Make three-eighths of a turn between 1 and 3, and three-eighths of a turn between 4 and 7.

*Footwork.* 1. T H. 2. H T. 3. T H. 4. H T. 5. T H. 6. T H. 7. T.

*General Notes.* Keep the hips well forward when taking the 3rd step. Relax the L knee well on 4. The body should be backing towards the wall on 5 and the 6th step will move slightly across the back of the body in a direction diagonally to the wall. Note that there is no foot rise on 6. When the RF commences to move back for the 7th step the heel must be in contact with the floor with the front toe released. (See diagram on page 173)

## REVERSE WAVE

### Man

The Reverse Wave has a variety of uses. A list of the positions from which it can be taken is given in the general notes.

It consists of the first four steps of the Reverse Turn (taken in a different direction), a Backward Three Step, and then a Heel Pull (5 and 6 of the Natural Turn). It is preceded by a Feather.

One of the most popular positions in which to use the Reverse Wave is described.

Commence facing the LOD. Finish facing diagonally to the centre.

1. LF forward, turning body to L.                                    S
2. RF to side, on same LOD.                                         Q
3. LF back, diag. to wall.                                         Q
4. RF back, diag. to wall, body turning to L.                      S
5. LF back, curving towards the LOD.                               Q
6. RF back, down LOD.                                              Q
7. LF back, down LOD, body turning to R.                           S
8. Pull RF back firmly, at the same time turning on
   L heel. Finish with RF at the side of LF, feet parallel
   and about 25 cm (ten inches) apart. Weight on RF.   S
9. LF forward, body turning to the L.                              S

*Contrary Body Movement.* CBM on 1, 4, 7, and 9.

*Rise and Fall (Body).* Rise at end of 1; up on 2 and 3. Lower at end of 3. Rise at end of 5; up on 6. Lower at end of 6.

*Body Sway.* Sway to L on 2 and 3. Sway to R on 5 and 6. Sway to L on 8.

*Amount of Turn.* The amount of turn on each part of the Reverse Wave is given in the notes below.

*Footwork.* 1. H T. 2. T. 3. T H. 4. T H. 5. T. 6. T H. 7. T H. 8. H, IE of foot, whole foot, then IE of LF. 9. H.

*General Notes.* When moving backwards the man must not let his poise or weight fall back. Note that the rise is taken from the ball of LF on 5. The L heel does not lower.

*Possible Alignments for the Reverse Wave.*

(a) Along side of room. Commence facing LOD. Turn three-eighths between 1 and 3 and take 4th step diagonally to wall. Make an eighth turn on 4, 5, 6 to back the LOD.

On steps 7, 8 turn three-eighths to R to face diagonally to centre. If at a corner, turn a quarter to face the new LOD or an eighth to face diagonally to centre of the new LOD.

(b) Round a corner. Commence facing LOD. Turn three-eighths between 1 and 3 and take 4th step diagonally to wall. Make a quarter turn on 4, 5, 6 to back diagonally to wall of the new LOD.

On steps 7, 8 turn a quarter to R to face diagonally to centre of the new LOD.

(c) Along side of room. Commence facing diagonally to wall. Make a half turn between 1 and 3 and take 4th step back diagonally to wall. Continue as in alignment (a) above.

(d) Round a corner. Commence facing diagonally to wall. Make a half turn between 1 and 3 and take 4th step back diagonally to wall. Continue as in alignment (b) above.

(e) Round a corner. Commence facing diagonally to centre. Make three-eighths turn between 1 and 3 and take 4th step down the LOD near a corner. Make a quarter turn on steps 4, 5, 6 to back the new LOD and then three-eighths to R on steps 7, 8 to face diagonally to centre of the new LOD.

Although the above are the accepted alignments for the Reverse Wave, the figure may be danced from practically any position. The main point to remember is that the turn must be gradual, and not abrupt between steps 4 and 6.

The Wave may be danced directly after a Reverse Turn or any Feather Finish ended diagonally to wall.

A Hover Feather may follow the 8th step. A Closed Impetus may be used after the 6th step and a Basic Weave is used after checking on the 4th step. (See diagram on page 177.)

## REVERSE WAVE

### Lady

The Reverse Wave consists of the first four steps of the Reverse Turn (taken in a different direction), a forward Three Step and then a Brush Step (5 and 6 of the Natural Turn). A chart appears on page 177.

The Reverse Wave can be taken from many positions. A list of these is given at the end of the notes on the man's steps. One of the most popular positions from which to use the Wave is described. It is preceded by a Feather, the last step of the Feather being the first of the Reverse Wave.

Commence with the back to the LOD. Finish with the back diagonally to the centre or to the new LOD.

1. RF back, turning body to L.                                      S
2. Close LF to RF turning on R heel (Heel Turn).
   Finish facing diag. to wall, weight on LF.                       Q
3. RF forward, diag. to wall.                                       Q
4. LF forward, diag. to wall, body turning to L.                    S
5. RF forward, curving towards the LOD.                             Q
6. LF forward, down LOD.                                            Q
7. RF forward, down LOD, turning body to R.                         S
8. LF to side, across the LOD.                                      S
9. Brush RF up to LF, and then step back with RF,
   body turning to L.                                               S

*Contrary Body Movement.* CBM on 1, 4, 7, and 9.

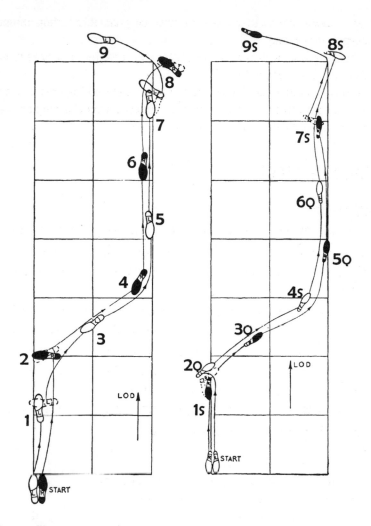

**Reverse Wave**
**Left: Man  Right: Lady**

*Rise and Fall (Body).* Rise slightly at end of 1 (NFR); continue to rise on 2; up on 3. Lower at end of 3. Rise at end of 5; up on 6. Lower at end of 6.

*Body Sway.* Sway to R on 2 and 3. Sway to L on 5 and 6. Sway to R on 8.

*Amount of Turn.* The amount of turn on each part together with possible uses of the Wave is given at the end of the notes on the man's steps.

*Footwork.* 1. T H. 2. H T. 3. T H. 4. H. 5. H T. 6. T H. 7. H T. 8. T H, then IE of T of RF. 9. T.

*General Notes.* The lady can materially assist the man's backward movement by keeping the hips well forward and rather "pressing" forward towards him from steps 4 to 7. The poise, however, must still be maintained.

# CHANGE OF DIRECTION

## Man

The Change of Direction actually consists of three steps only and is counted "Slow, Slow, Slow". In the description below the second step is divided into beats of the music to make it more easily understood.

It is preceded by a Feather, a Reverse Turn, or any figure ended with a Feather Finish, facing diagonally to wall.

1.  LF forward, turning body to L.                                    S
2.  RF diagonally forward, R side leading,
    sliding it along the floor on the inside
    edge of the toe.                               1st beat ⎫
    With the knees well relaxed, brush the LF                ⎬
    sharply to RF, at the same time turning up              ⎪
    to a half turn to L. Turn on ball of RF but             ⎪
    keep the R heel down.                          2nd beat ⎭  S
3.  LF forward, across the body.                                      S

*Contrary Body Movement.* CBM on 1 and 3. The 3rd step is placed in CBMP.

*Rise and Fall.* None.

*Body Sway.* Sway to L on 2.

*Amount of Turn.* The turn is governed by the following figure. Half a turn is the most effective. See notes below.

*Footwork.* 1. H. 2. IE of T, H, then IE of T of LF. 3. H.

*General Notes.* Although the 2nd step is termed diagonally forward, it must follow the line of the preceding step on the LF. The fact that the R side is leading slightly on this step accounts for it being diagonally forward. The turn must be sharp. Keep pressure on the inside edge of the toe of the LF as it closes, and close the L toe slightly in advance of the R toe.

*Amalgamations.* (a) Along the sides of the room. Dance a Reverse Turn and then a Change of Direction, make a quarter turn on the Change of Direction and follow with a Feather diagonally to centre into any Reverse figure.

(b) At a corner, after a Reverse Turn. Make three-eighths of a turn to finish facing the new LOD or a half turn to finish facing diagonally to centre of the new LOD.

*Note.* Some advanced dancers hold step 2 for an additional "Slow".

# CHANGE OF DIRECTION

## Lady

The Change of Direction actually consists of three steps only and is counted "Slow, Slow, Slow". In the description below the second step is divided into beats of the music to make it more easily understood.

It is usually preceded by a Feather, a Reverse Turn, or any figure ended with a Feather Finish.

| | | |
|---|---|---|
| 1. RF back, turning body to the L. | | S |
| 2. LF diagonally back L side leading. | 1st beat | |
| With the knees well relaxed, brush RF to LF, at the same time turning up to half a turn to L. Turn on ball of LF. | 2nd beat | S |
| 3. RF back, across the body. | | S |

*Contrary Body Movement.* CBM on 1 and 3. The 3rd step is placed in CBMP.
*Rise and Fall.* None.
*Body Sway.* Sway to R on 2.

*Amount of Turn.* The turn is governed by the following figure. Half a turn is the most effective.

*Footwork.* 1. T H. 2. T, IE of T, H, then IE of T of RF. 3. T.

*General Notes.* Although the 2nd step is termed diagonally back, it must follow the line of the preceding step on the RF. The fact that the L side is leading slightly on this step accounts for it being diagonally back.

The lady's 2nd step must not be quite as long as the man's, otherwise she will finish at his R side when the turn is completed.

When the RF brushes up to the LF the R toe will be level with the L instep, not toe to toe.

## CLOSED IMPETUS

### Man

This figure is very popular in the Foxtrot and is also used in other dances. It can be danced either at a corner or as a progressive figure along the sides of the room.

It is usually danced after the first three steps of the Natural Turn and is followed by a Feather Finish which is the last part of the Reverse Turn. It can be used after the 6th step of the Reverse Wave. A diagram appears on page 182.

Dance 1, 2 and 3 of the Natural Turn. SQQ. Finish with the back to the LOD. Continue:

1. LF back, turning body to the R.                              S
2. Close RF to LF turning on L heel. Finish with
   weight on RF facing diag. to centre. (Heel Turn.)           Q
3. Continue turning on ball of RF and step to side
   and slightly back with LF.                                  Q
4. RF back, diag. to centre against the LOD, turning
   to the L.                                                    S

Follow with 5, 6, 7 of a Reverse Turn, ending this diag. to centre, or, if at a corner, diag. to wall of the new LOD.

*Contrary Body Movement.* CBM on 1 and 4.

*Rise and Fall (Body)*. Rise at end of 2; up on 3. Lower at end of 3.

*Body Sway*. Sway to L on 2.

*Amount of Turn*. Make three-eighths of a turn on steps 1 and 2 and a quarter between 2 and 3. A quarter turn to the L is made between steps 4 and 7.

*Footwork*. 1. T H. 2. H T. 3. T H. 4. T.

*Leading*. As the LF is taken back on the 1st step, the man should begin to incline his body to the L, so that the lady's forward impetus is received on his R side. He must lead the lady firmly with his R hand as she steps forward with her RF to assist her forward swing. If this is done it will be found that the lady's impetus will create the turn with no further effort from the man.

*General Notes*. Advanced dancers tend to hurry the 1st step and thus get a "Hover" effect between steps 2 and 3. Although steps 1, 2 are a Heel Turn, there is no rise. The knees should be relaxed on 2 and the rise taken at the end of 2.

## CLOSED IMPETUS

### Lady

This figure may be danced either at a corner or along the sides of the room.

It is usually danced after the first three steps of the Natural Turn, and is followed by a Feather Finish, which is the last part of the Reverse Turn. It can be used after the 6th step of the Reverse Wave. A diagram appears on page 182.

Dance 1, 2, and 3 of the Natural Turn (SQQ). Finish facing the LOD. Continue as follows:

| | | |
|---|---|---|
| 1. RF forward, turning body to the R. | | S |
| 2. LF to side, across the LOD. | | Q |
| 3. Continue turning on ball of LF and take a small step diag. forward with RF, having brushed it to LF. | | Q |
| 4. LF forward, diag. to centre against the LOD, turning to L. | | S |

Follow with 5, 6, and 7 of the Reverse Turn QQS

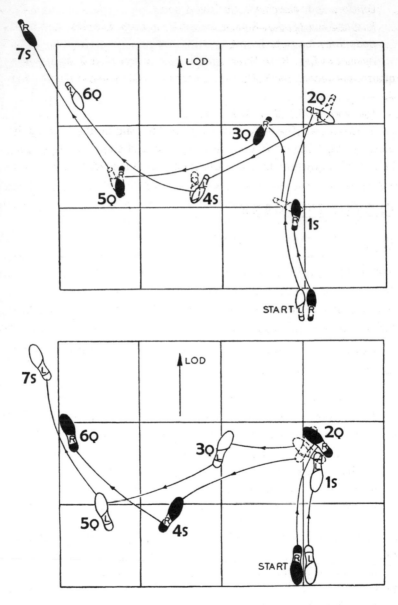

**Closed Impetus and Feather Finish**
**Top: Lady  Bottom: Man**

*Contrary Body Movement.* CBM on 1 and 4.
*Rise and Fall (Body).* Rise at end of 2; up on 3. Lower at end of 3.
*Body Sway.* Sway to R on 2.
*Amount of Turn.* Make three-eighths turn on the first 2 steps and a quarter between 2 and 3. Make a quarter turn to L between steps 4 and 7.
*Footwork.* 1. H T. 2. T. 3. T H. 4. H.
*General Notes.* The body must swing well forward on the 1st step, in order to assist the man's turn. Although the 2nd step is taken on the ball of the LF there is no rise until the end of this step.

# CLOSED TELEMARK

## Man

The Telemark is a very useful figure when space is limited, and can be used instead of a Reverse Turn.

It is usually preceded and followed by a Feather, the last Feather being commenced outside the partner.

Commence facing diagonally to the centre. Finish facing diagonally to the wall.

1. LF forward, turning body to the L.     S
2. RF to side, across the LOD.     Q
3. Continue turning on ball of RF, step to side and slightly forward with LF. Finish with LF pointing diag. to wall, body almost facing diag. to wall.     Q
4. RF forward, diag. to wall, outside partner.     S
Follow with 2, 3, and 4 of Feather. End facing diag. to wall. (QQS)

*Contrary Body Movement.* CBM on 1 and 4. The 4th step is placed in CBMP.
*Rise and Fall (Body).* Rise at end of 1; up on 2 and 3. Lower at end of 3.
*Body Sway.* Sway to L on 2.
*Amount of Turn.* Make three-quarters of a turn between 1 and 4, the body turning slightly less.
*Footwork.* 1. H T. 2. T. 3. T H. 4. H.

*General Notes.* Care should be taken not to get the feet too close together on the 3rd step, otherwise the body will overturn. The Telemark could be followed by a Natural Turn, the last step of the Telemark becoming the first of a Natural Turn. This is not to be generally recommended; as the man is commencing from an outside position, the lady would have difficulty in executing her heel turn.

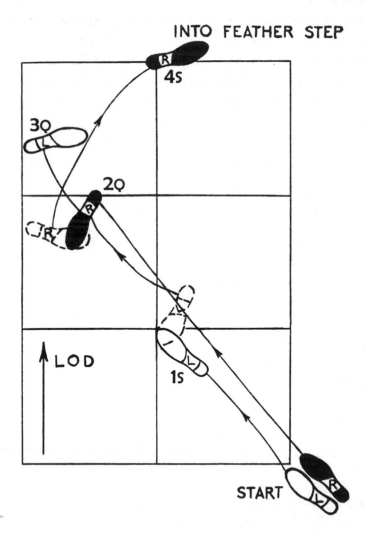

**Closed Telemark (Man)**

The second step should almost back the LOD, otherwise the lady will get left too much to man's R side on 3 and 4.

## CLOSED TELEMARK

### Lady

The Telemark is usually preceded by a Feather taken diagonally to the centre, and also followed by a Feather. The second Feather is commenced with the man outside the lady.

The last step of the preceding Feather will be the first of the Closed Telemark, and the last step of the Closed Telemark becomes the first of the following Feather.

Commence with the back to the centre diagonally. Finish with the back diagonally to the wall.

1. RF back, turning body to L.  S
2. Close LF to RF, turning on R heel. Finish facing LOD, weight on LF.  Q
3. Continue turning on ball of LF and step to side and slightly back with RF. Finish with feet backing diag. to wall, body almost backing diag. to wall.  Q
4. LF back, diag. to wall, partner outside.  S
   Follow with 2, 3, and 4 of Feather, finishing with back diag. to wall. (QQS)

*Contrary Body Movement.* CBM on 1 and 4. The 4th step is placed in CBMP.

*Rise and Fall (Body).* Rise slightly at end of 1 (NFR); continue to rise on 2; up on 3. Lower at end of 3.

*Body Sway.* Sway to R on 2.

*Amount of Turn.* Make three-quarters of a turn between 1 and 4, the body turning slightly less.

*General Notes.* The 3rd step should be quite long, otherwise the lady will get left too much at the side of the man when the 4th step is taken. (See diagram on page 186.)

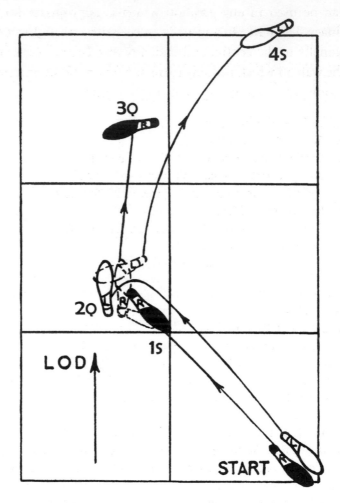

**Closed Telemark (Lady)**

## OPEN TELEMARK
### (With a Feather Ending)

### Man
The Open Telemark is a variation of the Closed Telemark in
which the 3rd and 4th steps are taken in Promenade Position.

It can be used in any position which is appropriate for the ordinary Telemark. It is usually preceded by a Feather taken diagonally to the centre, and ended with a Feather diagonally to the wall on which the lady turns square on the second step.

Commence facing diagonally to the centre.

1. LF forward, turning body to L.        S
2. RF to side, across the LOD.        Q
3. Continue turning on ball of RF until body is facing towards outside wall, and step to side and slightly forward with LF (Now in PP. See note.)        Q
4. RF forward, in PP, diag. to wall.        S
5. Turning lady square, step diagonally forward LF.        Q
6. RF forward, outside partner.        Q
7. LF forward, in line with partner (diag. to wall.)        S

*Contrary Body Movement.* CBM on 1 and 7. The 4th and 6th steps are placed in CBMP.

*Rise and Fall (Body).* Rise at end of 1 ; up on 2 and 3. Lower at end of 3. Rise at end of 4; up on 5 and 6. Lower at end of 6.

*Body Sway.* Sway to L on 2. Sway to R on 5 and 6.

*Amount of Turn.* The turn of man and lady differs in this figure. Open Telemark: man makes three-quarters of a turn, the body turning slightly less.

*Footwork.* 1. H T. 2. T. 3. T H. 4. H T. 5. T. 6. T H. 7. H.

*General Notes.* As the man continues to turn on his 2nd step he must guide the lady by applying pressure with the base of his R hand on her L side. He must endeavour to indicate that he is turning to the Promenade Position and that she is not to continue the turn with him. As he leads her into the 5th step the pressure will be transferred to the fingers, to indicate that the lady must turn to face him again.

A Natural Turn may follow the Open Telemark. Please see page 204.

## OPEN TELEMARK
### (With a Feather Ending)
### Lady

The Open Telemark is a variation of the Closed Telemark in which the 3rd and 4th steps are taken in Promenade Position. It is preceded by a Feather taken diagonally to the centre, and ended with a Feather taken back diagonally to the wall on which the lady turns square to partner on the 2nd step.

Commence with the back to the centre diagonally.

1. RF back, turning body to L.                                            S
2. Close LF to RF, turning on R heel. (Heel Turn.)
   Finish facing the LOD.                                                 Q
3. RF diag. forward in PP, R side leading. The R toe
   should be pointing to LOD.                                             Q
4. LF forward, across the body, in PP. Begin to turn to L.  S
5. Turning to the L until body is square to man,
   step to side and slightly back with RF.                               Q
6. LF back, partner outside (diag. to wall).                             Q
7. RF back.                                                              S

*Contrary Body Movement.* CBM on 1, 4, and 7. The 4th and 6th steps are placed in CBMP.

*Rise and Fall (Body).* Rise slightly at end of 1 (NFR); continue to rise on 2; up on 3. Lower at end of 3. Rise at end of 4; up on 5; up on 6 (NFR). Lower at end of 6.

*Body Sway.* Sway to R on 2. Sway to L on 5 and 6.

*Amount of Turn.* Make three-eighths turn on steps 1 and 2 and a slight body turn to L on 3. To regain normal position turn three-eighths to L on steps 4 to 7.

*Footwork.* 1. T H. 2. H T. 3. T H. 4. H T. 5. T H. 6. T H. 7. T.

*General Notes.* When the lady turns to PP it is more effective if she turns her head to face the direction of her 3rd step. Some ladies prefer to keep the head turned to the L. Either is correct. It is a matter of personal taste. The direction of steps 3 and 4 is diagonally to wall, although the feet are pointing to LOD.

# HOVER TELEMARK

## Man

The Hover Telemark is a most attractive type of standard variation. It is so named because instead of turning on the second step of a Telemark, the dancer "hovers" and replaces the 3rd step in approximately the same position as it started.

It is danced when the man is stepping forward with his LF. The last step of a Reverse Turn or any Feather Finish are good entries. It is used to change direction.

Dance six steps of a Reverse Turn. Finish facing diagonally to wall and continue as follows:

1. LF forward, diag. to wall, turning body to the L.     S
2. RF to side and let the LF close slightly towards the RF. Now facing the LOD.     Q
3. LF to side and slightly forward, LF pointing diag. to centre but body still facing the LOD.     Q
4. RF forward, outside partner, diag. to centre.     S

Continue by doing 2, 3, 4 of a Feather-step. (QQS.)

*Contrary Body Movement.* CBM on 1 and 4. The 4th step is placed in CBMP.

*Rise and Fall (Body).* Commence to rise at end of 1; continue to rise on 2; up on 3. Lower at end of 3.

*Body Sway.* Sway to the L on 2.

*Amount of Turn.* A quarter turn to the L, the body turning slightly less.

*Footwork.* 1. H T. 2. T (RF), then IE of T, of LF. 3. T H. 4. H.

*General Notes.* Care should be taken to rise very gradually between steps 1 and 2, reaching the greatest height when the LF has brushed towards the RF. The L knee should be relaxed and veering inwards at this point. Although the position of 3 is "side and slightly forward" the LF should tend to move more sideways. The man may turn lady to PP at the end of 2 and take steps 3 and 4 in PP.

# HOVER TELEMARK

## Lady

1. RF back, turning body to L.      S
2. Step to side with LF, letting RF close slightly towards the LF. Body backing the LOD.      Q
3. RF to side and slightly back, body still backing the LOD.      Q
4. LF back diag. to centre, partner outside.      S

Continue with 2, 3 and 4 of the Feather step. (QQS.)

*Contrary Body Movement.* CBM on 1 and 4. The 4th step is placed in CBMP.

*Rise and Fall (Body).* Commence to rise at end of 1 (NFR); continue to rise on 2; up on 3. Lower at end of 3.

*Body Sway.* Sway to R on 2.

*Amount of Turn.* A quarter turn to the L is made, the body turning slightly less.

*Footwork.* 1. T H. 2. T (LF), then IE of T of RF. 3. T H. 4. T.

# HOVER FEATHER

## Man

The Hover Feather consists of three steps, and is danced after the man has done a Heel Pull. The best positions in which to use it are given in the notes. It is described from the most popular position which is after the 5th step of a Natural Turn.

Dance steps 1 to 5 of the Natural Turn. Finish facing diagonally to the centre then continue as follows:

1. At the end of the Heel Pull (5th step of Natural Turn), rise to toes and place the LF diag. forward, with the L side leading and preparing to step outside partner.      Q
2. RF forward, outside partner.      Q

3. LF forward, diag., to centre.                                  S

Use the 3rd step as the 1st step of any Reverse figure.

*Contrary Body Movement.* CBM on 3. The 2nd step is placed in CBMP.

*Rise and Fall (Body).* Rise at the end of the preceding step. Up on 1 and 2. Lower at end of 2.

*Body Sway.* The body is swaying to the L on the Heel Pull. Sway to the L on 1 of Hover Feather.

*Amount of Turn.* There is no turn.

*Footwork.* 1. T. 2. T H. 3. H.

*General Notes.* When dancing the Heel Pull preceding a Hover Feather the body should be allowed to overturn slightly to the R as the rise is made. The L knee will then veer inwards towards the R knee without the L heel leaving the floor. Pressure is kept on the inside edge of the toe of LF to assist the balance.

The Hover Feather can be used after the 8th step of the Reverse Wave. It is also included as a part of the Natural Telemark and the Natural Twist Turn.

## HOVER FEATHER

### Lady

Dance steps 1 to 5 of the Natural Turn. Finish backing diagonally to the centre. Continue as follows:

As the 5th step of the Natural Turn is taken, the RF should brush to the LF. At the same time rise to the toes.

1. Place the RF diag. back, with the R side leading.      Q
2. LF back, partner outside.      Q
3. RF back, diag. to centre.      S

Step 3 will become the first step of any Reverse figure.

*Contrary Body Movement.* CBM on 3. The 2nd step is placed in CBMP.

*Rise and Fall (Body).* Rise at the end of the preceding step; up on 1; up on 2 (NFR). Lower at end of 2.

*Body Sway.* The body is swaying to the R on the Brush Step (5th step of Natural Turn). Sway to the R on 1 of Hover Feather.

*Amount of Turn.* There is no turn.

*Footwork.* 1. T H. 2. T H. 3 T.

*General Notes.* As the RF brushes to the LF on the preceding step the body should overturn slightly to the R. The rise is taken from the ball of the LF. The L heel does not touch the floor.

# NATURAL TELEMARK

## Man

The Natural Telemark is a comparatively easy and most useful figure, which can be used instead of a Natural Turn.

The easiest position to introduce it is at the corner of the room, but it is possible to use it along the side of the room. It is described as it would be used in the latter position.

Commence facing diagonally to the wall. Finish facing diagonally to the centre.

| | | |
|---|---|---|
| 1. | RF forward, turning body to the R. | S |
| 2. | LF to side, across the LOD. | Q |
| 3. | Continue turning on the ball of LF and take a small step to side with RF, on the toes. Now facing diag. to centre. | Q |
| 4. | LF diag. forward, preparing to step outside partner, L side leading. | Q |
| 5. | RF forward, outside partner. | Q |
| 6. | LF forward, diag. to centre. | S |

Step 6 will become the 1st step of any Reverse figure.

*Contrary Body Movement.* CBM on 1 and 6. The 5th step is placed in CBMP.

*Rise and Fall (Body).* Rise at end of 1; up on steps 2, 3, 4, and 5. Lower at end of 5.

*Body Sway.* Sway to the R on 2 and to the L on 4.

*Amount of Turn.* Make a quarter turn on the first 2 steps and a half turn between steps 2 and 3. At a corner make only a quarter turn on the last part to end facing diagonally to centre of the new LOD or three-eighths to face the new LOD.

*Footwork.* 1. H T. 2. T. 3. T. 4. T. 5. T H. 6. H.

*General Notes.* Do not hurry between Steps 2 and 3 otherwise the lady will be "pulled off" her Heel Turn.

*Amalgamations.* (a) Reverse Turn, followed by a Three Step continued in a direction diagonally to wall; Natural Telemark ending diagonally to centre. Follow with any Reverse figure.

(b) Feather, Three Step taken down the LOD and ending near a corner; Natural Telemark making five-eighths of a turn to end diagonally to centre of the new LOD. Follow with any Reverse figure.

# NATURAL TELEMARK

## Lady

A simple and most useful figure which can be used instead of a Natural Turn. Commence backing diagonally to the wall.

1. LF back, turning body to the R.                      S
2. Close RF to LF making a Heel Turn to face the LOD.    Q
3. Continue turning to the R on the ball of RF and step to side LF. Now backing diag. to centre. The RF will now move slightly towards LF                     Q
4. RF diag. back, R side leading.                   Q
5. LF back, partner outside.                       Q
6. RF back, diag. to centre.                        S

Step 6 will become the 1st step of any Reverse figure.

*Contrary Body Movement.* CBM on 1 and 6. The 5th step is placed in CBMP.

*Rise and Fall (Body).* Rise slightly at end of 1 (NFR); continue to rise on 2; up on 3 and 4; up on 5 (NFR). Lower at end of 5.

*Body Sway.* Sway to L on 2 and to R on 4.

*Amount of Turn.* Make three-eighths of a turn to R on 1 and 2 and three-eighths between 2 and 3. When danced at a corner, making only a half a turn on the complete figure, make three-eighths of a turn between 1 and 2 and an eighth between 2 and 3.

*Footwork.* 1. T H. 2. H T. 3. T. 4. T H. 5. T H. 6 T.

*General Notes.* Do not attempt to brush the RF up to LF on step 3 otherwise the continuity of the movement will be lost. The RF should move slightly towards LF but there is not sufficient time for it to brush completely to LF.

# NATURAL TWIST TURN

## Man

The Natural Twist Turn can be used instead of a Natural Turn. Although it can be danced by quite average dancers, it looks most effective when danced with the speed and polish that the more experienced dancer can give to a variation of this type.

It could be used at a corner but is better when used along the sides of the room. The latter method of dancing is described below.

Commence facing the LOD. Finish facing diagonally to the centre.

| | |
|---|---|
| 1. RF forward, turning body to the R. | S |
| 2. LF to side, across the LOD. | Q |
| 3. Continue turning slightly to R and take a small step back with the RF on the ball of the foot, crossing it behind the LF. Now backing the LOD. | "and" |
| 4, 5. Keeping the feet flat, twist on both feet for three-eighths of a turn to the R. Finish facing diag. to centre with feet apart as in a Heel Pull, then slowly rise to the toes. | QS |
| 6, 7, 8. LF diag. forward and go into a Hover Feather. | QQS |

*Contrary Body Movement.* CBM on 1 and 8. The 7th step is placed in CBMP.

*Rise and Fall (Body).* There is no rise on the first part. Rise on 5; up on 6 and 7. Lower at end of 7.

*Body Sway.* Sway to R on 2, 3. Sway to L on 5, 6.

*Amount of Turn.* Make seven-eighths of a turn to R between steps 1 and 5. When danced at a corner, it is better to end facing the new LOD or facing diagonally to the wall of the new LOD. The body will overturn slightly to the R on 5.

*Footwork.* 1. H T. 2. T H. 3. T. 4. Twist on T of RF, and H of LF, with feet flat. End with weight on whole of R. 5. T (RF) with pressure on IE of T of LF. 6. T. 7. T H. 8. H.

*General Notes.* After the man has taken his 2nd step he must lead the lady slightly to his R side so that she takes steps 3, 4, 5 moving round and outside him on his R. She will get square to him again at the end of her 5th step. The rise at the end of 5 must not be abrupt, and the L knee should veer inwards as the body overturns to the R. It should be noted that steps 2 and 3 have only a half beat each, and it is this quickening of the turn, followed by a slow rise and Hover, that makes the figure so attractive. The man should remember to move the RF quickly on 3, and not try to get speed by rushing the 2nd step. Do not rise until the turn is completed on step 5.

There is no rise on the first 2 steps, these being taken without the swing used in other Natural movements.

The normal entry to this figure is a Three Step down the LOD.

# NATURAL TWIST TURN

## Lady

This variation is commenced backing the LOD.

| | | |
|---|---|---|
| 1. | LF back, turning body to the R. | S |
| 2. | Close RF to LF, turning on the L heel (Heel Turn). | Q |
| 3. | Small step forward with LF, preparing to step outside partner, L side leading. | "and" |
| 4. | Small step forward with RF, outside partner and moving diag. to wall. | Q |
| 5. | LF to side, with body backing diag. to centre. Rise to toes and allow RF to brush to LF, body over-turning slightly to the R. | S |
| 6, 7, 8. | RF diag. back and go into a Hover Feather. | QQS |

*Contrary Body Movement.* CBM on 1, 4 and 8. The 4th and 7th steps are placed in CBMP.

*Rise and Fall (Body).* There is no rise on the first 4 steps. Rise on 5; up on 6; up on 7 (NFR). Lower at end of 7. Steps 3, 4, and 5 are taken on the balls of the feet.

*Body Sway.* Sway to the L on 2, 3. Sway to R on 5, 6.

*Amount of Turn.* Make seven-eighths of a turn to R between steps 1 and 5. Less turn will be made when danced at a corner.

*Footwork.* 1. T H. 2. H . 3. T. 4. T. 5. T and IE of T of RF. 6 T H. 7 T H. 8. T.

*General Notes.* If the man leads the figure properly the lady will feel his increased speed at the end of the second step and she must then move away from her Heel Turn very quickly. It should be noted that steps 2 and 3 have only a half beat each.

## BASIC WEAVE

### Man

This is a very popular movement. Normally it is used as a progressive figure, although it can be adapted for use at a corner. It is described as it would be used along the sides of the room.

Commence facing the LOD and dance steps 1 to 4 of the Reverse Wave. Finish backing diagonally to the wall, and commence the Basic Weave from this position.

1. Step forward on to LF, turning body to the L.    Q
2. RF to side, body backing the LOD.    Q
3. LF back, diag. to centre, partner outside.    Q
4. RF back, diag. to centre, partner in line. Body turning to the L.    Q
   (The next 3 steps are the same as steps 5, 6, 7 of the Reverse Turn.)
5. LF to side and slightly forward, body facing wall.    Q
6. RF forward, outside partner.    Q
7. LF forward, diag. to wall.    S

*Contrary Body Movement.* CBM on 1, 4, and 7. The 3rd and 6th steps are placed in CBMP.

*Rise and Fall (Body).* Rise at end of 1; up on steps 2, 3, 4, 5, and 6. Lower at end of 6.

*Body Sway.* Sway to the L on 2. 3. Sway to the R on 5, 6.

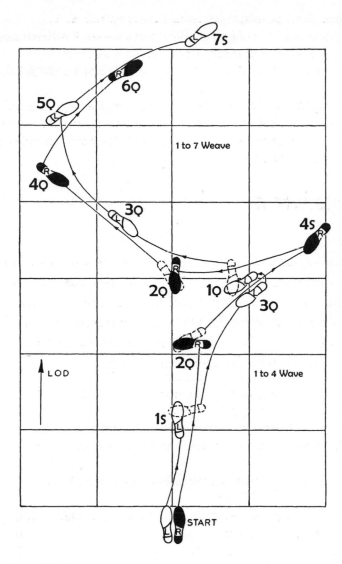

**Basic Weave (Man)**
**Following 1 to 4 of Reverse Wave**

*Amount of Turn.* Make a quarter turn between 1 and 3 and a quarter turn between 4 and 7.

*Footwork.* 1. H T. 2. T. 3. T. 4. T. 5. T. 6. T H. 7. H. (See note.)

*General Notes.* Care should be taken not to let the weight drop back too much on the 4th step of the preceding Reverse Wave, otherwise the entry to Weave will be forced.

On step 3 (LF) it is permissible to use the Footwork of T H and this will often result in a more soft and flowing movement.

The Basic Weave can be danced at a corner. Dance 1 to 4 of the Reverse Turn, finishing backing the LOD near a corner. Now turn a quarter turn to L on steps 1 to 3 of the Weave; take the 4th step down the new LOD and end the Feather finish diag. to the wall of the new LOD.

The Weave may be danced in the Waltz after the 4th step of a Reverse Turn taken back diag. to wall. See also the Weave from PP.

## BASIC WEAVE

### Lady

The Basic Weave is mostly used as a progressive figure and it is described as it would be danced along the sides of the room.

Commence backing the LOD and dance 1 to 4 of the Reverse Wave. Finish facing diagonally to the wall and commence the Basic Weave from this position.

1. Step back on to RF, turning the body to the L.                    Q
2. Small step to side with LF. Body now facing the LOD.         Q
3. RF forward, diag. to centre, outside partner.                      Q
4. LF forward, diag. to centre, body turning to L.                   Q
   (The next 3 steps are the same as steps 5, 6, 7 of
   the Reverse Turn.)
5. RF to side. Body backing towards the wall.                         Q
6. LF back, partner outside.                                                Q
7. RF back, diag. to wall.                                                     S

*Contrary Body Movement.* CBM on 1, 4, and 7. The 3rd and 6th steps are placed in CBMP.

*Rise and Fall (Body).* Rise at end of 1 (NFR); up on 2, 3, 4, 5; up on 6 (NFR). Lower at end or 6.

*Body Sway.* Sway to R on 2, 3. Sway to L on 5, 6.

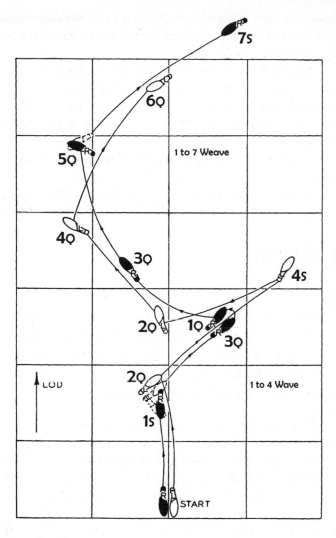

**Basic Weave (Lady)**
**Following 1 to 4 of Reverse Wave**

*Amount of Turn.* Make a quarter turn between 1 and 3 and a quarter turn between 4 and 7.

*Footwork.* 1. T H. 2. T. 3. T. 4. T. 5. T H. 6. T H. 7. T.

*General Notes.* When the man uses the alternative footwork on 3, the lady will still step forward on the toes on steps 3 and 4, although the rise will not be so pronounced.

## TOP SPIN

### Man

This variation is not only attractive to dance, but it is a very useful figure in a crowded room, and an experienced dancer will use it instinctively to change his direction when a collision is imminent. The Top Spin consists of two backward turning steps which are used after checking forward on the RF, these two steps being followed by 5, 6, 7 of a Reverse Turn.

It is possible to dance the Top Spin along the sides of the room, and a diagram of this is given. The following description is of a Top Spin danced at a corner.

Commence when near a corner.
Dance steps 1 to 6 of the Reverse Turn. Finish with the RF forward, outside partner.

Remain up on toes, body facing diag. to wall.    SQQSQQ

1. Turning the body to the L, move the LF slightly to the R, behind the RF and directly against the LOD. Partner outside.    Q

2. RF back, diag. to wall against the LOD. Partner in line. Body still turning to the L.    Q

(The next 3 steps are the same as steps 5, 6, 7 of the Reverse Turn.)

3. LF to side and slightly forward, body facing the new LOD.    Q

4. RF forward, diag. to centre of the new LOD, outside partner.    Q

5. LF forward, in line with lady, diag. to centre of new LOD.    S

*Contrary Body Movement.* CBM on 2 and 5. The 1st and 4th steps are placed in CBMP.

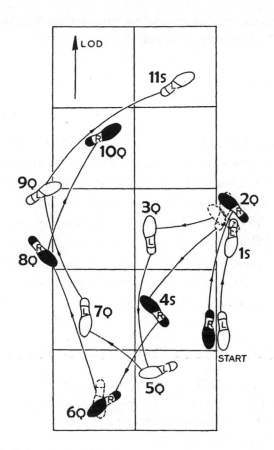

**Top Spin (Man)**
**Steps 1, 2, 3 are a Closed Impetus**
**Steps 4, 5, 6 are 4, 5, 6 of a Reverse Turn**
**Steps 7 to 11 are the Top Spin**

*Rise and Fall (Body).* Up on steps 1 to 4. Lower at end of 4.

*Body Sway.* Sway to the R on 3, 4.

*Amount of Turn.* Make an eighth of a turn between the preceding step and step 1; an eighth between 1 and 2 and a quarter between 2 and 5.

*Footwork.* 1. T. 2. T. 3. T. 4. T H. 5. H. Note: on step 1 the footwork of T H may be used and this will often result in a more soft and flowing movement.

*General Notes.* It should be noted that when the Top Spin follows the 6th step of a Reverse Turn, this step should be taken with the feet and body facing diagonally to wall. Normally on the 6th step of a Reverse Turn the RF is diagonally to wall, but the body has turned slightly less.

*Amalgamations.* (a) At a corner. The description shows the entry into Top Spin at a corner. It should be followed by any Reverse figure.

(b) Along the sides of the room. Dance 1, 2, 3 of a Natural Turn, followed by a Closed Impetus Turn (SQQSQQS). Make a half turn on the Impetus Turn so that the last step is taken back on RF in a direction against the LOD. Now dance steps 5, 6 of the Reverse Turn (QQ) finishing with the RF forward outside partner. The RF is taken in a direction diagonally to the centre against the LOD. Check on this step and continue with the Top Spin. The body will be backing the LOD on 1 of the Top Spin, backing diagonally to centre on 2, and facing diagonally to wall on 5. A diagram of this amalgamation is shown.

There are numerous other amalgamations, but these two are the most important. Any time that the RF has stepped forward outside partner in a Feather or a Feather Finish to any figure, the movement may be checked and followed by a Top Spin. The amount of turn would vary according to the position in the room. Remember that a half turn is the most comfortable amount of turn to make on the complete figure. If the dancer will visualize the Top Spin as two steps back, turning to the L and followed by 5, 6, 7 of the Reverse Turn, its introduction into the dance will be very much simplified.

## TOP SPIN

### Lady

The notes at the beginning of the man's steps and the general notes and amalgamations should be studied very carefully. The description that follows is of the Top Spin as danced at a corner. The diagram on page 203 shows the use of the Top Spin along the side of the room.

Commence near a corner.
Dance steps 1 to 6 of a Reverse Turn. Finish

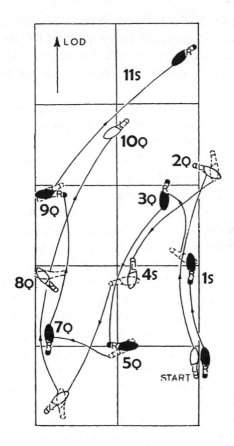

**Top Spin (Lady)**
**Steps 1, 2, 3 are closed a Closed Impetus**
**Steps 4, 5, 6 are 4, 5, 6 of a Reverse Turn Feather Finish**
**Steps 7 to 11 are the Top Spin**

with the LF back, partner outside. Remain up
on toes, body backing diag.to wall.                          SQQSQQ

1. Turning the body to the L move the RF to the
   L across the front of the LF outside partner.            Q

2. LF forward, diag. to wall against the LOD, still
   turning to L.                                            Q

(The next 3 steps are just the same as steps 5, 6, 7
of the Reverse Turn.)

3. RF to side, body backing the new LOD.            Q
4. LF back, diag. to centre of the new LOD,
    partner outside.            Q
5. RF back, partner now in line. diag. to centre of
    the new LOD.            S

*Contrary Body Movement.* CBM on 2 and 5. The 1st and 4th steps are placed in CBMP.

*Rise and Fall (Body).* Up on steps 1, 2, 3; up on 4 (NFR). Lower at end of 4.

*Body Sway.* Sway to the L on 3, 4.

*Amount of Turn.* Up to a half turn may be made on the complete figure. Make an eighth between the preceding step and 1, an eighth between 1 and 2, an eighth between 2 and 3, and an eighth between 3 and 4.

*Footwork.* 1. T. 2. T. 3. T H. 4. T H. 5. T.

*General Notes.* When checking on 6 of a Reverse Turn to follow with a Top Spin the lady will not lower her R heel on the 5th step of the Reverse. She should remain on her toes for steps 5 and 6 otherwise her weight will move too far back.

For other amalgamations of the Top Spin please see the man's notes.

## OUTSIDE SWIVEL
## (From the Open Telemark and Natural Turn)

### Man

The Outside Swivel consists of two steps only. It can be used from several positions, but it was in the amalgamation described that the figure first gained popularity.

Commence facing diagonally to the centre and dance 1, 2, 3 of a Feather. Continue as follows:

### Open Telemark

1. LF forward, turning body to L.            S
2. RF to side, across the LOD.            Q

3. Continue turning on ball of RF until body is
   backing diag. to centre and step sideways with LF.    Q
   Now in PP.

## Natural Turn

4. RF forward, across the body in PP, moving
   towards the wall, and begin to turn to R.              S
5. LF to side, body now backing the LOD and having
   turned square to partner.                             Q
6. Still turning slightly, step back RF, R side leading,
   now backing diag. to wall.                            Q

## Outside Swivel

7. LF back, diag. to wall, with the toe turned
   inwards, partner outside. As this step is taken,
   let the body continue to turn to the R as the RF
   is drawn back across the front of LF without weight
   on it. (See notes.) Both man and lady are now
   in PP. (The lady having swivelled to PP.) The man is
   facing diag. to centre.                               S
8. RF forward, across the body in PP towards centre.     S

## Feather Ending

9-11. Follow with steps 2. 3, 4 of a Feather, taken diag. to
   centre, and turning lady square on 2 of Feather.      QQS

*Contrary Body Movement.* CBM on 1, 4, 7, 8 and 11. Steps 4, 7, 8
and 11 are also placed in CBMP.

*Rise and Fall (Body).* Rise at end of 1, up on 2 and 3. Lower at end
of 3. Rise at end of 4; up on 5 and 6, Lower at end of 6. No rise on 7.
Rise at the end of 8; up on 9 and 10. Lower at end of 10.

*Body Sway.* Open Telemark: sway to L on 2. There is no sway on a
Natural Turn commenced in Promenade Position and no sway on the
Outside Swivel. Sway to L on 9 and 10.

*Amount of Turn.* Open Telemark: make a half turn to L. Natural Turn:
make a quarter turn between 4 and 6. Outside Swivel: body will turn a
quarter turn to R. The LF will turn inwards to point diagonally to centre
as the step is taken, but the turn of the body is gradual. There is no
turn on the Feather ending.

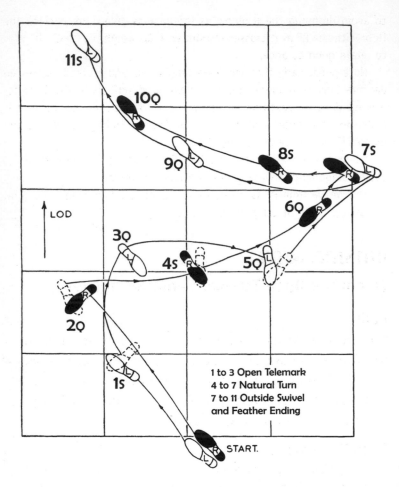

11s

10Q

9Q

8s

7s

LOD

3Q

4s

5Q

6Q

2Q

1s

1 to 3 Open Telemark
4 to 7 Natural Turn
7 to 11 Outside Swivel
and Feather Ending

START.

**Open Telemark, Natural Turn, Outside Swivel and Feather Ending (Man)**

*Footwork.* Open Telemark: 1. H T. 2 T. 3. T H. Natural Turn: 4. H T. 5. T. 6. T H. Outside Swivel: 7. T H with pressure on T of RF. Feather Ending: 8. H T. 9. T. 10 T H. 11. H

*General Notes.* When the man takes his LF back on the 1st step of the Outside Swivel, he must keep a firm pressure with his R hand on the lady's L side. He must check her forward impetus and continue pressure on her L side to lead her into the Outside Swivel. It is essential that his body should turn gradually as she turns. Care should be taken to avoid dropping the R elbow as this lead is given. Pressure on the floor with the RF as it crosses in front without weight will help the man to retain good balance.

Note particularly that the Open Telemark is underturned. Advanced dancers may turn more, but the position described is the best for average dancers. Less turn may be made on the Outside Swivel when it is danced at a corner, and the following Feather Ending would be taken diagonally to centre of the new LOD.

When dancing the Feather Ending after the Outside Swivel the LF is placed diagonally forward on 9, with L side leading.

The Weave from PP is an excellent figure to follow step 7. Turn on the Swivel could be adjusted if at a corner.

# OUTSIDE SWIVEL
## (From the Open Telemark and Natural Turn)
### Lady

The Outside Swivel consists of two steps only. It can be used from several positions, but it was in the amalgamation described below that the figure first gained popularity.

Commence backing diagonally to the centre and dance 1, 2, 3 of a Feather. Continue as follows:

### Open Telemark

| | | |
|---|---|---|
| 1. | RF back, turning body to L. | S |
| 2. | Close LF to RF, turning on R heel (Heel Turn). Finish facing diag. to wall. | Q |
| 3. | RF diag. forward in PP. | Q |

### Natural Turn

| | | |
|---|---|---|
| 4. | LF forward, across the body in PP, moving towards the wall, with LF pointing diag. to wall. | S |
| 5. | RF forward, between the man's feet, body square to man and facing diag. to wall. | Q |
| 6. | LF forward, preparing to step outside partner, L shoulder leading. | Q |

## Outside Swivel

7. RF forward, diag. to wall, outside partner. Swivel
   on the ball of the RF for a half turn to the R and
   at the same time close the LF to RF, slightly back,
   without weight on it. Finish in PP.                     S
8. LF forward, across the body in PP and turning body
   to L, moving towards Centre.                            S

## Feather Ending

9–11. Turn square to partner and follow with steps 2, 3, 4 of a
Feather as follows:

*Contrary Body Movement.* Open Telemark: CBM on 1. Natural Turn:
step 4 is placed in CBMP. Outside Swivel: CBM on 7 and 8. Both steps
are placed in CBMP. Feather Ending: CBM on 11 which is also placed in
CBMP.

*Rise and Fall (Body).* Open Telemark: Rise slightly at end of 1 (NFR);
continue to rise on 2; up on 3. Lower at end of 3. Natural Turn: Rise at
end of 4; up on 5 and 6. Lower at end of 6. Outside Swivel: no rise on
7. Feather Ending: Rise at the end of 8; up on 9; up on 10 (NFR). Lower
at the end of 10.

*Body Sway.* Open Telemark: sway to R on 2. There is no sway on a
Natural Turn commenced in Promenade Position, and no sway on the
Outside Swivel.

*Amount of Turn.* Open Telemark: make a quarter turn between 1 and
2. Natural Turn: there is no turn on this part of the figure. Outside
Swivel: make a half turn to R on 7. Less turn may be made at a corner.
Feather Ending: make a quarter turn to L.

*Footwork.* Open Telemark: 1. T H. 2. H T. 3. T H. Natural Turn: 4. H
T. 5. T. 6. T H. Outside Swivel: 7. H T H and pressure on IE of T of LF.
8. H T. Feather Ending: 9. T H. 10. T H. 11. T.

*General Notes.* Although the turn is made on the ball of RF in the
Outside Swivel the foot must be kept quite flat. The knees should be
relaxed. The pressure on the inside edge of the toe of the LF will
materially assist the balance.

When turning square to partner to take the Feather Ending to the
Outside Swivel, the RF should be placed to the side and slightly back,
backing the LOD for step 9, then turn to back diag. to centre for 10, 11.

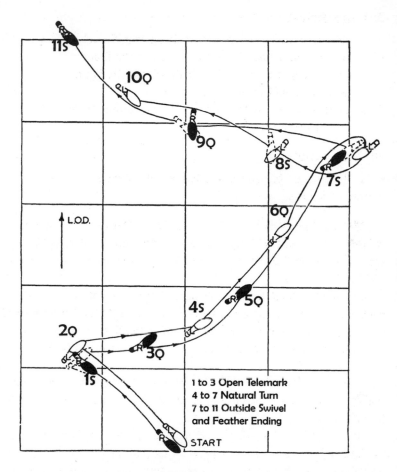

**Open Telemark, Natural Turn, Outside Swivel and Feather Ending (Lady)**

*Special Note.* The Weave from PP, described on pages 154-8 of the Waltz section, can be danced in the Foxtrot after the Outside Swivel. It is better to underturn the Outside Swivel and to move to centre for the first step of the Weave from PP. Rhythm in the Foxtrot will be QQQQQQS.

# NATURAL WEAVE

## Man

The Natural Weave is a delightful free moving figure which can be used as an alternative to the Natural Turn. Normally it is danced after a Three Step.

Commence facing the LOD

1. RF forward, turning to R.                                        S
2. LF to side, almost backing diag. to centre.                     Q
3. Still turning slightly to R step back RF diag.
   to centre, with R side leading.                                 Q
4. LF back, diag. to centre, partner outside.                      Q
5. RF back, partner in line and turning to L.                      Q
6. LF to side and slightly forward, body facing wall.              Q
7. RF forward, diag. to wall, outside partner.                     Q
8. LF forward, diag. to wall.                                      S

*Contrary Body Movement.* CBM on 1, 5, and 8. The 4th and 7th steps are placed in CBMP.

*Rise and Fall (Body).* Rise at end of 1; up on steps 2, 3, 4, 5, 6, 7. Lower at end of 7.

*Body Sway.* Sway to R on 2; to L on 4; to R on 6 and 7.

*Amount of Turn.* Make three-eighths of a turn to R between 1 and 3 and a quarter turn to L between 5 and 8.

*Footwork.* 1. H T. 2. T. 3. T. 4. T. 5. T. 6. T. 7. T H. 8. H.

*General Notes.* Note the slight continuance of the turn between steps 2 and 3 and also the quick change of sway on steps 2 and 4. When taking the 3rd step it is advisable to feel that it moves slightly rightwards. If it is taken back under the body, a common fault, an ugly body line will result. On step 4 it is permissible to use the Footwork of T H on LF. This often results in a softer movement.

The Natural Weave can be danced after a Three Step and can also be commenced in Promenade Position, when the man will turn square to lady as the 2nd step is danced. When commenced in PP the lady's 1st step will be forward and her 2nd step danced diagonally forward (making no Heel Turn). The Open Telemark is a good entry.

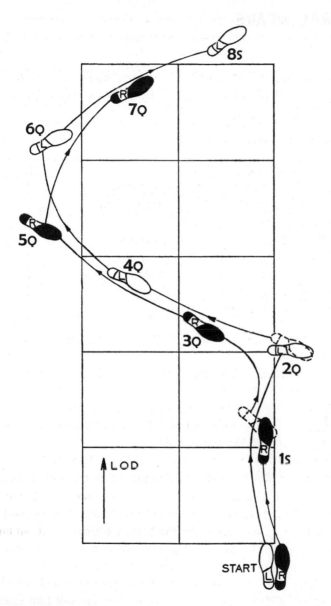

**Natural Weave (Man)**

# NATURAL WEAVE

## Lady
Commence backing the LOD.

1. LF back, turning to the R.    S
2. Close RF to LF turning on the L heel (Heel Turn). End facing diag. to centre.    Q
3. LF forward, diag. to centre, with L side leading and preparing to step outside partner.    Q
4. RF forward, outside partner.    Q
5. LF forward, diag. to centre, in line with partner, and turning to L.    Q
6. RF to side, body backing the wall.    Q
7. Still turning slightly to L step back LF, diag. to wall, partner outside.    Q
8. RF back, diag. to wall.    S

*Contrary Body Movement.* CBM on 1, 5, and 8. The 4th and 7th steps are placed in CBMP.

*Rise and Fall (Body).* Rise slightly at end of 1 (NFR) continue to rise on 2; up on steps 3, 4, 5, 6, up on 7 with NFR; Lower at end of 7.

*Body Sway.* Sway to L on 2; to R on 4; to L on 6 and 7.

*Amount of Turn.* Make three-eighths of a turn to R on steps 1 and 2 and a quarter turn to L between 5 and 8.

*Footwork.* 1. T H. 2. H T. 23. T. 4. T. 5. T. 6. T H. 7. T H. 8. T.

*General Notes.* See notes following the man's steps and diagram on page 213.

# WEAVE FROM PROMENADE POSITION

## Man
This beautiful variation is also described in the Waltz section but with a different alignment. The alignments are interchangeable and suggested entries are the Open Impetus (shown in the diagram on page 214) or the Hover Telemark

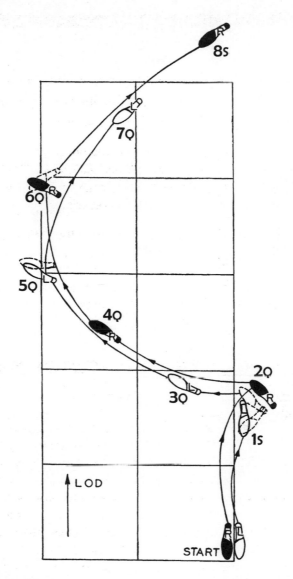

**Natural Weave (Lady)**

ended in Promenade Position.

Dance steps 1, 2, 3 of an Open Impetus. Count SQQ and

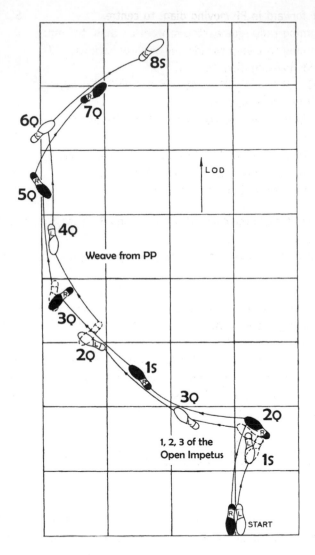

**8s**

**6Q**  **7Q**

LOD

**5Q**

**4Q**

Weave from PP

**3Q**

**2Q**

**1s**

**3Q**

**2Q**

1, 2, 3 of the
Open Impetus

**1s**

**R L**  START

**Weave from Promenade Position (Man)**
**From 1 to 3 of Open Impetus**

end in Promenade Position, moving diagonally to centre as shown in the diagram. Continue:

1. RF forward in PP moving diag. to centre.                          S
2. Turning Lady square, step forward LF, diag. to centre.            Q
3. Turning to L step to side and slightly back with RF
   body backing diag. to wall.                                       Q
4. Still turning slightly, step back LF, down the LOD
   with partner outside.                                             Q
5. RF back, down the LOD with lady in line and turning
   to the L.                                                         Q
6. LF to side and slightly forward, body facing wall.               Q
7. RF forward, diag. to wall, outside partner.                       Q
8. LF forward, in line with partner.                                 S

*Contrary Body Movement.* CBM on 2, 5, and 8. Steps 1, 4, and 7 are placed in CBMP.

*Rise and Fall (Body).* Rise at end of 1; up on steps 2 to 7; lower at end of 7.

*Body Sway.* Sway to L on 3 and 4. Sway to R on 6 and 7.

*Amount of Turn.* Make a quarter turn to L between 2 and 3 and an eighth between 3 and 4. Make three-eighths to L between 5 and 8.

*Footwork.* 1. H T. 2. T. 3. T. 4. T. 5. T. 6. T. 7. T H. 8 H.

*General Notes.* Some dancers find it easier to get a softer movement by lowering the L heel on step 4, but avoid completely lowering the body and getting an ugly "dipping" movement on step 5. Please also read the General Notes on this figure in the Waltz section.

# WEAVE FROM PROMENADE POSITION

## Lady

Although this delightful variation is described from an entry of the Open Impetus it can be used from any Promenade Position with similar alignment.

Dance steps 1, 2, 3 of an Open Impetus. Count SQQ and end in Promenade Position, moving diagonally to centre but with the RF pointing to centre, as shown in the diagram.

Continue:

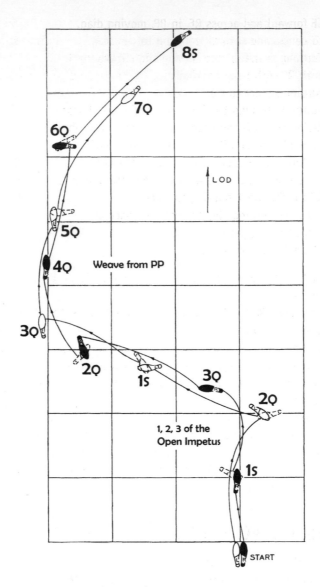

LOD

Weave from PP

8s

7Q

6Q

5Q

4Q

3Q

2Q

1s

3Q

2Q

1s

1, 2, 3 of the
Open Impetus

START

**Weave from Promenade Position (Lady)**
**From 1 to 3 of Open Impetus**

1. LF forward and across RF, in PP, moving diag. to centre and with LF pointing to centre.    S
2. Turning to the L, step to side and slightly back with RF with body backing diag. to centre and turning square to man.    Q
3. Continue turning to L on ball of RF until almost facing the LOD and then step to side and slightly forward with LF with L toe pointing to LOD.    Q
4. RF forward, outside partner, down the LOD.    Q
5. LF forward, in line with partner and turning to L.    Q
6. RF to side, body backing the wall.    Q
7. Continue turning slightly and step back LF, diag. to wall, partner outside.    Q
8. RF back, partner in line.    S

*Contrary Body Movement.* CBM on 1, 5, and 8. Steps 1, 4, and 7 are placed in CBMP.

*Rise and Fall (Body).* Rise at end of 1; up on steps 2 to 7 (with NFR on 7). Lower at end of 7.

*Body Sway.* Sway to R on 3 and 4. Sway to L on 6 and 7.

*Amount of Turn.* Make three-eighths to L between 1 and 2 and three-eighths between 2 and 3. Make a quarter to L between 5 and 6 and an eighth between 6 and 8.

*Footwork.* 1. H T. 2. T. 3. T. 4. T. 5. T. 6. T H. 7. T H. 8. T.

*General Notes.* Advanced lady dancers often keep the head turned to the R on steps 1 to 5, turning it back to its normal position as the Feather Finish is danced. Please also read the General Notes on this figure in the Waltz section.

## SUGGESTED FOXTROT AMALGAMATIONS

1. Feather–Three Step–Natural Turn.

2. Feather diagonally to centre–Reverse Turn–Three Step–Natural Turn into a corner–Finish facing the new LOD.

3. Feather–4 steps of Reverse Wave–Basic Weave–Change of Direction.

4. Feather–Three Step–1, 2, 3 of Natural Turn–Closed

Impetus followed by 5, 6, 7 of a Reverse Turn (Feather Finish) ending diagonally to the centre. Follow with any Reverse figure.

5. Feather diagonally to the centre–Reverse Turn–Straight into a Reverse Wave, ending with a Hover Feather taken diagonally to the centre–Open Telemark, Natural Turn and Outside Swivel–Weave from PP.

6. Feather–Three Step–Natural Weave–Change of Direction.

7. Feather–Three Step–1, 2, 3 of Natural Turn–Closed Impetus. Underturn the Closed Impetus and follow with 4, 5, 6 of a Reverse Turn (Feather Finish) ended moving diagonally to centre against LOD–Top Spin.

8. Feather–Reverse Turn–Hover Telemark ending in PP– Weave from PP–Three Step –Natural Turn.

9. Feather down LOD–First four steps of Reverse Wave–Basic Weave–Three Step–Natural Twist Turn, Natural Telemark, or Natural Weave.

# SECTION IV
# THE TANGO

The average Englishman looks upon the Tango as a dance full of eccentricities, and probably regards it as extremely difficult to acquire. Actually, the steps can be acquired much more easily than those of the Quickstep and Foxtrot, but the "style" and "character" of the Tango is very elusive – Tango "atmosphere" it is usually termed.

English dancers have endeavoured to capture this "atmosphere" by the introduction of an unnatural and rather cramped type of hold together with the use of a very relaxed movement, the resultant dance being both "creepy" and ungainly. The introduction of a more staccato action considerably enlivened the dance, and, although the tendency to exaggerate this action brought forth a certain amount of criticism, its influence remains.

Tango music is so attractive that the moderate dancer will be well repaid for the time spent in learning a few of the simple basic figures. The keen dancer who takes the trouble to acquire that elusive Tango atmosphere will find full compensation from the correct interpretation of what is undoubtedly one of the most fascinating dance rhythms.

**Promenade Position – Man's back view showing position of lady's hand throughout the Tango**

# GENERAL NOTES

*Time.* 2/4. Two beats in a bar. Both the 1st and 2nd beats are accented.

*Tempo.* Music played at 33 bars a minute.

*Basic Rhythms.* The figures consist of various combinations of "Slows" and "Quicks". As Tango music is in 2/4 time, each "Slow" has only one beat of music, and each "Quick" has a ½ beat.

*Figures.* Walk, Progressive Side Step, Rock Turn, Progressive Link, Closed Promenade, Open Promenade, Back Corté, Rocks, Open Reverse Turns, Basic Reverse Turn, Progressive Side Step Reverse Turn, Natural Twist Turn, Natural Promenade Turn, Promenade Link, Four Step, Fallaway Promenade, Outside Swivel and Brush Tap, Outside Swivel turning to L.

The Tango being an entirely different type of dance from the other standard dances, a detailed description of its chief characteristics is given in the following pages. The manner of approach depends very much upon the ability of the dancer, but it is advisable for all dancers to read the instructions on the Hold, the Placing of the Feet, and the characteristics of the Walk.

The construction of the Tango is comparatively simple owing to the fact that more walking steps are used, thus giving the dancer time to think which figure to use next. The following suggestions regarding the order in which to learn the basic figures should prove useful to the beginner.

*The Walk.* Learn this first. Approach it by means of a perfectly natural movement, afterwards trying to introduce points 1, 2 and 3 referred to in the notes on the Walk.

*Progressive Side Step.* Learn this figure, and then practise it, using three walking steps between each Progressive Side Step.

*Rock Turn.* Usually a Reverse Turn is introduced next, but the Rock Turn will be found easier and more useful.

*Closed Promenade, Open Promenade.* These figures will follow quite easily from the Rock Turn. First dance 2 Walks, LF, RF, then turn the lady to PP.

*Reverse Turn.* The Open Reverse Turn, lady outside, using the Closed Finish, is probably the most popular and should be learned next.

Notes on the general construction are given in the descriptions of the separate figures.

## The Hold

The hold in the Tango is rather more compact than in the moving dances. The lady is held slightly more on the man's R side, but this must not be exaggerated. The man's R arm will be slightly farther round the lady. To obtain the correct hold for the extended arms, stand in position and with the L arm held in the normal Foxtrot hold. The man should now bring his L hand slightly in towards him, and also lower it a little. These movements must be made from the elbow, the forearm only moving. To correspond with this alteration the lady should drop her elbow slightly as well as moving her hand. The man, however, should endeavour to keep his elbow in the normal position.

Owing to the position of her body in the Tango (slightly more to the man's R), the lady will find it more comfortable to place her L hand rather more at the back of the man's R arm or with the hand actually resting on the man's back, just under his arm-pit.

## Position in the Walk

Walking movements in the Tango are not taken with the man facing square to the LOD. When a step is taken down the LOD his feet and body will be facing almost diagonally to the centre, with his R hip and shoulder in advance of his L. In backward movements the reverse will apply. This positioning of the body at the commencement of the dance will affect the Walk in the following ways:

Each step taken forward with the LF will give the effect of moving across the body (called "Contrary Body Movement Position"). It is important that the L heel is placed on, not across, the line of the RF.

As a step is taken with the RF the *Right side is leading*. This term is used to describe this position in the following descriptions.

This action will result in the Walk taking the line of a wide curve to the man's L.

In backward movements the man's L side will lead, when stepping back with LF. RF back steps are placed in CBMP. The same rules apply to the lady's Walk.

*Further Characteristics of the Walk.* Although the balance and distribution of weight are similar to those in other dances, there are one or two important characteristics in the Tango Walk that should be noted.

*1. Knees.* The knees are kept slightly flexed throughout the dance. To realize the full meaning of this, the dancer must remember that in the other dances, when the leg is at the full extent of its stride, the knee is comparatively straight. In the Tango the feet are lifted slightly from the floor in the Walk (see Note 2), and when the foot meets the floor at the full extent of the stride, it does so with the knee slightly move flexed than in the moving dances, although the muscles of the leg are well toned to avoid any suggestion of "drop" or softness as the weight is taken on to the step. Naturally, the moving leg will flex more as it is passing through to its forward position, care must be taken not to relax the knee of the supporting leg further, otherwise a "lilting" or "up and down" movement will result.

2. *Placing of Feet.* All walking steps in the Tango picked up from the floor slightly and placed into position. This, of course, is in direct opposition to the gliding movement of other dances. Care must be taken not to exaggerate this action. It is preferable to keep the ball of the foot of the moving leg skimming over the floor until it nearly reaches the supporting foot, before lifting it slightly from the floor and placing it in position with a crisp action. The keen dancer will also observe that the curving of the Walk to the L will result in the weight being taken on the L edge of both feet in a forward movements and on the R edge in backward movements.

3. *Sharpness.* The crisp action of the Walk is obtained by delaying the movement of the foot that is not supporting the weight of the body. If a step forward has been taken with the RF, the moving of the LF should be delayed slightly, so that when it does move forward it must move quickly in order to be in position on the next beat of the music. Do not delay the back foot too long, as this would result in a loss of continuity in the movement of the body.

Whilst these three points apply also to the backward Walk, it must be admitted that it is much more difficult when doing a backward movement to "feel" the action referred to in Notes 2 and 3. This is owing to the fact that the toe will meet the floor first. One can get more character into a movement that is led with the heel first. No attempt must be made to lift the foot upwards at the full extent of the stride and then force it down to the floor in an effort to achieve sharpness of action in the backward walk.

All steps should be of medium length, not short. They will not be as long as in moving dances. The action of the step comes from the hip, not from the knee only, but the swinging action of the other dances is not used.

## The Turns

*Contrary Body Movement.* Although Contrary Body Movement is often used in turning figures in the Tango, the "swing" into the turns, to which I have referred in the moving dances, is almost completely absent. The turns in the Tango are less acute, and the R side lead adopted in this dance (referred to under "Position in the Walk") makes the entry into L turns much easier. Right-hand turns are often taken from Promenade Position or are so constructed that a conscious swing of the body is unnecessary.

*Contrary Body Movement Position.* This is referred to frequently in the descriptions of the Tango figures, and is the position achieved when the body is not turned but the leg placed across the body, so giving the appearance of Contrary Body Movement. Every normal step forward with the LF and back with the RF by both man and lady will be in Contrary Body Movement Position. It frequently happens that Contrary Body Movement is used on a Contrary Body Movement Position step. This is noted in the descriptions. The 2nd step of every promenade figure automatically results in Contrary Body Movement Position.

*Rise and Fall.* There is no Rise in the Tango. The absence of "swing" on the turns, and the fact that the feet are placed rather than swung into position, account for this difference from the moving dances. In one or two figures, steps are taken and swivels made on the ball of the foot, but there is no pronounced Rise, and the heel is kept close to the floor.

In the accompanying charts a few swivels of the feet have been shown but it is important to remember that in practically every case this swivel of the foot is made *after* the next step is in position.

## Body Sways

The reasons for the absence of Rise and Fall and body swing in the Tango also account for the lack of Body Sways. The shoulders should be kept as level as possible.

## Footwork

In the Tango, the word *Ball* instead of *Toe* is used in describing Footwork. Other terms used are *Inside edge of foot, Inside edge of Ball of foot,* and *Whole foot.* The correct footwork on each step is given following the descriptions of the figures, but some helpful rules to remember are:

1. All forward steps, whether taken in CBMP or with a side lead are described as *Heel*. It is not necessary to say *Heel, then Flat.* The first two steps of Promenade figures are also Heel. (It is taken for granted that the toe will then lower.)

2. All backward steps taken in CBMP are *Ball, Heel,* indicating that the step is taken on to the Ball, then lowering to the whole foot.

3. All backward steps taken with a L or R side lead are *Inside edge of Ball, Heel.* The reason for this is quite obvious.

4. The footwork of side steps varies. Some are *Inside edge of foot* indicating that the inside edge of the foot touches the floor first, before it flattens. Others are *Inside edge of Ball, Heel,* or just *Ball, Heel.* A few are *Whole Foot.* The use of these terms will be found consistent in all figures, and it will help the student to get a truer interpretation of the dance if the correct footwork is used.

5. The footwork of closing steps also varies. The majority are *Whole Foot,* but in some more advanced figures it will be found that a foot closes with the footwork of *Ball, Heel.*

## Alignment

It is important to remember that the alignment on forward and backward steps in the Tango descriptions is a *directional* term, and that the Right side lead used by the man in a forward walk, and the Left side lead used in a backward walk will result

in the feet and body having a different alignment from the
actual direction of the step.

The following examples will assist students to understand
this point:

1. *Step back LF, down the LOD.* The direction of the step will be
down the LOD but the L side lead will result in the feet and body
backing *diagonally to the centre.*

2. *Step forward RF, diag. to centre.* The direction of the step will be
diagonally to the centre, but the R side lead will result in the feet and
body facing the *centre.*

## Closing of the Feet

The feet are closed very frequently in the Tango, and much
more character can be given to the dance if the feet are closed
correctly.

The feet are usually closed after a step to the side, an example being: "LF to side and slightly forward. Close RF to LF". The
following details should be studied:

1. When stepping to the side with LF take the step on the inside
edge of the LF, with the L knee veering inwards. The whole foot will be
on the floor as the complete weight moves on to the foot.

2. Delay moving the RF and feel that the pressure is left on the
inside edge of the ball of the RF with the R heel almost touching the
floor. The R knee will tend to move towards the L knee.

3. Pick the RF very slightly off the floor and then close it
*deliberately,* but not very sharply, to the LF, placing it slightly back.

4. Do not close the feet tightly together. The R toe should be level
with the L instep and about 2 cm (an inch) away from it, but the knees
must be touching, with the R knee tucked slightly behind the L knee.
The RF should tend to turn *very slightly* inwards.

Anything in the nature of a "solid" closing of the feet with
knees straight should be avoided. The closing of the foot slightly
back instead of completely level with the LF will result in the

body assuming the same position as is used in a forward walk.

A similar movement is used by the lady when closing her LF to her RF. Differences are that her RF will be placed to the side with the inside edge of the *ball* of the foot making the first contact with the floor, and her LF will close, or rather nearly close, with the Left heel near the Right instep.

## Promenade Figures

Promenade figures are danced with the man's R side and the lady's L side in close contact, and with the opposite sides of the body "open" or apart, so that the bodies form a "V" shape.

Normally, if a Promenade is taken along the LOD the man will be facing diagonally to the wall, and the lady will face diagonally to the centre. It is, however, advisable to keep the position slightly more compact with the bodies.

The position of the lady's head in Promenade figures is a matter of personal taste. The normal position is for the lady to turn her head to the Right so that she is facing the direction of the Promenade. Some ladies prefer to keep the head in the usual position or even turn it more to the Left.

It is advisable to use the position which feels most comfortable.

## THE WALK FORWARD

Notes on the characteristics of the Walk are given on the preceding pages. It should be noted that each Walk occupies only one beat of music, but it is easiest to count it "Slow" as the slow tempo of the music makes the step of the same duration as a "Slow" in the Foxtrot. The actual movement of the feet is as follows:

Take a natural-length step forward with the RF, placing the foot heel first and going immediately on to the flat foot. Bring the rear foot forward with the toe skimming the floor. Lift this foot slightly from the floor just before it reaches the supporting foot, and then continue forward to repeat the Walk on the LF.

Note that the heel of the supporting foot is always released just after the moving foot passes the supporting foot.

As the RF commences to move forward the weight is on the supporting (L) foot. When the RF is placed, the weight is central for a moment, and then taken forward on to the RF. The body must be kept moving all the time, and any tendency to "sit back" on the supporting foot must be avoided.

## THE WALK BACKWARD

Take a natural-length step backward with the LF, placing the toe first and lowering to the ball of the foot. Commence to move the front foot back with the heel skimming the floor, and lower the heel of the supporting (L) foot as the moving foot passes to continue with another Walk.

It should be noted that in actual practice the heel of the supporting foot tends to lower slightly earlier than it does in the Walk used in the Quickstep and Foxtrot.

As the LF commences to move back the weight is on the supporting (R) foot. When the LF is placed back the weight is central for a moment, and then taken on to the back foot.

## PROGRESSIVE SIDE STEP

### Man

The Progressive Side Step might be termed a quickening of the Walk in which the second step is taken sideways. This figure can be taken in any forward direction, and should tend to curve slightly to the L.

1. LF forward, across the body.                             Q
2. RF to the side and slightly back.*                       Q

(The ball of the RF should be level with the L instep.)

* See note on page 231.

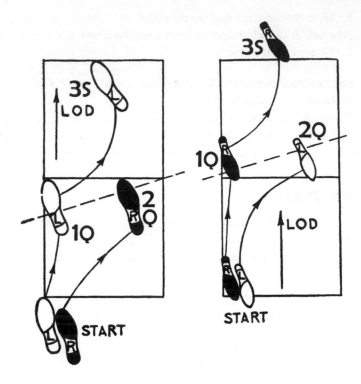

**Progressive Side Step**
**Left: Man  Right: Lady**

3. LF forward, across the body.     S

*Contrary Body Movement Position.* Steps 1 and 3 are in CBMP.
*Footwork.* 1. H. 2. IE of foot. 3. H.
*General Notes.* Although the man's 2nd step is to the side and slightly back in relation to the body, it will progress further along the LOD than the LF if the figure is turned. This step should be placed sharply, using the inside edge of the foot.

One or three walking steps should be used before the Progressive Side Step is repeated.

## Lady

1. RF back, across the body.     Q

2. LF to the side and slightly forward.*      Q
(The ball of the RF should be level with the L instep.)
3. RF. back, across the body.      S

*Contrary Body Movement Position.* Steps 1 and 3 are in CBMP.
*Footwork.* 1. B H. 2. IE of B, H. 3. B.
*General Notes.* When the 2nd step is placed on the inside edge of the Ball of the LF, the L Heel should be quite close to the floor. If the L Heel is raised too much a "bouncing" movement will result.

# ROCK TURN

## Man

A simple and useful figure comprising the Rock and a Closed Finish.

This figure can be commenced diagonally to the wall or down the LOD. Finish facing diagonally to the wall.

1. RF forward, turning body to the R.      S
2. LF to side and slightly back. Backing centre.      Q
3. Still turning body to the R, rock forward on to RF, R side leading.      Q
4. LF back, lengthening the step a little, moving diag. to centre with the L side leading.      S
5. RF back (to centre) turning body to L.      Q
6. LF to side, and slightly forward.      Q
7. Close RF to LF, slightly back. Face diag. to wall.      S

*Contrary Body Movement and Position.* CBM on 1 (slight) and 5. 5 is also taken in CBMP.
*Footwork.* 1. H. 2. IE of B H. 3. IE of B H. 4. IE of B H. 5. B H. 6. IE of foot. 7. Whole foot.
*Amount of Turn.* Make a quarter turn to the R between 1 and 3, and a quarter turn to L between 3 and 6.
*General Notes.* On the first step no swivel is made on RF. As the LF moves sideways for the 2nd step, the R Heel will be released from the

---

* Although in the diagrams the 1st and 2nd steps appear to toe the same line, the position described is correct in relation to the body, as indicated by the dotted line.

floor. Pressure is then felt on the IE of the ball of the RF before the heel is replaced on the 3rd step. Alternatively the RF may be picked up slightly and then replaced on the heel and then the flat foot. The knees must be kept well relaxed in the Rock. Do not release the toe of RF when commencing to move it back for step 5 or control will be lost.

*Amalgamation.* A good elementary amalgamation is:
Commence facing diag. to wall.

| | |
|---|---:|
| Walk – LF, RF | SS |
| Progressive Side Step. | QQS |
| Rock Turn. | SQQSQQS |

Finish diag. to wall to continue with Walk.

The Rock Turn may follow the Natural Promenade Turn. The man will not turn the lady to PP on the 4th step of the Natural Promenade Turn. (See General Notes, Natural Promenade Turn.)

## ROCK TURN

### Lady

This figure can be commenced diagonally to a wall or down the LOD. It is usually ended with the lady backing the wall diagonally.

1. LF back, turning body to the R.
2. Move RF slightly rightwards, leaving it forward, slightly between man's feet.                                    Q
3. Still turning to R, rock back on to the LF moving it slightly leftwards, L side leading.                         Q
4. RF forward, lengthening the step a little. Moving diag. to centre, R side leading.                               S
5. LF forward (to centre), turning body to L.                                                                       Q
6. RF to side and slightly back.                                                                                    Q
7. Close LF to RF, slightly forward.                                                                                S

*Contrary Body Movement and Position.* CBM on 1 (slight), and 5. 5 is also taken in CBMP.

*Amount of Turn.* Make a quarter turn to the R between 1 and 3, and a quarter turn to the L between 3 and 6.

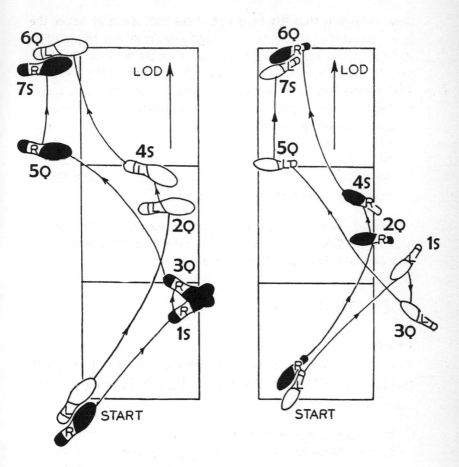

**Rock Turn**
**Left: Man  Right: Lady**

*Footwork.* 1. B H. 2. H. 3. IE of B H. 4. H. 5. H. 6 IE of B H. 7. Whole foot.

*General Notes.* On the actual Rock Turn (steps 1 to 4) the lady is on the inside of the turn. As the RF is moving rightwards, it is kept between the man's feet as he, being on the outside of the turn, steps round her with his LF. The knees must be kept well relaxed in the Rock.

*Amalgamations.* A useful amalgamation is given in the notes on the man's steps.

## WALK INTO PROMENADE POSITION

The descriptions of the Closed and Open Promenades are given in the following pages. Methods of turning to commence these figures from a Walk should be studied.

The normal position to dance a Promenade is sideways along the LOD. Assuming the dancer has just completed a figure such as the Rock Turn, or a Reverse Turn with a Closed Finish, he would be facing diagonally to the wall with the feet closed. After a step forward with the LF the procedure would be:

(1) Step forward with the RF more in line with the LF than a normal RF walk, and at the same time turn the lady to Promenade Position by applying pressure with the base of the R hand on the L side of her back. The man will have practically no turn to make as he is already in a diagonal position.

On the latter part of the "Slow" count on which this step is made, the man should place the LF to side, without weight, before stepping to the side for the 1st step of the Promenade figure. It is helpful to count "and" as the LF is placed.

It is not good style to "brush" the LF past the RF and go straight into a Promenade figure. The LF should make a slight pause before moving sideways for the first step of the Promenade, and the inside edge of the ball of the LF should be in contact with the floor at this point.

The lady should place her RF to the side, without weight, before stepping to the side. The notes in the two preceding paragraphs also apply to the lady's RF.

(2) If a Promenade figure is taken following a Walk when moving along the LOD it is better to dance the entire Promenade in a direction diagonally to the centre. The step following the Promenade is taken forward with the LF down the LOD.

(3) A more advanced entry to Promenade figures is the Progressive Link. This is described next.

# PROGRESSIVE LINK

## Man

This figure is a the most popular entry into a Promenade figure although the Walk to Promenade Position is a little easier for the beginner. It can be commenced diagonally to the wall or facing the LOD.

1. LF forward, across the body.                                    Q
2. RF to side and slightly back. (See note below.)       Q
With LF continue by stepping sideways into a Promenade figure.

*Contrary Body Movement Position.* The 1st step is placed in CBMP.
*Footwork.* 1. H. 2. IE of foot and IE edge of B of LF.
*General Notes.* As the 2nd step is taken, the man should bring the R side of the body slightly back, and at the same time turn the lady to PP. If the Progressive Link is commenced facing the LOD the following Promenade figure should be taken diagonally to centre. If it is commenced facing diagonally to wall, the Promenade figure will be taken along the LOD. The 2nd step is short.

The Progressive Link can be danced following a Walk on the RF or after a Closed Promenade or any Closed Finish. It is also used directly following a Promenade Link.

# PROGRESSIVE LINK

## Lady

Commence backing diagonally to the wall or the LOD.

1. RF back, across the body.                                      Q
2. As the man turns lady to PP she will step to
   the side and slightly back with LF (short step).      Q
Finish in PP and follow with a Promenade figure.

*Contrary Body Movement Position.* The 1st step is placed in CBMP.
*Amount of Turn.* Make a quarter turn to R.
*Footwork.* 1. B H. 2. IE of B H and IE of B of RF.

*General Notes.* Although the 2nd step is termed "to side and slightly back" it should be noted that this refers to its position in relation to the body and the RF. It is actually placed on the same line of dance as the 1st step.

# CLOSED PROMENADE

## Man

The Closed Promenade can be danced moving sideways along the LOD, or in a direction diagonally to the centre. Methods of entry from the Walk are given on the previous page.

As previously mentioned, in Promenade figures the man's R side and the lady's L side are kept close together, whilst the opposite hips and shoulders are apart, the two bodies thus forming a "V".

| | |
|---|---|
| 1. LF to side in PP. | S |
| 2. RF forward and across in PP. | Q |
| 3. LF to side and slightly forward. | Q |
| 4. Close RF to LF slightly back. | S |

*Contrary Body Movement Position.* Step 2 is in CBMP.
*Footwork.* 1. H. 2. H. 3. IE of foot. 4. Whole foot.
*General Notes.* Note that the first step is quite long. The 3rd step should be placed crisply on the inside edge of LF and with the L knee veering inwards before taking the weight on to the whole foot. As the RF closes, the L side will tend to move slightly back.

Although the bodies lose contact on one side, the Promenade Position must be kept compact. This will be found easier if the lady is held with her L hip slightly behind the man's R hip.

The man must lead the lady with his R hand to turn her square on the 3rd step.

Whilst beginners will find it useful to practise a succession of Promenades, the more advanced dancer should never dance more than one Promenade figure in succession. It is also better style to take the Promenade from a Walk or a Progressive Link, and not after a figure that has ended with the feet closed.

Follow the Closed Promenade with a LF Walk taken diagonally to the wall.

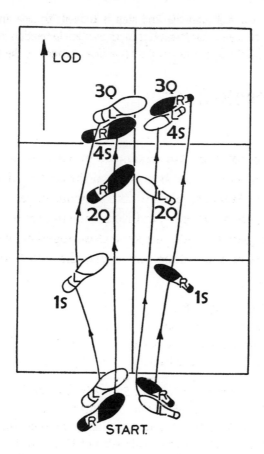

**Closed Promenade**
**Left: Man   Right: Lady**

# CLOSED PROMENADE

## Lady

The Closed Promenade can be danced moving sideways along the LOD, or in a direction diagonally to the centre. Method of entry from the Walk is given on a previous page.

As stated previously, the Closed Promenade is danced with the bodies in a "V" position, the lady's L side being close to the man's R side, and opposite hips and shoulders are apart. When dancing a Promenade along the LOD the lady's feet will be facing diagonally to the centre.

1. RF to side in PP.                                                 S
2. LF forward and across in PP.                                      Q
3. RF to side and slightly back, and at the same
   time turning square to partner.                                  Q
4. Close LF to RF, slightly forward.                                S
   Finish with back diagonally to the wall.

*Contrary Body Movement and Position.* CBM and CBMP on 2.
*Footwork.* 1. H. 2. H. 3. IE of B H. 4. Whole foot.
*General Notes.* The 1st step should be quite long. The bodies should not turn more outwards as the 2nd step moves across.

The lady turns square to man as she takes her 3rd step. This step is placed on the inside edge of the ball of RF before lowering the heel, but there must be no rise. The R knee should veer inwards as this step is taken.

When dancing a Closed Promenade the lady may turn her head to the R to face along the LOD or leave it in the normal position. Both methods are correct and it is a matter of personal taste.

## OPEN PROMENADE

### Man

The Open Promenade is similar to the Closed Promenade, but the 4th step is taken forward outside the partner. It is usually danced sideways along the LOD.

Commence in Promenade Position, after a Walk forward on the RF or a Progressive Link. Finish facing almost diagonally to the wall.

1. LF to side in PP.                                                S
2. RF forward and across in PP, and commence
   to turn to R.                                                    Q

3. Short step to side and slightly forward with LF, turning partner square.  Q
4. RF forward, outside partner.  S

*Contrary Body Movement and Position.* Steps 2 and 4 are in CBMP and slight CBM is used on 2.

*Footwork.* 1. H. 2. H. 3. IE of foot. 4. H.

*General Notes.* As the 3rd step is taken to the side, it is advisable to turn very slightly to the right so that the body is almost square to the wall, otherwise an ugly hip movement is likely to result when the 4th step is taken forward across the body.

The weight is slightly more forward on the 3rd step of an Open Promenade than on the 3rd step of a Closed Promenade, and this will give a clear indication to the lady as to which Promenade is being danced. The direction of the 4th step will be between the wall and diagonally to wall.

Follow with:

(1) Progressive Side Step. Step immediately forward with LF rather across the front of the body to get into line with the partner, and dance the Progressive Side Step.

(2) After stepping forward with RF, transfer weight back to LF and dance a LF Rock, taken outside partner, each step being placed in CBMP. Make up to just under a quarter turn to R on the Rock, then bring the lady in line as you step back on RF into a Closed Finish. End facing diag. to wall. Count "QQS QQS". The Rock may also be danced without turn, then turn the Closed Finish to end facing diag. to centre to follow with a Reverse Turn, or two Walks and a Reverse Turn.

(3) Back Corté (see page 240). After stepping forward with the RF transfer the weight back to the LF, turning the body slightly to the R (S); then dance 2, 3, and 4 of the Back Corté, making very little turn to the L to end facing diag. to wall (QQS). The lady gets into line on the 2nd step of the Back Corté.

(4) Outside Swivel.

# OPEN PROMENADE

## Lady

The Open Promenade is similar to the Closed Promenade, but

the lady takes the 4th step back with the partner outside instead of closing it to RF.

It is usually danced along the LOD.

Commence in Promenade Position, after a Walk backward on the LF or a Progressive Link. Finish backing almost diagonally to the wall.

1. RF to side in PP.                                           S
2. LF forward and across in PP, and commence to
   turn to L.                                                  Q
3. RF to side and slightly back, having turned
   square to the man.                                          Q
4. LF back, partner outside.                                   S

*Contrary Body Movement and Position.* CBM on 2. Steps 2 and 4 are placed in CBMP.

*Footwork.* 1. H. 2. H. 3. IE of B H. 4. B.

*General Notes.* The 3rd step should not be too short, otherwise the lady will be left too much at the R side of the man on the outside step. The 4th step is taken in a direction between the wall and diagonally to wall.

Please refer to man's General Notes for appropriate following figures.

## BACK CORTÉ

### Man

The Back Corté is used chiefly when the man is moving backwards to the LOD and wishes to turn to a forward direction.

It consists of a step back with LF followed by the Closed Finish.

Commence backing diagonally to the centre. Finish facing diagonally to the wall.

1. LF back down the LOD, L side leading.                       S
2. RF back, turning body to L.                                 Q
3. LF to side and slightly forward.                            Q
4. Close RF to LF, slightly back. Finish diag. to wall.        S

*Contrary Body Movement and Position.* CBM on 2, which is also placed in CBMP.

*Amount of Turn.* A quarter turn to L may be made.

*Footwork.* 1. IE of B H. 2. B H. 3. IE of foot. 4. Whole foot.

*General Notes.* Do not release the toe of RF when commencing to move it back for step 2 or control will be lost. It is important to remember the normal L side lead on the 1st step, otherwise the turn to the L will be abrupt. If the 1st step is taken down the LOD with the body backing diagonally to centre, the direction of the 2nd step will be diagonally to centre and the 3rd step will point diagonally to wall with the body facing wall. The L side will move back as the RF closes. Follow with a Walk forward diagonally to the wall with the LF.

The Back Corté can be used in the following positions:

(1) After a Closed Promenade or any figure that has a Closed Finish ended facing diag. to wall. Take step 1 of the Back Corté to centre. End facing diag. to centre to go into a Reverse figure. (When at a corner step 1 will move down the new LOD. End facing diag. to wall.)

(2) After the Open Promenade or any figure that has an Open Finish. When taken from this position step 1 of the Back Corté will be in CBMP with lady outside. Make a slight turn to R on this step, then bring lady in line and commence to turn body to L on 2, taking this step to the centre. End facing diag. to wall. (Alternatively make no turn on step 1, then turn L to end facing diag. to centre.)

(3) After the first four steps of the Progressive Side Step Reverse Turn, in place of the normal LF Rock and Closed Finish.

(4) After a RF Rock.

(5) After the Natural Twist Turn (see page 255. Overturn the twist to end backing diag. to centre, having turned square to lady.

# BACK CORTÉ

## Lady

The Back Corté is used when the man is moving backwards to the LOD and wishes to turn to a forward direction.

It consists of a step forward with the RF, followed by a Closed Finish.

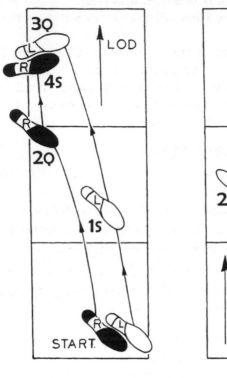

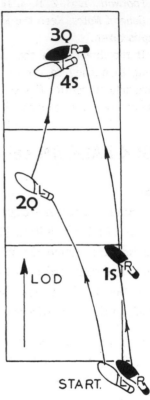

**Back Corté**
**Left: Man  Right: Lady**

Commence facing diagonally to the centre. Finish backing diagonally to the wall.

| | |
|---|---|
| 1. RF forward down the LOD, R side leading. | S |
| 2. LF forward, turning the body to L. | Q |
| 3. RF to side and slightly back. | Q |
| 4. Close LF to RF, slightly forward. | S |

*Contrary Body Movement and Position.* CBM on 2, which is also placed in CBMP.

*Amount of Turn.* A quarter turn to L may be made.

*Footwork.* 1. H. 2. H. 3. IE of B H. 4. Whole foot.

*General Notes.* Keep the R hip well towards the partner as the 3rd step is taken.

If the direction of the 1st step is down the LOD with the body facing diagonally to centre, the direction of the 2nd step will be diagonally to centre. The RF will be backing diagonally to wall on 3, but the body will complete the turn as the LF closes on 4.

## ROCK BACK ON LEFT FOOT

### Man

The Rock is used frequently in the Tango, and danced mainly with the LF leading first. The most popular way of introducing this figure is when the man is moving backwards down the LOD. The standard positions from which to use the Rock are given below. Commence with the back diagonally to centre. Finish in the same direction.

1. LF back down the LOD, L side leading.                   Q
2. Rock forward on to RF, R side leading.                  Q
3. LF back, lengthening the step slightly, L side leading. S

There is no CBM. Normally there is no turn, but a slight turn to the R may be made when the LF Rock is danced outside partner following an Open Promenade or Open Finish.

*Footwork.* 1. IE of B H. 2. H. 3. IE of B H.

*General Notes.* The important points to remember are:

The first step must not be too long, and the foot must be placed on the inside edge of the ball of foot before lowering the heel. Do not release the toe of RF when commencing to move it back for the following step or control will be lost.

When stepping back on to the LF on step 3 this step must always be lengthened slightly. A good rule to remember is always move the 3rd step of a Rock towards the direction in which you intend to move afterwards.

The LF Rock may be used in place of the Back Corté. It is also steps 5, 6, 7 of the Progressive Side Step Reverse Turn.

# ROCK FORWARD ON RIGHT FOOT

## Lady

The Rock is a very popular figure in the Tango and is mostly danced by the lady with her RF leading first, and facing diagonally to the centre.

1. RF forward down the LOD, R side leading          Q
2. Rock back on to LF, L side leading.          Q
3. RF forward, lengthening the step slightly,
   R side leading.          S

There is no CBM. Normally, there is no turn, but a slight turn to the R may be made when danced outside partner.

*Footwork.* 1. H. 2. IE of B H. 3. H.

*General Notes.* The first step must not be too long. When stepping forward on the RF on step 3 the step must always be lengthened slightly.

# ROCK BACK ON RIGHT FOOT (LADY ROCK FORWARD LF)

The Rock can be danced with the man leading on the RF back. The description is the same as for the LF Rock, but it should be remembered that, as the man usually adopts a L side lead when moving backward, all steps will be in CBMP. This applies to both man and lady.

The RF Rock is often used directly following a LF Rock. It could be used from any of the positions given for the LF Rock, substituting a RF Rock instead of the Open or Closed Reverse Finish.

Follow the RF Rock with a Back Corté.

*Footwork.* Man: 1. B H. 2. H. 3. B (H). Lady: 1. H. 2. B H. 3. H.

# OPEN REVERSE TURN, LADY IN LINE

## Man

The Open Reverse Turn is probably the easiest Reverse Turn

for the beginner to learn first, the steps being somewhat similar to the first three steps of the Foxtrot Reverse Turn. The figure is preceded by a Walk forward on the RF.

Commence facing diagonally to the centre. Finish facing diagonally to the wall.

1. LF forward, across the body, turning to L.                          Q
2. RF to side and slightly back, body backing the LOD.        Q
3. LF back down the LOD, L side leading.                           S
Now continue with the Closed Finish as follows:
4. RF back, diag. to centre, turning to L.                           Q
5. LF to side and slightly forward.                                     Q
6. Close RF to LF, slightly back. Facing diag. to wall.         S

*Contrary Body Movement and Position.* CBM on 1 and 4. Both of these steps are placed in CBMP.

*Amount of Turn.* Three-quarters of a turn on the complete figure.

*Footwork.* 1. H. 2. B H. 3. IE of B H. 4. B H. 5. IE of foot. 6. Whole foot.

*General Notes.* The turn must be made without the "Body swing" that is used in the moving dances.

The Open Finish (see page 248) may be used in place of the Closed Finish.

Follow with a LF Walk or Progressive Side Step.

# OPEN REVERSE TURN, LADY IN LINE

## Lady

This Reverse Turn is similar to the Reverse Turn of the Foxtrot, and is, perhaps, the most generally used.

It is preceded by a step back on the LF.

Commence backing the centre diagonally. Finish backing diagonally to the wall.

1. RF back, across the body, turning to L.                           Q
2. Close L heel to R heel with the toe pointing
to the LOD.                                                                     Q

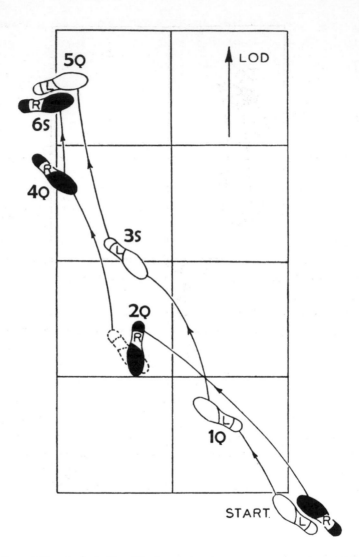

**Open Reverse Turn Lady in Line (Man)**

3. RF forward, down the LOD, R side leading.　　　　　　S
Now continue with the Closed Finish as follows:
4. LF forward, diag. to centre, turning to the L.　　　　Q
5. RF to side and slightly back.　　　　　　　　　　　Q

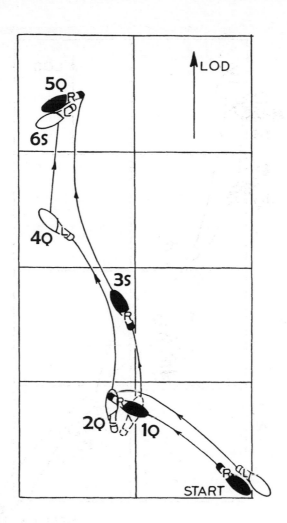

**Open Reverse Turn Lady in Line (Lady)**

6. Close LF to RF slightly forward. Back diag. to wall.    S

*Contrary Body Movement and Position.* CBM on 1 and 4. Both of these steps are placed in CBMP.

*Amount of Turn.* Three-quarters of a turn on the complete figure.

*Footwork.* 1. B H. 2. Whole foot. 3. H. 4. H. 5. IE of B H. 6. Whole foot.

*General Notes.* Although the position of the 2nd step might be termed an "untidy" Heel Turn, no attempt must be made to turn on the R heel. When the RF moves back it is placed on the ball of foot and the RF will then turn inwards as the weight is taken on to it, until it is finally pointing diagonally to wall.

An Open Finish may be used in place of the Closed Finish (see page 250).

## OPEN REVERSE TURN, LADY OUTSIDE

### Man

This method of dancing the Open Reverse Turn is to lead the lady outside on the third step. The normal ending is the Closed Finish (see page 245), but an Open Finish in which the man steps forward with the RF outside the lady, instead of closing his feet on the last step, may be used. This method is given in the description and diagram.

It is preceded by a step forward on RF.

Commence facing diagonally to the centre. Finish facing almost diagonally to the wall.

1. LF forward, across the body, turning to the L.            Q
2. RF to side, body backing diag. to wall.                   Q
3. LF back down the LOD, with partner outside.               S

Now continue with the Open Finish as follows:

4. RF back down the LOD, turning to the L, lady in line.     Q
5. LF to side and slightly forward.                          Q
6. RF forward, outside partner, in a direction between
   the wall and diag. to wall.                               S

*Contrary Body Movement and Position.* CBM on 1 and 4. The 1st, 3rd, and 6th steps are placed in CBMP.

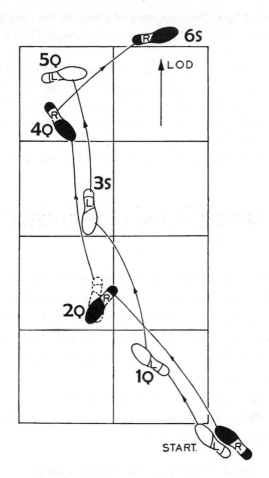

**Open Reverse Turn Lady Outside (Man)**
**Shown with Open Finish**

*Amount of Turn.* Just under three-quarters of a turn on the complete figure.

*Footwork.* 1. H. 2. B H. 3. B H. 4. B H. 5. IE of foot. 6. H.

*General Notes.* Note that less turn is made between the first 2 steps when the partner is to step outside on 3. Also note that the turn between steps 4 and 5 is slightly less than in a Closed Finish. This will help to keep contact with lady on the outside step and give a better body line. The 3rd step is taken straight back down the LOD in CBMP, and not with the usual L side lead. Because of this the 4th step will move down the LOD instead of diagonally to centre.

The Open Finish could be followed by any of the endings used after the Open Promenade and given on page 239.

## OPEN REVERSE TURN, LADY OUTSIDE

### Lady

In this Reverse Turn, the lady steps outside the man on the 3rd step and the normal ending is the Closed Finish. Alternatively an Open Finish may be used, in which the man steps outside the lady on the last step. This method is given in the description and diagram.

It is preceded by a step backward on the LF.

Commence backing diagonally to the centre. Finish backing almost diagonally to the wall.

1. RF back across the body, turning to the L.                    Q
2. LF to side and slightly forward, with the toe
   pointing to LOD, but body turning slightly less.              Q
3. RF forward down the LOD and outside partner.                  S
Now continue with the Open Finish as follows:
4. LF forward down the LOD, in line with man and
   turning to the L.                                             Q
5. RF to side and slightly back.                                 Q
6. LF back, partner outside, in a direction between
   wall and diag. to wall.                                       S

*Contrary Body Movement and Position.* CBM on 1 and 4. The 1st, 3rd, and 6th steps are placed in CBMP.

*Amount of Turn.* Just under three-quarters of a turn on the complete figure.

*Footwork.* 1. B H. 2. Whole foot. 3. H. 4. H. 5. IE of B H. 6. B.

*General Notes.* It will be noted that the 2nd step moves to side and slightly forward when the lady is stepping outside on the 3rd step.

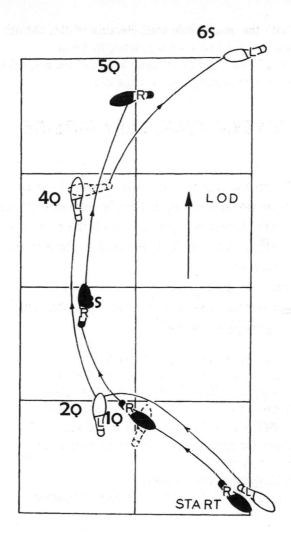

**Open Reverse Turn Lady Outside (Lady)**
**Shown with Open Finish**

# BASIC REVERSE TURN

## Man

The Basic Reverse Turn is easy to dance although beginners find it a little difficult to lead. The second half of this turn is a

Closed Finish. This could be replaced with an Open Finish. It is preceded by a Walk forward on the RF.

Commence facing diagonally to the centre. Finish facing diagonally to the wall.

| | |
|---|---|
| 1. LF forward across the body, turning to L. | Q |
| 2. RF to side and slightly back, across LOD. | Q |
| 3. Cross LF in front of RF. Backing the LOD. | S |
| 4. RF back, down LOD, turning body to L. | Q |
| 5. LF to side and slightly forward. | Q |
| 6. Close RF to LF, slightly back. | S |

*Contrary Body Movement and Position.* CBM on 1 and 4. CBMP on 1 only.
*Amount of Turn.* Three-quarters of a turn to L.
*Footwork.* 1. H. 2. B H. 3. Whole foot. 4. B H. 5. IE of foot. 6. Whole foot.
*General Notes.* The 2nd step should be placed with the toe turning inwards.
Follow with a LF Walk or Progressive Side Step.

## BASIC REVERSE TURN

### Lady

| | |
|---|---|
| 1. RF back across the body, turning to L Diag. to centre. | Q |
| 2. LF to side and slightly forward. | Q |
| 3. Close RF to LF, slightly back. Facing the LOD. | S |
| 4. LF forward, down LOD, turning body to L. | Q |
| 5. RF to side and slightly back. | Q |
| 6. Close LF to RF, slightly forward. | S |

*Contrary Body Movement and Position.* CBM on 1 and 4. CBMP on 1 only.
*Amount of Turn.* Three-quarters of a turn to L.
*Footwork.* 1. B H. 2. Whole foot. 3. Whole foot. 4. H. 5. IE of B H. 6. Whole foot.
*General Notes.* The 2nd step must be placed with the toe pointing down the LOD. There is no swivel as the 3rd step is closed. Keep the R hip well towards the partner as the 5th step is taken.

# PROGRESSIVE SIDE STEP REVERSE TURN

## Man

This figure consists of the Progressive Side Step danced with a strong turn to the left, a Walk on RF taken against the LOD, a Rock Back on LF, and the Closed Finish. (An Open Finish could be used.)

It is preceded by a Walk on the RF.

Commence facing diagonally to the centre. Finish facing diagonally to the wall.

1. LF forward across the body, turning to the L.                Q
2. RF to side and slightly back, across the LOD.                Q
3. LF forward across the body, almost against the LOD.          S
4. RF forward against the LOD, R shoulder leading.              S

Now continue with the LF Rock as follows:

5. Transfer weight back to LF, L side leading.                  Q
6. Rock forward on to RF, R shoulder leading.                   Q
7. LF back, lengthening the step slightly,
   with L side leading. Moving down the LOD.                    S
8. RF back, diag. to centre, turning to the L.                  Q
9. LF to side and slightly forward.                            Q
10. Close RF to LF, slightly back. Facing diag. to wall.        S

*Contrary Body Movement and Position.* CBM on 1, 3, and 8. These steps are also placed in CBMP.

*Amount of Turn.* Three-quarters of a turn to L on the complete figure.

*Footwork.* 1. H. 2. IE of foot. 3. H. 4. H. 5. IE of B H. 6. H. 7. IE of B H. 8. B H. 9. IE of foot. 10. Whole foot.

*General Notes.* When the 4th step is taken against the LOD the body will be backing diagonally to centre and will remain in that position until the Rock is completed.

After dancing the first 4 steps the following alternative endings may be used:

(1) Back Corté. LF back, slightly lengthening step, into the Back Corté. (SQQS) Finish facing diagonally to wall.

(2) Double Rock. Transfer weight back to LF and dance a LF Rock (QQS). Step back RF well under the body and down the LOD to dance a RF Rock (QQS). Follow with the Back Corté (SQQS).

## PROGRESSIVE SIDE STEP REVERSE TURN

### Lady

This is an attractive Reverse Turn, consisting of a Progressive Side Step danced with a strong turn to the Left, a Walk on LF, a Rock Forward on RF, and the Closed Finish.

It is preceded by a Walk backwards on the LF.

Commence backing diagonally to the centre. Finish backing diagonally to the wall.

|    |                                                                            |   |
|----|----------------------------------------------------------------------------|---|
| 1. | RF back, across the body, turning to the L.                                 | Q |
| 2. | LF to side and slightly foward, across the LOD.                             | Q |
| 3. | RF back, across the body. Almost against the LOD.                           | S |
| 4. | LF back against the LOD, L side leading.                                    | S |
| 5. | Transfer weight forward to RF, R side leading.                              | Q |
| 6. | Rock back on to LF, L side leading.                                         |   |
| 7. | RF forward, lengthening the step slightly, with R side leading, moving down the LOD. | S |
| 8. | LF forward, diag. to centre, turning to the L.                             | Q |
| 9. | RF to side and slightly back.                                              | Q |
| 10. | Close LF to RF slightly forward. Backing diag. to wall.                   | S |

*Contrary Body Movement and Position.* CBM on 1, 3, and 8. These steps are also placed in CBMP.

*Amount of Turn.* Three-quarters of a turn to L on the complete figure.

*Footwork.* 1. B H. 2. IE of foot. 3. B H. 4. IE of B H. 5. H. 6. IE of B H. 7. H. 8. H. 9. IE of B H. 10. Whole foot.

*General Notes.* Care should be taken to place the 2nd step to the side and slightly forward, with the L hip pressed firmly towards the man otherwise the character of the figure will be lost.

*Amalgamations.* Particulars of alternative endings to the first 4 steps of this figure are given in the notes on the man's steps.

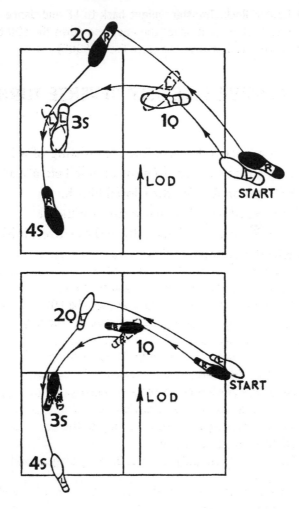

**Steps 1 to 4 of Progressive Side Step Reverse Turn**
**Top: Man Bottom: Lady**

# NATURAL TWIST TURN

## Man

This is a more advanced figure, but very attractive to dance. It commences in Promenade Position and is danced along the

LOD. It can be finished facing diagonally to wall, the LOD or diagonally to the centre. (See notes below.)

1. LF to side in PP along LOD.                                                S
2. RF forward and across in PP, turning to R.                               Q
3. LF to side, across LOD, backing diag. to centre.                        Q
4. Cross RF behind, and a few inches away from LF.                         S
   (Now backing the LOD.)
5. Turning on the ball of the RF and heel of the LF,
6. Twist just over a half turn to the R. Finish in the
   normal PP with the feet nearly together and the
   weight on the RF. Now facing diag. to wall.                             QQ
Continue along the LOD into a Closed Promenade with LF. (SQQS).

*Contrary Body Movement and Position.* The 2nd step is placed in CBMP, and CBM is also used.

*Amount of Turn.* Make a complete turn to the R on the whole figure. The amount of turn on the twist (steps 5 and 6) depends on the following figure. (See General Notes.)

*Footwork.* 1. H. 2. H. 3. B H. 4. B. 5, 6. Commence to twist on B of RF and H of LF. End on whole of RF and IE of B of LF.

*General Notes.* Keep the feet flat during the twist. It is better to finish the twist with the feet slightly apart and with the L knee veering inwards towards the R knee.

Alternative endings are:

(1) Make a half turn only on the actual twist and finish facing the LOD. Take the following Promenade diagonally to centre.

(2) Back Corté. Turn an additional quarter of a turn on the twist to square up to lady and back diag. to centre, and follow with a Back Corté. The first step of the Back Corté will move down the LOD and the second step diagonally to centre.

(3) LF Rock. Finish the twist backing diagonally to centre as in (2), and follow with a LF Back Rock and a Closed Finish (QQSQQS).

(4) At a corner. Turn only three-eighths on the twist and take the following Promenade along the new LOD.

(5) At a corner. Turn five-eighths to R on the twist to face lady and back diag. to centre of the new LOD. Follow with the Back Corté or Rock and Closed Finish.

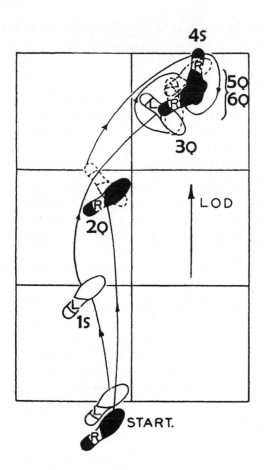

**Natural Twist Turn (Man)**

The first step of the Back Corté will move down the new LOD. End facing diag. to wall.

# NATURAL TWIST TURN

## Lady

This is a more advanced figure that is very attractive to dance. It is commenced in Promenade Position and danced along the LOD. It can be finished facing diagonally to the centre or LOD.

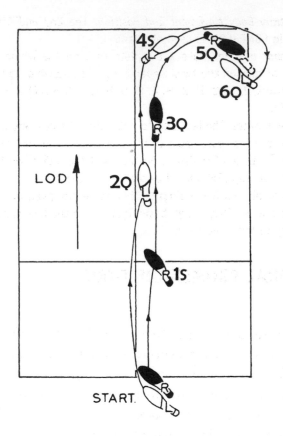

**Natural Twist Turn (Lady)**

1. RF to side in PP.                                                     S
2. LF forward and across in PP with foot pointing
   down the LOD.                                                        Q
3. RF forward between partner's feet.                                   Q
4. LF forward, preparing to step outside partner,
   L side leading.                                                      S
5. RF forward, outside partner, towards wall.                          Q
6. Turn on the ball of RF to face diag. to centre
   and place LF to side, small step, without weight in PP. Q
Continue along the LOD into a Closed Promenade with RF (SQQS).

*Contrary Body Movement and Position.* The 2nd and 5th steps are placed in CBMP. CBM is used on 3 and 5.

*Amount of Turn.* Make a complete turn on the whole figure. The amount of turn on the twist depends on the following figure.

*Footwork.* 1. H. 2. H. 3. H. 4. H. 5. H B. 6. B H (LF) and inside edge of B (RF).

*General Notes.* The lady should note, that she has very little turn to make on the first part, most of the turn being made by the man, who is on the outside of the turn. On the Twist the lady is on the outside, and her 5th step (RF) should be well round the man.

Several alternative endings to this figure are given in the notes on the man's steps. They are all basic figures, and the lady should have no difficulty in following them.

## NATURAL PROMENADE TURN

### Man

This is a simple Natural Turn taken from Promenade Position and should be used at a corner. It could be used when moving along the LOD, when it should be ended in a direction diagonally to the centre, to move to centre on the following Promenade (see General Notes).

Commence in Promenade Position, moving towards a corner. Finish in Promenade Position facing diag. to wall of the new LOD.

1. LF to side in PP along LOD.                                    S
2. RF forward in PP moving diag. to wall and
   turning to R.                                                  Q
3. LF to side and slightly back, body backing the LOD.   Q
4. Continue turning on the ball of LF for three-eighths
   of a turn to R, keeping the RF extended in
   front of LF and then step forward with RF diag.
   to wall of the new LOD.                                        S

Man then turns the lady to PP as he places the LF to the side of RF, without weight, ready to continue along the new LOD into a Closed Promenade (SQQS).

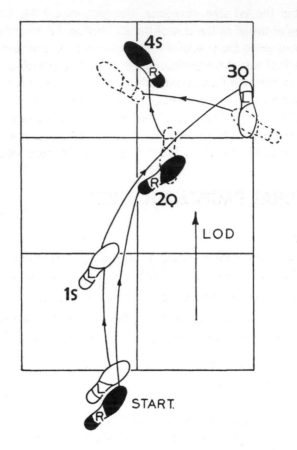

**Natural Promenade Turn (Man)**

*Contrary Body Movement and Position.* CBM on 2 and 4. Both steps are placed in CBMP.

*Amount of Turn.* Three-quarters of a turn to R is made on the complete figure.

*Footwork.* 1. H. 2. H. 3. B H B. 4. H, then IE of B of LF.

*General Notes.* If the Natural Promenade Turn is danced along the side of the room, make three-quarters of a turn to R. It is better to turn body slightly to R as LF is placed to the side of RF on 4, to allow the following Promenade to be taken diagonally to centre.

An attractive ending to the Natural Promenade Turn is to make the

4th step the 1st step of a Rock Turn (see page 231), omitting the placing of the LF to the side of the RF. This can be danced either at a corner or along the side of the room, when more turn could be made on the first part of the Rock Turn. The normal amount of turn would be made on the Rock Turn to end facing diag. to centre. A half turn could be made on 1, 2, 3 of the Rock Turn to achieve the normal alignment.

Note that the 2nd step of the Promenade Turn is forward, in a direction diagonally to wall. It is not taken across the body in a direction along the LOD as is the case with most Promenade figures.

## NATURAL PROMENADE TURN

### Lady

This is a simple Natural Turn taken from Promenade Position, and should be used at a corner. When used along the LOD, the following Promenade will move towards the centre.

Commence in Promenade Position, moving towards a corner. Finish in Promenade Position along the new LOD.

1. RF to side in PP along LOD.                                           S
2. LF forward and across in PP with foot pointing
   down the LOD.                                                         Q
3. RF forward, between partner's feet.                                   Q
4. Still turning to R, step to side and slightly back
   with the LF, with body backing diag. to wall of the
   new LOD.                                                              S

Lady will then continue to turn on the ball of LF until facing diag. to centre of new LOD in PP, and will place the RF to the side of LF, without weight, ready to continue along the new LOD into a Closed Promenade (SQQS).

*Contrary Body Movement and Position.* CBM is used on step 3. The 2nd step is placed in CBMP.

*Amount of Turn.* Three-quarters of a turn is made on the complete figure.

*Footwork.* 1. H. 2. H. 3. H. 4. B H, then IE of B of RF. (The L heel will lower after the turn is made.)

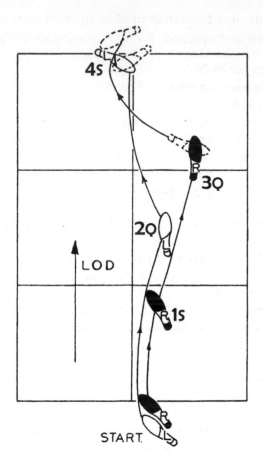

**Natural Promenade Turn (Lady)**

*General Notes.* Please refer to the man's General Notes. When the Rock Turn follows the 4th step of the Natural Promenade Turn (see man's notes) the placing of the RF to the side of LF will be omitted.

# PROMENADE LINK

## Man
This figure is used to change from a Promenade figure to a for-

ward figure. It is frequently used as an entry to the Four Step. Commence in Promenade Position moving along the LOD.

1. LF to side in PP.                                                S
2. RF forward and across in PP and commence to
   turn to R.                                                      Q
3. Turning to R to face wall, place the LF to the
   side of RF without weight. At the same time turn
   lady square.                                                    Q

Continue by stepping forward LF towards wall into a Four Step, Progressive Side Step or a Walk.

*Contrary Body Movement and Position.* CBM on 2, which is also placed in CBMP.

*Amount of Turn.* Turn an eighth to the R.

*Footwork.* 1. H. 2. H B (foot flat). 3. IE of B.

*General Notes.* Two other useful alignments are:

(1) Commence along LOD and make no turn. Lady will then make a quarter turn to L to get square to man. Follow with any of the endings given above, but commencing diagonally to wall. The Brush Tap is a good follow.

(2) Reverse Promenade Link. Commence facing the LOD and take the first 2 steps in a direction diagonally to centre. Man will then make an eighth of a turn to the Left, and lady will turn three-eighths to the L. Finish facing diagonally to centre and follow immediately with any Reverse figure. When this alignment is used the RF will point diagonally to centre on the 2nd step. The body only will turn on the 3rd step.

## PROMENADE LINK

### Lady

Commence in Promenade Position moving along the LOD.

1. RF to side in PP.                                               S
2. LF forward and across in PP and commence
   to turn to L.                                                   Q
3. Turning to L to back the wall, place the RF to
   the side of LF without weight. Now square to man.   Q

Continue by stepping back on RF into a Four Step, a
Progressive Side Step or a Progressive Link.

*Contrary Body Movement and Position.* CBM on 2, which is also
placed in CBMP.
*Amount of Turn.* Turn an eighth to the L.
*Footwork.* 1. H. 2. H B (foot flat). 3. IE of B.
*General Notes.* Other alignments are given in the man's notes. When
alignment (2) is used, the RF will point towards centre on 1 and 2.
Three-eighths of a turn to the L will be made between 2 and 3 to end
backing diag. to centre.

## FOUR STEP

### Man

This figure is very popular and is often danced after the
Promenade Link.

Commence facing the wall, with weight on RF.

1. LF forward, slightly across the body.                      Q
2. RF to side and slightly back. Now facing diag. to wall.  Q
3. LF back, partner outside and moving back diag. to
   centre against the LOD.                                    Q
4. Close RF to LF, slightly back, and at the same time
   turn the lady to PP.                                       Q

Continue by stepping to side with LF, along the LOD into a
Promenade figure.

*Contrary Body Movement and Position.* CBM on 1. The 1st and 3rd
steps are placed in CBMP.
*Amount of Turn.* In the alignment above an eighth of a turn to L is
used. Up to a quarter or no turn may be used.
*Footwork.* 1. H. 2. B H. 3. B H. 4. B H.
*General Notes.* Although the 2nd step is placed on the ball of the
foot the RF should be almost flat. Beginners may find a tendency to
jump or rise between steps 1 and 2.
A very good amalgamation is: dance the Progressive Link, the

Promenade Link, then the Four Step. Follow the Four Step with the Fallaway Promenade. The Four Step can also follow any Closed Finish, Closed Promenade, Open Promenade or Open Finish.

# FOUR STEP

## Lady

This figure is often danced after the Promenade Link.

Commence backing towards wall, with the weight on LF.

1. RF back, slightly across the body.                         Q
2. LF to side and slightly forward, with the foot
   pointing diag. to centre against the LOD.                  Q
3. RF forward, outside partner.                               Q
4. Turn to R on ball of RF to end in PP, facing diag.
   to centre, then close LF to RF, slightly back.             Q

Continue by stepping to side with RF along the LOD into any Promenade figure.

*Contrary Body Movement and Position*. CBM on 1 and 3. CBMP is also used on these steps.

*Amount of Turn*. Make an eighth turn to L between 1 and 2 and a quarter turn to R between 3 and 4. Up to a quarter turn to L (or no turn) may be used between 1 and 2.

*Footwork*. 1. B H. 2. Whole foot. 3. H B (Foot flat). 4. B H.

*General Notes*. Although the LF is pointing diagonally to centre against the LOD on 2, the body should be facing centre. Any attempt to turn the body too much to the L will result in loss of contact and a bad body line on the 3rd step.

# FALLAWAY PROMENADE

## Man

The Fallaway Promenade is a most attractive and not very difficult Standard Variation. It should be noted that both the man and lady remain in Promenade Position throughout. The term "Fallaway" is used when moving back in Promenade Position.

Commence in Promenade Position, along the LOD.

| | |
|---|---|
| 1. LF to side in PP. | S |
| 2. RF forward and across in PP, turning slightly to R. | Q |
| 3. LF to side in PP, now backing almost diag. centre. | Q |
| 4. RF back, towards centre in Fallaway. R side leading and body backing diag. to centre. | S |
| 5. LF back, towards centre in Fallaway and with LF pointing towards the wall. | Q |
| 6. Close RF to LF, slightly back in PP and body facing the wall. | Q |

With LF continue into a Promenade figure, moving diag. to wall.

*Contrary Body Movement and Position.* CBM on 2. The 2nd and 5th steps are placed in CBMP.

*Amount of Turn.* Make a quarter to R between 1 and 4 and an eighth to L between 4 and 5, body completing the turn on 6.

*Footwork.* 1. H. 2. H. 3. B H. 4. IWE of B H. 5. B H. 6. B H.

*General Notes.* Care must be taken to keep contact with lady on the 4th step by taking this in an "open" position, and on the 5th step by placing the LF back well under the body in CBMP. It will be noted that, although the body is backing diagonally to centre on 4, the 5th step is placed with the LF pointing to the wall. Thus, when the RF closes on 6, the body will automatically turn to face the wall, which is the correct position to take the following Promenade diagonally to wall. The Natural Promenade Turn is a good figure to follow the Fallaway Promenade.

## FALLAWAY PROMENADE

### Lady

Commence in Promenade Position, moving along the LOD. (The term "Fallaway" is used when moving back in Promenade Position.)

| | |
|---|---|
| 1. RF to side in PP. | S |
| 2. LF forward and across in PP, pointing down the LOD and turning slightly to R. | Q |

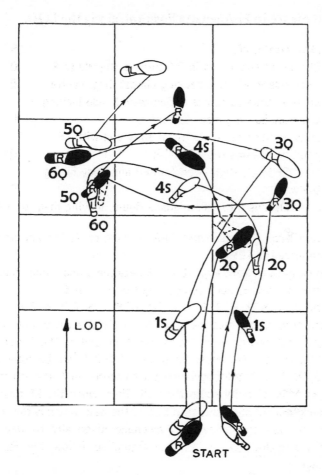

**Fallaway Promenade (Man & Lady)**

3. RF forward in PP, commencing to move down the but end facing almost diag. to wall.      LOD Q

4. Still turning to the R step back LF, towards centre in Fallaway, L side leading. Body backing diag. to centre against the LOD.      S

5. RF back, towards centre in Fallaway.      Q

6. Turning slightly to the L, close LF to RF, slightly back. End in PP with body facing the LOD.      Q

With RF continue into a Promenade figure, moving diag. to wall.

*Contrary Body Movement and Position.* CBM is used on 3 and 5. Steps 2, 3, and 5 are placed in CBMP.

*Amount of Turn.* A quarter to R, between 1 and 4. An eighth to L between 5 and 6.

*Footwork.* 1. H. 2. H. 3. H. 4. IE of B H. 5. B H. 6. Whole foot.

*General Notes.* The turn on step 5 is made on the ball of RF. The heel will lower after the turn is made. Note that the 3rd step commences to move in a direction down the LOD but will end with the RF and the body facing almost diagonally to wall. This will result in the step ending in CBMP.

## OUTSIDE SWIVEL AND BRUSH TAP
### (From an Open Promenade or Open Finish)

### Man

The Outside Swivel and the Brush Tap are two separate figures and both have a variety of uses. They are, however, often used as a complete variation after an Open Promenade, when they are joined together by steps 2 and 3 of a Promenade Link. This amalgamation is described below and notes on further uses of the figures are given under General Notes. The Reverse Outside Swivel, a more difficult variation, is described on page 271.

Dance an Open Promenade along the LOD. End with the RF forward, outside partner, in a direction between the wall and diagonally to wall. Then:

### Outside Swivel

1. Turning body to R, take weight back to LF with toe turned in and partner outside, then cross RF in front of LF without weight. End in PP facing wall.    S

Now continue with 2 and 3 of the Reverse Promenade Link as follows:

2. Turning body to R, move the RF forward and across

the LF in PP in a direction diag. to wall, RF pointing
diag. to wall. Q
3. Turning body to face diag. to wall, place the LF to
the side of RF without weight, small step. At the
same time turn the lady square. Q

## Brush Tap

1. LF forward, diag. to wall, in line with partner. Q
2. Turning to L step to side RF, now facing LOD. Q
3. Brush LF swiftly to RF without weight. &
4. Place the LF to the side, a small step, without weight. S

The next step is a forward step with LF. Note that steps 2 and 3
are danced to the time of one Q.

*Contrary Body Movement and Position.* Outside Swivel: CBM on 1.
Steps 1 and 2 are placed in CBMP. Brush Tap: CBM on 1, which is also
placed in CBMP.

*Amount of Turn.* Outside Swivel: there is a slight turn to R on step
1, and one eighth turn to L on step 2, the body completing the turn
on step 3. Brush Tap: one-eighth turn to L between steps 1 and 2.

Footwork. Outside Swivel: 1. B H, with pressure on B of RF. 2. H. 3.
IE of B. Brush Tap: 1. H. 2. B H. 3. Foot slightly off the floor. 4. IE of B.

*General Notes.* When leading the Outside Swivel it is advisable to
allow the R side of the body to move back as the lady turns. This will
avoid a cramped position on the Swivel. Some advanced dancers prefer
to leave the RF forward and not cross it in front as the lady turns. Make
sure that the RF is pointing diag. to wall on step 2. There must be no
swivel on this foot as the lady turns square.

An advanced method of dancing the Outside Swivel is for the man
to turn to the L. When the weight is taken back to the LF on step 1,
the LF will move under the body and step back in a direction against
the LOD and the RF, instead of crossing in front, will move leftwards
across the front of LF. Step 2 will then move in a direction diag. to
centre and at the end of the Link (step 3) man will be facing diag. to
centre. Man will continue by stepping forward LF into a Reverse figure.

When turning the Outside Swivel to the L after an Open Promenade
or Open Finish it is advisable to end these two figures diag. to wall.

## OUTSIDE SWIVEL AND BRUSH TAP
### (From an Open Promenade or Open Finish)

### Lady

Although the Outside Swivel and the Brush Tap can be used as two separate figures they are described below as a complete variation, joined together by steps 2 and 3 of the Promenade Link.

Dance an Open Promenade along the LOD. End with the LF back, in a direction between the wall and diagonally to wall. Then:

### Outside Swivel

1. Take the weight forward to RF outside partner and swivel to R on RF to face the LOD, allowing the LF to close to RF, slightly back, without weight. End in PP.                                                    S

Now continue with 2 and 3 of the Reverse Promenade Link as follows:

2. LF forward in PP, moving in a direction diag. to wall.   Q
3. Turning to L to get square to man, place the RF to the side of LF without weight, small step. Now backing diag. to wall.                                           Q

### Brush Tap

1. RF back, diag. to wall.                                          Q
2. Turning to L, step to side LF. Backing LOD.            Q
3. Brush RF swiftly to LF without weight.                     &
4. Place the RF to side, a small step, without weight.    S

The next step is a backward step with RF. Note that steps 2 and 3 are danced to the time of one Q.

*Contrary Body Movement and Position.* Outside Swivel: CBM on 1 and 2 which are also placed in CBMP.

*Amount of Turn.* Outside Swivel. Turn just over a quarter turn to R on step 1 and three-eighths of a turn to L between 2 and 3. Brush Tap:

Slight turn to L between steps 1 and 2.

Footwork. Outside Swivel: 1. H B (Foot flat) and IE of B of LF. 2. H B (Foot flat). 3. IE of B. Brush Tap: 1. B H. 2. Whole foot. 3. Foot slightly off the floor. 4. IE of B.

*General Notes.* When dancing the Outside Swivel some advanced dancers lift the LF from the floor as the swivel is made on RF. When this "flick" of the foot is used, the knees should be kept in contact. The lady may turn her head to the R at the end of the Swivel and then back to normal position as the Link is danced. When the "flick" of the LF is used it is smarter to keep the head turned well to the L throughout. Remember to keep in contact with partner on the swivel and to keep the hips well forward.

# REVERSE OUTSIDE SWIVEL

## Man

This is a far more advanced method of dancing the Outside Swivel but is most effective and enjoyable to dance. It consists of 1, 2 of an Open Reverse Turn, the Outside Swivel turning to L, and 2 and 3 of the Reverse Promenade Link.

Commence facing diagonally to centre after a Walk on RF or after a Reverse Promenade Link ended diagonally to centre.

1. LF forward, across the body, turning to L.                                  Q
2. RF to side, backing diag. to wall.                                         Q
3. Turning to L with a sharp swivel on the RF, step back
   LF, diag. to centre, with the partner outside. As the
   weight moves on to LF, the RF will be kept forward
   and will move leftwards across the front of LF. End
   in PP with body facing diag. to wall against the LOD.
   Keep weight on LF.                                                         S
4. RF forward in PP, with RF pointing and moving
   towards wall.                                                              Q
5. Turn lady square and place LF to side of RF
   without weight. Turn the body to L to face wall.          Q
With LF, continue by stepping forward into a Four Step.

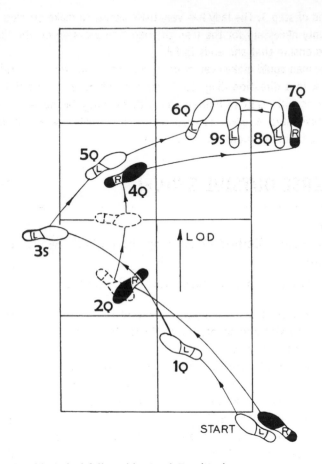

**Reverse Outside Swivel followed by Brush Tap (Man)**

*Contrary Body Movement and Position.* CBM is used on 1. Steps 1, 3 and 4 are placed in CBMP.

*Amount of Turn.* Make a half turn to L between 1 and 3 and one-eighth turn to L on steps 4, 5.

*Footwork.* 1. H. 2. B H. 3. B H with pressure on B of RF. 4. H. 5. IE of B.

*General Notes.* There must be a sharp and obvious swivel on the ball of RF as the LF swings back, well under the body for the Swivel. Note that the RF remains forward and does not cross tightly in front of LF at the end of step 3. The lady has very little swivel to make on step 3 and it is only necessary for the man to keep firm pressure on the lady's L side to ensure that she ends in PP.

The man could make even more turn to the L on step 3 and take the LF back in a direction diag. to centre but with the L Toe pointing to wall. This will result in him ending with his body facing wall. He will then take step 4 diag. to wall and follow with the Brush Tap as described. This is shown in the diagram.

# REVERSE OUTSIDE SWIVEL

## Lady

This effective method of dancing the Outside Swivel is more difficult.

Commence backing diagonally to the centre.

1. RF back, across the body, turning to L.                        Q
2. LF to side and slightly forward with the L toe pointing to LOD.                                       Q
3. RF forward, diag. to centre, outside partner, and swivel to R on ball of RF to face diag. to wall, allowing the LF to close to RF, slightly back, without weight. End in PP.                             S
4. LF forward, towards the wall in PP, but with the L toe pointing diag. to wall.                             Q
5. Turning to L to get square to man place the RF to the side of LF without weight. Small step. Now backing wall.                                          Q

With RF continue by stepping back into a Four Step.

*Contrary Body Movement and Position.* Steps 1, 3, and 4 are placed in CBMP and CBM is used on these steps.

*Amount of Turn.* Make three-eighths of a turn to L between 1 and 2 and a slight turn to L as step 3 is taken. Make a quarter turn to R on 3 to end in PP. Make three-eights of a turn to L between 4 and 5.

*Footwork.* 1. B H. 2. Whole foot. 3. H B (foot flat) and IE of B of LF. 4. H B (Foot flat). 5. IE of B.

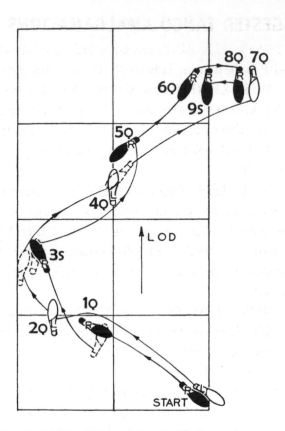

**Reverse Outside Swivel followed by Brush Tap (Lady)**

*General Notes.* It will be noted that the LF is pointing down the LOD on Step 2 and the lady will then step across this alignment to take the 3rd step diag. to centre. Although there is a quarter turn to R to the swivel (step 3) to end in PP it is better to underturn than overturn, as too much turn will make the Promenade Position too open and result in an ugly hip line. When the man overturns on his 3rd step to face the wall, the swivel of the lady will be negligible. See diagram.

## SUGGESTED TANGO AMALGAMATIONS

1. 2 Walks, LF, RF–Progressive Side Step–Rock Turn–LF Walk–RF Walk turning lady to PP–Closed Promenade.

2. 2 Walks, LF, RF–Progressive Side Step, turning slightly to L–RF Walk, diagonally to centre–Open Reverse Turn, lady outside, with Open Finish–LF Rock outside partner turning slightly to R–Closed Finish turning slightly to L to face diagonally to wall.

3. 2 Walks, LF, R–Progressive Side Step, turning slightly to L–RF Walk, diagonally to centre–first 4 steps of Progressive Side Step Reverse Turn ended with LF Rock, then RF Rock and Back Corté–2 Walks, LF, RF–Progressive Link, Natural Promenade Turn (at a corner or on side of room)–Closed Promenade.

4. 2 Walks, LF, RF–Progressive Side Step, turning slightly to L–RF Walk, diagonally to centre–Progressive Side Step Reverse Turn–Progressive Link–Natural Twist Turn–Open Promenade –Outside Swivel–Brush Tap.

5. Progressive Link–Promenade Link–Four Step–Fallaway Promenade – Natural Promenade Turn into Rock Turn.

6. Open Promenade ended diagonally to wall–Outside Swivel turning to L to end facing diagonally to centre–Open Reverse Turn, Lady in Line.

7. LF Walk–Rock Turn–Four Step, turning one eighth to L to face the LOD, ready to move diagonally to centre–Reverse Promenade Link to end facing diagonally to centre–Reverse Outside Swivel, ended facing diagonally to wall–Brush Tap.

# SECTION V

## RHYTHM DANCING (SOCIAL FOXTROT AND QUICKSTEP)

Rhythm Dancing is the name given to the type of dancing that is used in crowded ballrooms. It has, of course, existed for many years, and was frequently referred to as "Crush Dancing". There is nothing new in the figures used in this type of dancing, and they were, in the first place, only standardized as a guide to candidates in Amateur Tests.

It will be noted that many of the figures resemble those described in the Quickstep section of this book, but no attempt should be made to adhere to the strict rules of alignment that are so necessary in this dance. Very often the figures have to be danced with the absolute minimum of movement and with practically no progression; consequently, it is advisable to practise such figures as the Natural Pivot Turn and Chassé Reverse Turn in the form of a square, making no progress along the room at all.

The manner of expressing *rhythm* in these figures is most important since the execution of a set of basic figures with a complete absence of movement and body swing will tend to be very boring. The experienced dancer, with an inborn sense of rhythm, will interpret them with various types of rhythm, but easily the most popular, and possibly the easiest for the beginner to master, is the Charleston, and an appreciation of this subtle rhythm is essential if the dancer is to obtain the full enjoyment from Rhythm Dancing. The Charleston rhythm can be learned quite quickly if the following exercise is practised:

Commence with the feet together, and with the knees slightly relaxed.

|  | | Beats |
|---|---|---|
| 1. | Take a small step to the side with the LF – knees straight. | 1 |
| 2. | Relax knees slightly. | 2 |
| 3. | Close RF to LF without weight – knees straight. | 3 |
| 4. | Relax knees slightly. | 4 |
| 5. | Take a small step to the side with the RF – knees straight. | 1 |
| 6. | Relax knees slightly. | 2 |
| 7. | Close LF to RF without weight. | 3 |
| 8. | Relax knees slightly. | 4 |

Then step to side with the LF to repeat.

In practising this movement the dancer should give a slightly longer time value to the 1st and 3rd beats in each bar. Thus the step to the side and the closing will be held rather firmly, and the subsequent relaxing of the knees taken rather sharply. Unless this is done there will be a strong tendency to bend at once as the step to the side is made.

When the rhythm of the Charleston has been mastered, this action should be softened considerably, as it is not good form to use an obvious or staccato Charleston action in Rhythm Dancing. When using the Charleston as a progressive figure, the RF should be taken forward and the LF to the side alternately.

*Rise and Fall.* Rises are not used in Rhythm Dancing, the rhythmic relaxing and straightening of the knees being used instead.

The standardized figures in both Quick and Slow Rhythm Dancing are given, together with a few notes on their uses.

## QUICK TEMPO

*Time.* 4/4 Four beats in a bar. The 1st and 3rd beats are accented.

*Tempo.* Music should be played at about 50 bars a minute although the following figures can be danced to any 4/4 music that is faster than 40 bars a minute.

### Standardized Figures

1. Walk.
2. Quarter Turns to Right and Left.
3. Chassé Reverse Turn.
4. Natural Pivot Turn.
5. Reverse Pivot Turn.
6. Back Corté.
7. Change of Direction.
8. Side Step.

The man's steps are described, lady always dancing the normal opposite.

### 1. The Walk

The steps must be short, and a lilting movement should be used. The action of the Charleston may be introduced in the Walk. Forward steps may be taken as in the Quickstep Walk, with the ball of the foot and then the heel skimming the floor, or the foot may be kept practically flat throughout. In the backward Walk, the ball of the foot meets the floor first, the heel lowering as the moving foot passes. Each Walk takes 2 beats of music.

### 2. Quarter Turns to Right and Left

The design of the Quarter Turns is the same as in the Quickstep. Chassé movements are very small, and it is immaterial whether the feet are closed right together, or an Open Chassé, in which the closing foot moves only halfway towards the side step, is used. Steps 2 and 3 of the Quarter Turn to L are danced as a very small chassé.

## 3. Chassé Reverse Turn

The description of this figure is the same as in the Quickstep. It can be taken following the Quarter Turn to L or the Change of Direction. End with 4, 5, 6 of the Quarter Turn to L. Very little turn should be made over these 6 steps and the side steps should be short. Repeat the figure two or three times to make a complete turn.

## 4. Natural Pivot Turn

The description of this figure is the same as in the Quickstep. Keep all steps very short, and repeat two or three times to make a complete turn. The 4th step should tend to be more sideways than back, and the turn continued on the ball of the LF. The lady's 4th step will be forward, between the man's feet.

## 5. Reverse Pivot Turn

This figure is best taken after the 3rd step of the Quarter Turn to L. It can be used once at a corner to change the dancer's direction to the new LOD, or it can be danced three or four times to make a complete turn in one position.

| | | |
|---|---|---|
| 1. | LF. forward, pivoting very slightly to the L and keeping the RF behind in CBMP. | S |
| 2. | Balance back on to the RF, still turning slightly. | S |
| 3, 4. | Very small step to side LF, then close RF to LF. LF forward, to repeat. | QQ |

*Note.* The lady's steps are the normal opposite.

## 6. Back Corté

In this figure the man progresses backwards diagonally to centre. It can be taken after the first four steps of the Quarter Turn to R.

| | |
|---|---|
| 1. RF back, turning body very slightly to L. | S |
| 2, 3. LF to side, very small step, then close RF to LF, still turning body very slightly to L. | QQ |
| 4. LF back, turning body slightly to R. | S |

*Note.* The lady does a small Chassé on the 2nd and 3rd steps.

## 7. Change of Direction

The description of this figure is the same as in the Foxtrot, counting SSSS. It is best taken after the Quarter Turn to L, and used as a lead into the Chassé Reverse Turn. In Rhythm Dancing the step "diagonally forward" (lady diagonally back) on the RF tends to be placed more sideways, and less turn is made. The last step becomes the first of the Chassé Reverse Turn.

## 8. Side Step

Perhaps the most useful figure to use in a crowded room. It is taken sideways along the LOD, the man facing towards the wall and the lady facing centre.

| | |
|---|---|
| 1. Short step to side with LF. | Q |
| 2. Close RF half-way towards LF. | Q |
| 3. LF to side. | S |
| 4. Close RF to LF. | S |

This figure can be repeated several times. It can be ended by stepping forward with the LF into the Walk, or by the man turning slightly to the R as the LF is taken to the side on the 3rd step, and then stepping back with the RF, diagonally to the centre, into the Back Corté, or the Quarter Turn to L.

## SLOW TEMPO

*Time.* 4/4. Four beats to a bar. The 1st and 3rd beats are accented.

*Tempo.* Music should be played at about 30 bars a minute although the following figures can be danced to any 4/4 music that is slower than 40 bars a minute.

### Standardized Figures

1. Walk.
2. Side Chassé on the RF.
3. Quarter Turns to Right and Left.
4. Natural Pivot Turn.
5. Chassé Reverse Turn.
6. Back Corté.
7. Side Step.

It will be observed that the standardized figures for the slow tempo are similar to those in the quick tempo, with the exception of the Side Chassé on the RF, and the Side Step.

The whole dance should appear "lazy", and the relaxing of the knees should be much softer than in the quick tempo.

### The Side Step

In Slow Rhythm Dancing a different type of Side Step is used and this is described below. It is danced moving sideways along the LOD with the man facing wall and the lady facing centre.

| | |
|---|---|
| 1. Small step to side LF, along the LOD. | Q |
| 2. Close RF half-way towards LF. | Q |
| 3. Small step to side LF, along the LOD, and let RF move half-way towards it without weight. | S |
| 4. Move RF sideways against the LOD (to its position on step 2), and let LF close half-way towards it without weight. | S |

Repeat two or three times. There are several other ways of dancing this figure.

(1) When more rhythmic or staccato music is played, a better interpretation of the music will be achieved by dancing the first 3 steps counting QQQ, then close RF to LF without weight, counting Q. Move the RF sideways against the LOD counting Q, and then count another Q as LF closes to RF without weight.

(2) On step 4, instead of moving RF sideways against the LOD step forward and across with RF, along the LOD in Promenade Position, having turned slightly to L. The lady will step forward and across with LF along the LOD in Promenade Position on the 4th step. This variation of the Side Step is often referred to as "Conversation Piece". It can be repeated, and ended by the man turning the lady slightly to her L to bring her square as he dances the Chassé (steps 1, 2) and then stepping forward LF into a Walk. Alternatively the man could turn slightly to R on steps 1, 2, 3 to get square to lady and continue with the Quarter Turn to L.

The additional figure is given below.

### Side Chassé on the RF

This is taken after a step forward on the LF, counted "S".

| | |
|---|---|
| 1. RF to side, short step. | Q |
| 2. Close LF, to RF. | Q |
| 3. RF to side, and brush LF up to it. | S |
| LF forward to repeat. | |

In both slow and quick tempo, such figures as the Outside Spin, Natural Spin Turn, Cross Chassé, etc., can be introduced, but they should be attempted only by experienced dancers as it requires a certain amount of skill to use them without inconvenience to other dancers.

# SECTION VI

# THE VIENNESE WALTZ

The Viennese Waltz is one of the most attractive of the ball-room dances and has been a popular dance on the Continent for many years.

The Viennese Waltz must be used in all ballroom championships. Only seven figures are accepted: the Reverse and Natural Turns, the Forward and Backward Changes, the Reverse and Natural Fleckerls and the Check from Reverse to Natural Fleckerl. The description of these figures is given in chart form.

When danced in competitions and tests this Continental version of the dance must be used and other variations are not permitted.

The music is inspiring and the dance is beautiful to watch.

## GENERAL NOTES

*Time.* 3/4. Three beats in a bar. The 1st beat is accented.

*Tempo.* Music should be played at 60 bars a minute. (A little latitude is allowed for Amateur Tests between 50 and 60 bars per minute is permissable.)

*Figures.* Reverse Turn, Natural Turn, Forward and Backward Change Steps, Reverse Fleckerl, Natural Fleckerl, Check from Reverse Fleckerl to Natural Fleckerl.

The following special notes should be studied as they apply to practically all figures throughout the dance.

*Rise and Fall.* The rise in Reverse and Natural Turns and the Change Steps is a little more abrupt than in the slow Waltz and is quite shallow. The quicker music will make a full relaxation of the knee on the 1st step impracticable, and this alone will result in the rise being taken earlier. The normal rise is "Rise at the end of 1, up on 2 and 3, lower at the end of 3."

*Footwork.* All leading forward steps are taken with a heel lead, lowering immediately to the flat foot.

*Sway.* When the leading step of a turn is taken with the RF, sway will be used to the Right on the following two steps. It should be noted, however, that the Sway will commence early – as the 1st step is taken, and this sway will be felt far more from the waist upwards than from any inclination of the body from the feet upwards. A similar sway to the Left will be used after a leading step with the LF.

*Basic Amalgamation.* The basis of the dance is a series of Reverse Turns followed by a Change Step, then a series of Natural Turns followed by a Change Step. Advanced dancers will always time the changes so that they take place at the end of an eight bar phrase of the music, thus giving the dance a far better rhythmic interpretation.

## REVERSE TURN

### Man

Commence facing diagonally to wall.

| | | | |
|---|---|---|---|
| 1. LF forward | Facing LOD | 1/8 to L between preceding step and 1 | Rise E/O 1 |
| 2. RF to side and slightly back | Backing wall | 1/4 L between 1 and 2 | Up on 2 |

| 3 Cross LF in front of RF | Backing DW | $1/8$ L between 2 and 3 | Up on 3, lower E/O 3 |
|---|---|---|---|
| 4. RF back and slightly to side | Backing LOD | $1/8$ L between 3 and 4 | Rise E/O 4 NFR |
| 5. LF to side | Pointing DW | $3/8$ L between 4 and 5, body turns less | Body rise between 5 and 6 |
| 6. Close RF to LF | Facing DW | Body completes turn | Lower E/O 6 |

*Footwork.* 1. H T. 2. T. 3. T H. 4. T H. 5. T. 6. Flat.

*Body Sway.* SLL SRR. Note: The man may hold the preceding sway slightly at the beginning of steps 1 and 4.

*Contrary Body Movement.* CBM on 1 and 4.

*Precedes.* RF Change Step. Reverse Turn. Reverse Fleckerl. 1–3 Reverse Fleckerl then 4–6 of Reverse Turn. 1–3 of Natural Turn followed by a LF Backward Change Step, then 4–6 of Reverse Turn.

*Follows.* LF Forward Change Step. Reverse Turn. Reverse Fleckerl. Contra Check. 1–3 Reverse Turn followed by a RF Backward Change Step then 4–6 of Natural Turn.

Note that although the Reverse Turn is commenced facing diagonally to wall, the first step will move down LOD.

## Lady

Commence backing diagonally to wall.

| 1. RF back and slightly to side | Backing LOD | $1/8$ to L between preceding step and 1 | Rise E/O 1, NFR |
|---|---|---|---|
| 2. LF to side | Pointing DW | $3/8$ L between 1 and 2, body turns less | Body rise between 2 and 3 |
| 3. Close RF to LF | Facing DW | Body completes turn | Lower E/O 3 |
| 4. LF forward | Facing LOD | $1/8$ L between 3 and 4 | Rise E/O 4 |
| 5. RF to side | Backing wall | $1/4$ L between 4 and 5 | Up on 5 |
| 6. Cross LF in front of RF | Backing DW | $1/8$ L between 5 and 6 | Up on 6, lower E/O 6 |

*Footwork.* 1. T H. 2. T. 3. Flat. 4. H T. 5. T. 6. T H.

*Body Sway.* SRR SLL. The lady may hold the preceding sway slightly at the beginning of steps 1 and 4.

*Contrary Body Movement.* CBM on 1 and 4.

For Precedes and Follows see Man's Steps.

# NATURAL TURN

## Man

Commence facing diagonally to centre.

| 1. RF forward | Facing LOD | 1/8 to R between preceding step and 1 | Rise E/O 1 |
|---|---|---|---|
| 2. LF to side | Backing centre | 1/4 R between 1 and 2 | Up on 2 |
| 3. Close RF to LF | Backing DC | 1/8 R between 2 and 3 | Up on 3, lower E/O 3 |
| 4. LF back and slightly to side | Backing LOD | 1/8 R between 3 and 4 | Rise E/O 4, NFR |
| 5. RF to side | Pointing DC | 3/8 R between 4 and 5, body turns less | Body rise between 5 and 6 |
| 6. Close LF to RF | Facing DC | Body completes turn | Lower E/O 6 |

*Footwork.* 1. H T. 2. T. 3. T H. 4. T H. 5. T. 6. Foot flat.

*Body Sway.* SRR SLL. The man may hold the preceding sway slightly at the beginning of steps 1 and 4. Note that although the Natural Turn is commenced facing diagonally to centre, the first step will move down LOD.

*Contrary Body Movement.* CBM on 1 and 4. Note: The man may hold the preceding sway slightly at the beginning of steps 1 and 4.

*Precedes.* LF Change Step. Natural Turn. Natural Fleckerl. 1–3 Natural Fleckerl then 4–6 of Natural Turn. Contra Check. 1–3 of Reverse Turn followed by Backward Change Step then 4–6 of Natural Turn.

*Follows.* RF Change Step. Natural Turn. Natural Fleckerl. 1–3 Natural Turn followed by Backward Change Step then 4–6 of Reverse Turn.

## Lady

Commence backing diagonally to centre.

| | | | |
|---|---|---|---|
| 1. LF back and slightly to side | Backing LOD | $1/8$ to R between preceding step and 1 | Rise E/O 1, NFR |
| 2. RF to side | Pointing DC | $3/8$ R between 1 and 2, body turns less | Body rise between 2 and 3 |
| 3. Close LF to RF | Facing DC | Body completes turn | Lower E/O 3 |
| 4. RF forward | Facing LOD | $1/8$ R between 3 and 4 | Rise E/O 4 |
| 5. LF to side | Backing centre | $1/4$ R between 4 and 5 | Up on 5 |
| 6. Close RF to LF | Backing DC | $1/8$ R between 5 and 6 | Up on 6, lower E/O 6 |

*Footwork.* 1. T H. 2. T. 3. Flat. 4. H T. 5. T. 6. T H.

*Body Sway.* SLL SRR. The lady may hold the preceding sway slightly at the beginning of steps 1 and 4.

*Contrary Body Movement.* CBM on 1 and 4.

For Precedes and Follows see Man's steps.

# RF FORWARD CHANGE STEP – Natural to Reverse

## Man or Lady

Commence facing diagonally to centre.

| | | | |
|---|---|---|---|
| 1. RF forward | Facing LOD | $1/8$ to R between preceding step and 1 | Rise E/O 1 |
| 2. LF diagonally forward | Facing DW | $1/8$ R between 1 and 2 | Up on 2 |
| 3. Close RF to LF | Facing DW | | Up on 3, lower E/O 3 |

*Footwork.* 1. H T. 2. T. 3. T H.
*Body Sway.* SRR.
*Contrary Body Movement.* CBM on 1.
*Precede.* Natural Turn.
*Follow.* Reverse Turn.

## LF FORWARD CHANGE STEP – Reverse to Natural

### Man or Lady

Commence facing diagonally to wall.

| 1. LF fwd | Facing LOD | $1/8$ to L between preceding step and 1 | Rise E/O 1 |
| 2. RF diagonally fwd | Facing DC | $1/8$ L between 1 and 2 | Up on 2 |
| 3. Close LF to RF | Facing DC | | Up on 3, lower E/O 3 |

*Footwork.* 1. H T. 2. T. 3. T H.
*Body Sway.* SLL.
*Contrary Body Movement.* CBM on 1
*Precede.* Reverse Turn.
*Follow.* Natural Turn.

## LF BACKWARD CHANGE STEP – Natural to Reverse

### Man or Lady

Commence backing diagonally to centre.

| 1. LF back | Backing LOD | $1/8$ to R between preceding step and 1 | Rise E/O 1. NFR |
| 2. RF diagonally back | Backing DW | $1/8$ R between 1 and 2 | Up on 2 |
| 3. Close LF to RF | Backing DW | | Up on 3, lower E/O 3 |

*Footwork.* 1. T H. 2. T. 3. T H.
*Body Sway.* SLL.
*Contrary Body Movement.* CBM on step 1.
*Precede.* Natural Turn.
*Follow.* Reverse Turn.

# RF BACKWARD CHANGE STEP – Reverse to Natural

## Man or Lady

Commence backing diagonally to wall.

| 1. RF back | Backing LOD | $1/8$ to L between preceding step and 1 | Rise E/O 1. NFR |
|---|---|---|---|
| 2. LF diagonally back | Backing DC | $1/8$ L between 1 and 2 | Up on 2 |
| 3. Close RF to LF | Backing DC | | Up on 3, lower E/O 3 |

*Footwork.* 1. T H. 2. T. 3. T H.
*Body Sway.* SRR.
*Contrary Body Movement.* CBM on 1.
*Precede.* Reverse Turn.
*Follow.* Natural Turn.

# FLECKERLS

The Fleckerls are very difficult to master. As they are danced on the spot and repeated several times it is usual to move the preceding turns into the centre of the room so that the progression of the other couples is not impeded. Move to the outside of the room again during the following turns. (Note that the abbreviation B (ball of foot) replaces T (toes).

# REVERSE FLECKERL

## Man

Commence facing LOD (any other alignment is possible).

| | | |
|---|---|---|
| 1. LF fwd (small step) toe turned out | Pointing centre | $1/4$ to L between preceding step and 1, body turns less |
| 2. RF to side and slightly back with $1/2$ weight | Facing DW against LOD | $3/8$ L between 1 and 2 |
| 3. Cross LF in front of RF | Facing LOD | $3/8$ L between 2 and 3 |
| 4. RF to side and slightly back to inside edge of lady's LF | Facing DC | $1/8$ L between 3 and 4 |
| 5. Cross LF behind RF, $1/2$ weight (a type of twist turn) | Facing DW against LOD | $1/2$ L between 4 and 5 |
| 6. End weight on RF | Facing LOD | $3/8$ L between 5 and 6 |

*Note 1.* There is no rise.

*Footwork.* 1. H B. 2. B. 3. B H. 4. B H B. 5. B. 6. B H.

*Body Sway.* There is no sway.

*Contrary Body Movement.* CBM on step 1.

*Note 2.* When the steps are repeated, the Man will dance step 1 as lady's step 4 (draw LF back to RF, L heel closes to inside edge of RF).

*Note 3.* Because of the strong rotation there must be a foot swivel on the ball of the flat foot on each step.

*Precedes.* Reverse Turn, Reverse Fleckerl.

*Follows.* Reverse Turn, Reverse Fleckerl, 1-3 Reverse Fleckerl into 4-6 of Reverse Turn. Check to Natural Fleckerl.

## Lady

Commence backing LOD (any other alignment is possible).

| | | |
|---|---|---|
| 1. RF to side and slightly back to inside edge of Man's LF | Facing DW against LOD | $1/8$ to L between preceding step and 1 |
| 2. Cross LF behind RF, $1/2$ weight (a type of twist turn) | Facing DC | $1/2$ L between 1 and 2 |
| 3. End weight on RF | Facing against LOD | $3/8$ L between 2 and 3 |
| 4. Draw LF back to RF | Pointing to wall | $1/4$ L between 3 and 4 body turns less |
| 5. RF to side and slightly back with $1/2$ weight | Facing DC | $3/8$ L between 4 and 5 |
| 6. Cross LF in front of RF | Facing against LOD | $3/8$ L between 5 and 6 |

*Note 1.* There is no rise.

*Footwork.* 1. B H B. 2. B. 3. B H. 4. B H B. 5. B. 6 B H.

*Body Sway.* There is no sway.

*Contrary Body Movement.* CBM on 4.

*Note 2.* Because of the strong rotation there must be a foot swivel on the ball of the flat foot on each step.

For Precedes and Follows see Man's steps.

# NATURAL FLECKERL

## Man

Commence facing LOD (any other alignment is possible).

| | | |
|---|---|---|
| 1. RF forward between lady's feet | Facing DW | $1/8$ to R between preceding step and 1 |

| | | |
|---|---|---|
| 2. LF to side and slightly forward with $1/2$ weight, continuing to turn on RF | Facing DC against LOD | $1/2$ R between 1 and 2 |
| 3. Continue to turn on RF and take full weight on RF with LF held behind RF | Facing LOD | $3/8$ R between 2 and 3 |
| 4. LF to side and slightly forward | Facing DW | $1/8$ R between 3 and 4 |
| 5. Cross RF behind LF, $1/2$ weight (a type of twist turn) | Facing DC against LOD | $1/2$ R between 4 and 5 |
| 6. Untwist on RF then LF to side, small step | Facing LOD | $3/8$ R between 5 and 6 |

*Note 1.* There is no rise.

*Footwork.* 1. H B. 2. B. 3. B H. 4. H B. 5. B. 6. B H.

*Body Sway.* There is no sway.

*Contrary Body Movement.* CBM on 1.

*Note 2.* Because of the strong rotation there must be a foot swivel on the ball of the flat foot on each step.

*Precedes.* Natural Turn. Check from Reverse Fleckerl. Natural Fleckerl.

*Follows.* Natural Fleckerl. Natural Turn. 1–3 Natural Fleckerl into 4–6 of Natural Turn.

## Lady

Commence backing LOD (any other alignment is possible).

| | | |
|---|---|---|
| 1. LF to side and slightly forward | Facing DC against LOD | $1/8$ to R between preceding step and 1 |
| 2. Cross RF behind LF, $1/2$ weight weight (a type of twist turn) | Facing DW | $1/2$ R between 1 and 2 |

| | | |
|---|---|---|
| 3. Untwist on RF then LF to side, small step | Facing against LOD | $3/8$ R between 2 and 3 |
| 4. RF forward between man's feet | Facing DC against LOD | $1/8$ R between 3 and 4 |
| 5. LF to side and slightly forward with $1/2$ weight | Facing DW | $1/2$ R between 4 and 5 |
| 6. Cross RF in front of LF | Facing against LOD | $3/8$ R between 5 and 6 |

*Note 1.* There is no rise.

*Footwork.* 1. H B. 2. B. 3. B H. 4. H B. 5. B. 6. B H.

*Body Sway.* There is no sway.

*Contrary Body Movement.* CBM on 4.

*Note 2.* Because of the strong rotation there must be a foot swivel on the ball of the flat foot on each step.

For Precedes and Follows see Man's Steps.

# CHECK FROM REVERSE FLECKERL TO NATURAL FLECKERL

## Man

Commence facing LOD (any other alignment is possible)

| | | |
|---|---|---|
| 1. LF forward in CBMP, small step | Facing DC | $1/8$ to L between preceding step and 1 |
| 2. Transfer weight back to RF | Backing against LOD | $1/8$ R between 1 and 2 |
| 3. LF back and slightly to side, small step with toe turned in (pivot) | Backing DC, end facing against LOD | $3/8$ R between 2 and 3, and 1/8 R on 3 |

*Note.* There is no rise.
*Footwork.* 1. Foot flat. 2. T. 3. T H T.
*Body Sway.* There is no sway.
*Contrary Body Movement.* CBM on 1 and 3. Step 1 is placed in CBMP.
*Precedes.* Reverse Fleckerl. Reverse Turn.
*Follows.* Natural Fleckerl. Natural Turn.

## Lady

Commence backing LOD (any other alignment is possible).

| | | |
|---|---|---|
| 1. RF back in CBMP, small step | Backing DC | 1/8 to L between preceding step and 1 |
| 2. Transfer weight forward to LF | Facing against LOD | 1/8 R between 1 and 2 |
| 3. RF forward between Man's feet, small step | Facing DC ending backing against LOD | 3/8 R between 2 and 3 and 1/8 R on 3 |

*Note.* There is no rise.
*Footwork.* 1. T. 2. Foot flat. 3. T H.
*Body Sway.* There is no sway.
*Contrary Body Movement.* CBM on 1 and 3. Step 1 is placed in CBMP.
For Precedes and Follows see Man's Steps.

# SECTION VII

# FOR THE KEEN DANCER

## AMATEUR MEDAL TESTS

In most sports and recreations it is possible to make a fairly accurate assessment of one's progress. Yet for many years devotees of ballroom dancing, unless they belonged to the comparative few who compete in public dance halls, possessed no yardstick against which to measure their prowess. Today we have Amateur Medal Tests. There is no doubt that the general standard of ballroom dancing in this country has improved enormously since the leading professional associations and societies instituted these tests.

A few years ago the majority of pupils were content to reach a standard that would enable them to move round a ballroom without undue inconvenience to themselves or their partners; now the majority are only too glad to learn more thoroughly and to record their progress through the tests conducted by well-known professional examiners.

Since the adoption of these tests thousands of dancers have taken advantage of them. This is quite understandable, for ballroom dancing is such a delightful recreation, and the social atmosphere in most schools of dancing is so pleasant that to reach a reasonable standard is neither laborious nor expensive. Few other recreations provide such pleasure at such little cost.

I strongly recommend Medal Tests to every amateur who finds pleasure in dancing. It is easier to improve when there is an incentive to work, and when that first medal has been won the dancer will derive confidence and pleasure, not only from the progress itself, but also from the knowledge that experts have acknowledged and set a seal to that progress.

Between Medal tests and competition dancing there is a large gulf. The "flare" and movement expected from the competition dancer is not expected in these tests, indeed, when used, it is liable to look out of place. The main points to concentrate on are:

1. Neat and correct footwork.
2. A good upright poise and a correct hold.
3. A *quiet* interpretation of the basic and standard figures and a soft movement.

In advanced tests consideration must be given to style and other technical details, but a careful study of the points enumerated above is sufficient for success in the Bronze and Silver grades.

Remember, it is not what you do, but how you do it. Although most societies issue a syllabus of figures for each grade, marks are not lost through the omission of a figure in any dance, but they are lost when a candidate dances a figure badly.

Any qualified teacher can train and enter you for a Medal Test.

## COMPETITION DANCING

Keen dancers who have reached Silver or Gold Medal Test standard will often turn their thoughts to competition dancing. Far more glamour and excitement prevail in a competition at a well-known venue than in a Medal Test where one's efforts are seen by none but the examiner.

Many medallists jump to the conclusion that if they have succeeded in passing the Gold test or above of one of the leading Societies they should have little difficulty in reaching one of the final places in a competition. Unfortunately this is far from true.

In Medal Tests the examiner looks for technical accuracy, good poise and movement, and style that does not offend, even if it does not attract. The candidate is not dancing *against* another couple but to a set general standard of dancing, viewed by that examiner over a given period.

The dancer who passes the highest grade Medal Test can be sure that his dancing is technically sound and that he moves correctly and with good style. Such knowledge is a necessary basis for competition dancing, but is not enough to make a first-class competition dancer. The movement of the competition dancer must be free and flowing and effortless. A figure or group of figures which have been danced well enough to please an examiner must now be danced with the rhythmic expression to make them appear completely alive. The style of the dancer or the couple must be more than correct – it must *attract*. More difficult groups of figures must be learned and the man, who is responsible for leading them, must know how and when he may underturn or overturn them for effect – or to avoid another couple. Seventy-five per cent of competition success comes from experience and training. There is no short cut to success, but the following notes should help the young competition dancer to avoid some of the more obvious faults which have ruined the chances of so many young couples.

## The Hold

This is of vital importance. The general appearance of a couple will always strike the judge before he sees them actually dancing. Points to watch are:

The man's L arm should be angled with the forearm inclined slightly forward, showing an unbroken line from elbow to hand. Watch the grouping of the fingers of the L hand and make sure that the hand does not droop downwards from the wrist. The knuckles of the L hand should be slightly higher than the wrist.

The R elbow must not drop down when leading the lady, especially when leading her into Promenade figures. The R forearm should slope downwards from the elbow to the R hand. If the R hand is held too high on the lady's back, there will be a tendency to drop the R elbow. Many men keep the most pressure on the R wrist when holding the lady, and when this is done, the R hand, not being used, will dangle downwards from the wrist and will often move away from the partner's back. This fault ruins the appearance of the couple. Avoid this by keeping a little pressure on the lady's back with the index finger of the R hand. Study the illustrations in this book.

Ladies should watch the grouping of the fingers of the L hand. They should not be completely straight and stiff but grouped naturally, with the fingers slightly bent.

## Dress

The appearance of a couple will obviously be enhanced if the lady has an attractive dress. Dress fashions for ladies alter so much that it would be unwise to make too many comments, however, the dress should always "move" and flow with the dancer. Nowadays, many businesses specialise in dance wear. Ask your teacher for advice. It can just as obviously be ruined if the man is badly dressed. A really good evening dress suit is very difficult to make and the competition dancer would be advised to seek the advice of an expert before ordering a suit for dancing. Here are some points to watch.

When the arms are raised the coat should not lift from the shoulders. A good shoulder line is essential and it should be possible to see at least a little of the white collar even when the arms are raised. A coat that lifts and covers the white collar gives an appearance of raised shoulders. It is equally important that a little of the white cuff should be seen. The sleeves of the coat should be narrow to give a smart arm line, and a narrow sleeve will grip the white cuff of the shirt and keep it in the same position at all times. The coat "tails" should reach to the top of the calf. Tails that are too short look rather silly; when too long they look untidy, and spoil the line.

One of the worst faults is to wear the trousers too short or too narrow. When standing normally the trouser leg should reach to the heel of the shoe. It is inevitable that when dancing some figures it may tend to touch the floor, but that is far better than having a short trouser leg that rises almost to the ankles when a long step is taken. If they are worn too narrow they give a man the appearance of dancing with bent knees. If worn too wide they look clumsy.

## General

Presentation is a word very frequently used in connection with demonstration dancing by professionals, but presentation also plays its part in competition dancing. For example, the manner in which the lady uses her head in promenade figures can make a big difference to the picture presented by a couple in such variations as the Whisk and the Wing. Some ladies prefer to turn their heads to the right when in promenade, others keep the head turned to the left. Both are correct. The lady should use the method that looks most attractive, but the most annoying fault is that of affectation. Very often a lady who does not turn the head into the promenade position will turn it more to the left and at the same time raise the left shoulder with a rather coy expression. This type of affectation is annoying to watch and should be avoided. The ladies whose dancing is the most pleasing to watch are those who can use their heads naturally, and make them appear as a part of the body – and the picture.

Facial expression should also be studied. It is absurd to grin like a Cheshire cat throughout the contest. It is equally absurd to wear a grim expression. By all means open the mouth when smiling, but do not keep it open all the time.

The man should keep his head still and not move it from side to side as he turns or sways. Only when he leads his partner into a very open Fallaway position and a few other advanced figures should he turn to look at her.

## Position

One of the most common faults in competition dancing is for the lady to dance too much on the man's right side. The popularity of outside figures tends to make her slip to the man's right side, and she often remains there. It is impossible to dance completely in front of the man but it will ruin the picture of a couple if the lady consistently dances on the man's right hip.

The habit of many ladies of leaning well back from the hips, so that contact with the man is felt only at the hips instead of from the hips upwards, is a bad one, and tends to restrict the man's movement. It also makes it very difficult for the man to step outside his partner without losing contact with her. Many points are lost in competitions through this fault.

Inadequate contact while executing outside steps is sometimes the fault of the man holding his weight too far back. The body must follow through with the foot. This will also help the man to avoid that "sitting down" effect so often seen on outside steps.

## Variations

The inexperienced competition dancer often thinks that if half a dozen really difficult and "flashy" variations are included in each dance the judge will be impressed. Perhaps the best advice that can be given is to assure him that whereas a variation, no matter how difficult, will very seldom gain a point for a couple, a variation badly danced will inevitably lose them several points. In a competition where the standard of the couples is nearly even, the judges find it far easier to notice something they dislike than to be impressed by something they do like. Do not take risks. Choose a few figures that can be danced well and without the risk of faulty contact and unattractive body lines, and repeat these several times rather than risk employing a figure of which some part might displease the judge. If you have what you consider is a beautiful variation which you feel you can dance well, make sure that it is used between some sound basic work. A jewel in a plain setting will look far more attractive than a jewel in an ornate setting that can only detract from its beauty.

The keen competition dancer should also read the following section on "Expression in Dancing".

## EXPRESSION IN DANCING

There are hundreds of dancers who have a good floor appearance, correct technique and reasonably good movement, and yet they do not achieve greatness. What do they lack? Perhaps the most important differences between the good dancer and the outstanding dancer are in Softness and Expression.

Most dancers know that the correct softening of the knee on a step such as the first step of any Waltz turn will give their dance a more pleasing appearance, and they strive to acquire it. Fewer competitors realize that to give their dancing better rhythmic expression means the difference between the ordinary and the great.

A few rather obvious examples will help to convey what is meant by expression.

Watch the manner in which some dancers place the third step behind in the Whisk. It can be placed there rather quickly, dead on the beat, in which case there will most possibly be a jolt as the weight moves on to the step – or it can be almost "caressed" into position, slowly, with firm control, perhaps arriving slightly late but with good rhythmic expression. The last three steps of the Natural Spin Turn in the Waltz can be danced with the strict timing of one beat for each step or a little speeding of the movement on the fourth step can result in almost hanging on the fifth step with a rather late and light sixth step which completely alters the character of the movement. The Feather and Three Step in the Foxtrot can be given their correct technical timing; or a delayed timing of the previous step on the Left foot (last step of the Natural Turn) can be followed by a bold swing on the first step of the Feather and a slightly delayed third step, which will completely alter the expression. There are dozens of other instances where playing with the timing, achieved through the movement of the body rather than the placing of the feet, can make the dancing fascinating to watch and intensely satisfying to the dancer.

How is it done? Can it be acquired? It is done by stealing time from one step to give a hovering effect to the next; by softening the knees, and by appreciating that if the lady is given the correct lead she will help to create the impetus to gain this effect without obvious effort. All this can be acquired by any skilled dancer who has a strong sense of rhythm, good balance and the patience to practise so that it appears as an integral part of the dance. The unrhythmic dancer will fail at first, but there is nothing to prevent the acquisition of such rhythmic interpretation by anyone who has shown sufficient ability to become an intelligent average dancer.

Possibly the best amalgamation to practise is the Natural Turn ending with the Closed Impetus in the Foxtrot. Here are some hints for the man.

Dance 1, 2, 3 of the Natural Turn and then continue into the Closed Impetus in the following way:

As the LF is taken back on the 4th step, give the lady a firm but not too strong, lead with the R hand so that she swings well forward against your R side. Soften the knees and count this step "Q" (not the usual "S").

Dance the Heel Turn without worrying whether the feet are closed tightly together, and with the knees still soft. Keep the feet parallel even if they are not quite closed. Count this step "S". It will be noticed that the lady's forward movement will make you turn. Do not try to turn yourself.

Keep a firm hold of the lady to stop her swinging away from you. Do not try to rise. The speed of the lady's movement will cause you to rise without any effort on your part.

On the 4th beat move the LF to the side and rather more back than in standard technique. Make sure that it is actually placed on a *late* count of "Q", and placed lightly with the weight forward, before stepping back on the RF, diagonally to centre against the LOD for the normal "S" count, to continue with the Feather Finish, diagonally to centre.

Thus the timing has been altered from SQQS to QSQS. The effect will be to get early speed, then a Hover, and this expression will be found far more pleasing and attractive than the standard timing.

If, when practising the figure, it is noticed that the effort to quicken the movement between the first and second steps of the Closed Impetus can be seen, you can be sure that it is bad and that you have not mastered the lead. The speed must be gained without obvious effort.

Another extraordinarily good amalgamation to practise is the Open Impetus, followed by the Weave in the Waltz. The Weave from Promenade Position is described on pages 212–217 and is very much used by advanced dancers. Important points to watch are as follows:

Dance 1, 2, 3 of the Natural Turn (Waltz) and then take the 1st step of the Open Impetus back, again giving the lady a firm lead with the R hand to swing her forward against your R side.

The lady's impetus will now compel you to continue to turn to the R and rise to the toes after the heel turn. Keep firm pressure on the lady's back to prevent her from overturning, and hover as long as possible before placing weight on to the LF, moving diagonally to centre on a late count of "6".

The attractive Weave ending should be danced as follows:

Step forward with the RF, diagonally to centre in PP, and as this step is taken, give the lady a *very firm lead* to swing her well across the front of you as you step forward on the LF (on ball of foot), moving almost to centre. On this step (2) the lady will take a long step to side with the RF on the ball of foot, having turned square to the man, but with her head still turned to the R.

The swing given to the lady on the first step will cause her to continue to turn on the ball of RF until facing the LOD, when her LF is placed to the side (3). This swing will also result in the man and lady rising from the ball of foot on the 2nd step, and the man will endeavour to hold this rise with a hover effect, before placing his 3rd step (RF) to side with the body backing the LOD.

The Weave is continued by the man stepping back with LF down the LOD with the lady outside (4).

On the 5th step the man takes the RF back rather quickly, giving the lady a firm lead forward. Lady will step forward LF in line with man. Both man and lady use the ball of foot on 5.

With the body turning to the L press upwards from the ball of foot (this will be assisted by the lady's forward swing) and get a slight hover effect before placing the LF to side, with the body facing wall on 6. Take this step slightly late, and lightly.

The next step will be taken outside lady with the RF; remember to lower the L heel and release it again as the weight moves forward over the RF to continue into a Natural figure.

There are many other figures in which better expression can be gained by stealing time from one step and adding that time to the next. The Hover Telemark will look infinitely better if, instead of giving it the strict SQQS rhythm, the time is distributed to the approximate value of 1½ beats, 1½ beats, 1 beat, 2 beats.

The really first-class dancer will know whether an unusual rhythmic interpretation is justified on artistic grounds by the *feel* of it. The less experienced dancer should seek the advice of a professional who can tell at once whether an unusual interpretation is advisable.

# SECTION VIII

# BALLROOM PARTY DANCES

At both public and private dances it is a good idea to introduce one or two party dances, especially when such dances result in an interchange of partners. Some of the most popular of these are described below.

## PAUL JONES

This is one of the most popular novelty dances in England, and is frequently used at social dances to effect an interchange of partners and to create a friendly atmosphere.

### Description

The MC, DJ, or leader of the band announces a "Paul Jones" and the band then plays a bright tune. The dancers then form two large circles, the men on the inside and facing outwards, the ladies on the outside and facing inwards, that is, towards the men.

With hands joined the two circles move to the right so that they are moving in opposite directions. When the music stops, the man claims the lady directly in front of him and dances. There should then be a short pause in the music to permit the men to take their partners and then play a Waltz, Quickstep, Foxtrot, etc., or a Sequence or Latin American dance. After playing about 32 bars the music is stopped, the circle is formed as before, and continued as described above.

It is sometimes advisable to commence by playing a Waltz or Quickstep and then when all the dancers are on the floor, to announce a Paul Jones and immediately break into the Call tune. This ensures that all couples will take part.

## "EXCUSE ME" DANCE

Three or more men and ladies are given cards with "Excuse me" written on them. A popular tune is then played and all the couples dance. Those persons with the cards stand in the centre of the floor. A man with an "Excuse me" card is permitted to present it to any other man and claim his partner, whilst a lady can present a card to any other lady.

When a partner has been taken from a person it is not permissible for him or her to reclaim that partner immediately. The card must be presented as soon as possible to one of another couple.

Alternatively, if no cards are used, the person claiming a partner can tap his or her partner on the back, saying "Excuse me".

## SPOT DANCE

This is a good way of distributing a few prizes to the dancers at a social dance or party. The organiser of the dance arranges for a few "spots", such as under certain electric lights or near a column or post in the ballroom. Music for a popular dance is played and then the music is stopped. The couple standing nearest to the selected spot are given a prize. Another way of doing this is for the MC to announce (when the music stops) that the winners are the couple standing nearest to Mr or Mrs – (a prominent person).

Where "spotlights" are available it is a good idea for the spotlight to play on the dancers during the dance, and then when the music stops, the couple standing in the direct ray of the spotlight are the winners.